"*Whose Money Is It Anyway?* could well become the handbook of a revived movement to induce reluctant companies — and governments — to improve the benefits available to retired Canadians."
The Toronto Star

"No matter where you stand in the political spectrum or what your attitude toward pensions, you should read this book."
Star Phoenix (Saskatoon)

"Finlayson weaves together a fascinating account of public pension policy, the uncertain future of the Canadian Pension Plan and the management of private funds...a particularly important read for oil patchers in the early stages of their careers."
The Calgary Sun

"*Whose Money Is It Anyway?* is a disturbing book that challenges complacency and attacks many popular beliefs about the Canadian pension system."
The Ottawa Citizen

"Every now and then...a book comes along that we ought to read because it's good for us. On rare occasions, such a book will be well written and easy to read, too. Such an occasion is Ann Finlayson's *Whose Money Is It Anyway?*"
The Pembroke Observer

"If you didn't get this book in your Christmas stocking, go out and buy it. You'll need it."
The Hamilton Spectator

PENGUIN BOOKS

Whose Money Is It Anyway?

Ann Finlayson, a former writer at *Maclean's* magazine in
Toronto, was born in Iowa. She attended Smith College,
the University of Edinburgh and Boston University, and
holds Master's degrees from Harvard and the University of
Toronto. In addition to working as a writer, reporter and
researcher, she has taught at York University and in the
Magazine Journalism program at Ryerson Polytechnical
Institute. Ann Finlayson lives in downtown Toronto
with her family.

WHOSE MONEY
IS IT ANYWAY?

THE SHOWDOWN

ON PENSIONS

ANN FINLAYSON

Penguin Books

PENGUIN BOOKS
Published by the Penguin Group
Penguin Books Canada Ltd, 2801 John Street, Markham, Ontario L3R 1B4
Penguin Books Ltd, 27 Wrights Lane, London W8 5TZ, England
Viking Penguin Inc., 40 West 23rd Street, New York, New York 10010, USA
Penguin Books Australia Ltd, Ringwood, Victoria, Australia
Penguin Books (NZ) Ltd, 182-190 Wairau Road, Auckland 10, New Zealand

Penguin Books Ltd, Registered Offices: Harmondsworth, Middlesex, England

First published in Viking by Penguin Books Canada Limited, 1988

Published in Penguin Books, 1989

1 3 5 7 9 10 8 6 4 2

The following are used by permission:
Dingman, Harold, "Pension poverty." In *Maclean's*, March 1, 1949.
Mercer, William, "We're going haywire in our security plans."
In *Maclean's*, July 20, 1957.

*Queries regarding radio broadcasting, motion picture, video cassette,
television and translation rights should be directed to the author's
representative: Peter Livingston Associates, Inc., 120 Carlton St., Suite 304,
Toronto, Ontario, Canada M5A 4K2.*

Manufactured in Canada

Canadian Cataloguing in Publication Data

Finlayson, Ann, 1941-
Whose money is it anyway?

Bibliography: p.
Includes index.
ISBN 0-14-011178-6

1. Pensions — Canada.   2. Old age pensions — Canada.   I. Title.

HD7129.F56 1989   331.25'2'0971   C88-094444-7

For Michael

::

ACKNOWLEDGEMENTS

::

I owe a great debt of gratitude to my husband, Michael, without whose constant support, incisive interventions and occasionally insufferable enthusiasm this book would never have gotten off the ground. I am also grateful for the sufferance of my children who have all acquired a profound new respect for the words "deadline" and "you'll just have to do it yourself." Nor would this book have been possible without the enthusiasm of, as far as I can tell, the entire staff at Penguin Books whose good cheer and kind words were invaluable to me. I especially thank David Kilgour, who understood from the beginning that pensions are anything but dull, and my editor, Iris Skeoch, who inherited a project well underway with enormous grace and boundless interest. Both of them, and my copy editor, Kathleen Richards, were a joy to work with.

I wish also to acknowledge the enthusiasm of Peter Livingston and David Johnston, the helpful comments of David Short, Sam Gindin and Jeff Boloten and the kindness of *Maclean's* magazine in granting me a leave of absence in which to complete the book. The expert assistance of Linda Bailey, Sherri Aikenhead and John Daly, all of whom found time outside their busy workdays to provide help with the mountain of research any discussion of pensions requires, was invaluable to me as was the wizardry of Norman Zacour, who launched a rescue mission whenever my sometimes errant computer threatened to devour the book's chapters in their entirety.

It would have been quite impossible to cover the historical background of the Canadian pension system today without leaning heavily upon the pioneering work of economist Kenneth Bryden, Professor Emeritus at the University of Toronto, and historian Desmond Morton, Principal of the University of Toronto's Erindale College, or to do justice to the "women's question" without relying upon the work of Louise Dulude, past president of the National Action Committee on the Status of Women, whose paradigm-shattering perspectives ensured that women's difficulties with the pension system would never again be brushed aside. I fully acknowledge my debt to them.

To Marty Friedland, whose task force was operating on the front lines of a nasty skirmish in a larger war, I can say only that I appreciate his making the report and research studies available to me promptly and I hope we are still friends. I regret the fact that Conrad Black never returned my calls. To the dozens of people who did return my calls and kindly agreed to take the time to explain, instruct, speculate and provide, I am grateful. Without them, this book could not have been written. To the handful who extemporized, obfuscated and demurred, may their patronizing ways come back to haunt them and may all their employees ask to use the photocopier at once.

Finally, I must acknowledge the inspiration I derived from the words of the late Judy LaMarsh, whose sense of vague discomfiture when moving through the predominantly male world of pensions I have sometimes shared. The fight for the CPP took a heavy toll on Judy LaMarsh. "It took the shine off politics for me," she admitted. "In the minds of many it stamped me for a quarrelsome, stubborn, heavy-handed fighter. That's an unpleasant public image for anyone, especially a woman, and I resented it." To the scrappy, determined and fair-minded woman who understood full well that even the banks have a better reputation than the politicians for being trustworthy in the handling of other people's money and that the insurance industry is even worse: R.I.P.

CONTENTS

::

..

Whose Money
Is It Anyway?

THE SHOWDOWN

ON PENSIONS

..

ANN FINLAYSON

::

Introduction

::

The word "pensions" evokes many images: elderly women at supermarket check-outs with a tin or two of Campbell's soup and a loaf of day-old bread in their shopping carts; Bob White and the Canadian Auto Workers on strike against Chrysler because they want their pensions indexed; furious Dominion Stores employees complaining publicly that Toronto financier Conrad Black had raided their pension fund and stolen their futures; angry grandmothers on Parliament Hill protesting the government's attempt to de-index their old-age-security benefits; grim-faced economists predicting that the Canada Pension Plan would soon go broke; vast pension funds controlling billions and billions of dollars careering around the Canadian economy like behemoths run amok.

Yet despite the high drama which periodically engulfs pension issues, thinking deeply about pension matters is not an activity at which most Canadians excel. Because pensions are synonymous with growing old, most of us prefer to ignore them until retirement day approaches. Indeed, many Canadians don't have a clue about how the country's pension system works — or about exactly what they themselves can expect to receive one day from the various pension schemes in which they are involved, from RRSPs to company plans to the Quebec or Canada Pension Plan.

The chaotic and sometimes incomprehensible images swirling around pensions meant little more to me than they did to everyone else until the day I asked to see a copy of my own pension plan at work. I had no special expertise in pensions, but I was curious, mainly because I was approaching that mystical date — ten years' service and age forty-five — when my pension would be "vested." All I wanted to know was a little bit about the plan and a little bit about what had become of my money.

For nearly ten years Maclean Hunter, Canada's venerable publishing and communications giant, had deducted a chunk of my salary at *Maclean's* magazine and routed it into the company's compulsory pension plan. And for nearly ten years, I had not given that money much thought. I knew, of course, that at some point I would reap the benefits of Maclean Hunter's efforts on my behalf and I *had* received periodic communications about my contributions and the benefits I might expect in the future. But I knew next to nothing about the pension plan itself. So out of curiosity — I had been reading about Conrad Black too — I wrote a letter to Maclean Hunter and asked for a copy of the plan.

Almost a month passed with no reply. I phoned Maclean Hunter's affable personnel director Charles Lee who said that the documents would be available in his office shortly. There was, however, one hitch. The legislation stated that an employee is entitled to review pension documents one time only in any twelve-month period and it was not clear from my conversation with Charles Lee whether or not copies would be provided. So I wrote a second letter. Would copies, in fact, be provided? And, if not, what arrangements could I make to photocopy sections of some or all of the documents?

It was a simple request and, seemingly, one with the force of law behind it. Section 27.(1) of the Ontario Pension Benefits Act stated, unambiguously it seemed, that:

> At the written request of an employee who is a member of the plan or his agent authorized in writing, the employer within thirty days receipt of the request, shall make available to the member or his agent copies of any of the following documents or information requested.

The Act then listed the same documents I had requested in my initial letter.

But, alas, everything was not clear after all. The trouble lay with the phrase "shall make available . . . copies." Did that mean that copies of the documents would be provided? If not, did it mean that the documents could be photocopied? According to Maclean Hunter, it meant neither. "On two separate occasions," Charles Lee wrote back, "we have contacted the Pension Commission of Ontario who have indicated to us quite clearly that they interpret the phrase "shall make available" to mean that we are not required to issue copies of the documents to the plan member." My subsequent calls to the Pension Commission suggested that, against all logic, this might indeed be so.

Interpretations varied, depending on the voice on the other end of the line at the Pension Commission. Yes, it was possible to make photocopies, but there might be a small charge. No, it was not my right to make photocopies, even if I was willing to pay for them. Yes, the legislation seemed to say that copies would be provided. No, that did not necessarily mean that copies would be provided. The only consensus seemed to be that handwritten extracts could be taken and that, as a member of the plan, I could stare at the documents indefinitely — as long as I asked to do so only once a year.

It all seemed silly to me, so I tried again. The person to speak with at the Commission, the person who could give me a definitive answer on this matter, I was told, was Sheila Fish. The Maclean Hunter pension plan was Sheila's territory. And she, co-operation incarnate on the other end of the telephone line, was happy to discuss my problem. We spoke of "interpretation bulletins" and of "waiting for new rulings expected daily." Was it not straightforward?, I asked. Does "shall make available" not mean shall make available? Does "copies" not mean copies? Would the documents be so clear to an employee who had never seen them before that copies were unnecessary? "Well," said Sheila with an air of finality, "they would be clear to me. But then I've got the advantage of knowing how to read them." With that, she confirmed that, as she understood the matter in light of the latest interpretation bulletin, Charles Lee was right.

It was probably time to give in. But the impasse raised some interesting questions. Why would a respectable company like Maclean Hunter want to place such an obstacle in the way of an employee? And why would a company that prides itself on its benefits plans go out of its way, not once but twice, to obtain a ruling that prevented me from photocopying the documents — when the intent of the legislation clearly was to guarantee me that right? Sheila had the answer. "It could tie up their photocopier, interfere with their business," she said. "And," she added sternly, "some employers just don't feel that they want to allow employees to have access at that level. You've got to look at the worst situation. What if four thousand employees wanted copies all at once? Then what?"

Then what, to be sure. The perils of thousands of aging Maclean Hunter employees storming Charles Lee's office on, say, a busy Tuesday afternoon, each one demanding to use the photocopier, made some sense. After all, one straightforward request for a copy of the pension plan initiated by one curious employee had set off alarm bells somewhere deep in Maclean Hunter's corporate soul, doubtless interfering with somebody's business. Perhaps it really did look like the beginning of a stampede.

New provincial regulations took effect on January 1, 1987 spelling out even more clearly my right to have the documents. Yet even then — even in light of rules specifically designed to prevent employers from behaving as Maclean Hunter had behaved — the company capitulated with reluctance. After two more attempts, I finally got the copies, a tiny victory as victories go. Still, my surprise and dismay that Maclean Hunter would go to such ridiculous lengths to deny me or any employee easy access to pension information to which I was clearly entitled provided both the impetus and the energy for this book. And the deeper I dug into the current state of Canadians' pension arrangements, the more evidence I found to confirm my growing suspicion that all is not as it may seem in the high-powered world of pensions.

Maclean Hunter, I soon discovered, was not unique in its reluctance to broadcast the details of its pension plan. Many respected Canadian corporations shroud their plans in secrecy, offering their employees incomplete or misleading information about how their pension fund operates and what they can expect when they retire. Moreover, when employees do ask questions, the answers are invariably couched in the impenetrable jargon of the pension industry and based on unstated assumptions which are extremely difficult, if not impossible, for anyone who is not an "expert" to challenge. Pensions, it would seem, are for employers to bestow and the rest of us to receive with gratitude and humility.

Yet in the last decade it has become very clear to many critics of the private pension system that there are as many, if not more, reasons to mistrust employers when they make pension promises as to be grateful to them. Far too many older Canadians have learned that lesson the hard way when they discovered that the pensions on which they depended began to vanish into thin air on the day after they retired.

At the same time, after countless rounds of pension reform, Canadians had been told that in the course of the next twenty-five years, their compulsory contributions to the Canada Pension Plan would double while the level of benefits most of them could expect to receive from the plan would remain about the same as before. Moreover, new RRSP rules suggested that it would be necessary for people earning an average salary to save eighteen percent of their earnings over their entire working lifetime if they hoped to be comfortable when they retired.

These were troubling developments and they seemed to me to demand an explanation. If Canadians were going to have to pay nearly one-fifth of their entire lifetime earnings to secure a modest income in their later years, surely they should be able to rest easy in the knowledge that they would receive what they had paid for. Canada had just emerged from more than a decade of continuous attempts to reform the country's pension system to achieve precisely that end. And Canadians had been assured that the reform process is now virtually complete. Now, after the system had been "reformed," I wondered, have all of the problems finally been solved? Certainly the pension industry would have us believe that they have.

In September 1987, for example, Ronald Anderson of the Toronto *Globe and Mail* wrote a financial column which bore the soothing headline, "Pension reforms have eased major stresses." Anderson informed *Globe* readers that the changes in pension legislation made in the past few years indicate that "in most disputed areas" the reformers had actually won all of the major battles.

Anderson based his comments on the assessments of *The Mercer Bulletin*, a monthly newsletter of William M. Mercer Limited, the influential firm of actuarial consultants whose clients include many of Canada's largest corporations. The pension reformers, according to Mercer, had won the battle on three of the four major issues that had dominated the debate over occupational pensions since 1981, when the federal government sponsored a huge conference on pensions designed to reach a national consensus on reform. Of the four big issues — the inadequate pension coverage of the work force, the erosion of benefits by inflation, the poor treatment of women by the system, and the loss of entitlements by mobile (or laid-off) workers — the bulletin said, only inflation protection for pensioners remained an issue.

Yet, while it is true that some changes have been made which will make the system as a whole fairer for most Canadians, that assessment of the current state of pension reform, I discovered, was both premature and superficial. In fact, inflation protection is *the* critical issue in pension reform and it is a long way from being resolved. On top of that, the reforms which could have made the system better for every Canadian have run into roadblocks which could prevent their implementation in many provinces for years to come.

In the coming months and years, Canadians will witness a showdown over pensions. Its outcome will directly affect their own lives and their own futures — and the lives and futures of their children. It will be a battle over political ideology and a battle over power. Above all, it will be a battle over money. And this time, the critical question we should all be asking is: Just whose money is it, anyway?

..

PART ONE

PUBLIC PENSIONS:
A GATHERING CRISIS

::

· 1 ·

BRIAN MULRONEY
AND THE SACRED TRUST

::

"When the background of the present system of social security is considered, it is not surprising that it has many deficiencies."

Canadian economist Harry Cassidy, 1943

..

In the heat of the 1984 federal election campaign, Liberal Prime Minister John Turner levelled a sweeping accusation at Tory leader Brian Mulroney. A Progressive Conservative government in Ottawa, Turner charged, would "slash existing social programs", and implement a means test to ensure that only the very poorest Canadians would qualify for financial assistance under the Old Age Security and the Family Allowance plans. Nonsense, countered Mulroney. It was the Liberals themselves who had spoken in the past of abandoning universality in Canada's social programs. Tories, Mulroney insisted gravely, understood full well that Canada's universal social welfare programs constituted a "sacred trust." No Progressive Conservative government, he vowed, would dream of "tampering" with them.

Mulroney's political adversaries were plainly sceptical of his assurances and it was not hard to see why. A Tory policy convention two years earlier had openly questioned the wisdom of providing both of these benefits to all eligible Canadians regardless of their income levels. Furthermore, government-sponsored social programs were under heavy fire by conservative governments in both the United States and Great Britain. No philosophical soul mate of Margaret Thatcher and Ronald Reagan, the argument ran, could be expected to leave Canada's "sacred trust" alone.

There was more than a hint of hypocrisy in the ensuing mighty uproar over Brian Mulroney's "sacred trust" and his dogged insistence that the Tories harboured no hidden agenda for dismantling the country's social welfare system. Indeed, in the past both Liberals and New Democrats had been heard to wonder aloud whether the principle of universality was worth defending. In 1982, the same year pre-Mulroney Tory policy makers began to toy seriously with making a public commitment to putting an end to universality in some programs, for example, Liberal finance minister Marc Lalonde had said publicly that the Liberals too might well want to take a hard look at the principle with a view to reform.

Lalonde's comments echoed earlier remarks by Pierre Trudeau who had vowed during the 1968 election campaign that there would be no more of "this free stuff." And only that June, Liberal leadership candidate Donald Johnston had suggested that Canadians might be better served by a guaranteed-annual-income scheme than by the universal programs. Even the New Democrats had been heard to question the wisdom of universality. NDP welfare critic Margaret Mitchell had said as recently as that July that not only did her party support higher tax rates for upper-income Canadians, but New Democrats would be prepared to "tax back their old age pensions as well."

In the slanging match over the sincerity of Mulroney's pledge to protect the "sacred trust," though, it seemed that no one was eager to examine what, exactly, that sacred trust amounted to for older Canadians. The metaphor simply hovered over the debate, shimmering with the aura of sanctimony bestowed upon it by Mulroney's reverent tones. And soon every politician in the land was scrambling to bask in its reflected light. Liberals, said John Turner, would "never surrender" the principle of universality. The New Democratic Party, declared party leader Ed Broadbent, was the prime mover and the only true guardian of the sacred trust. Out of the blue, universality had become a potent issue in an otherwise predictable election campaign.

But in the rush to occupy the moral high ground, little attention was paid to the reality of Canada's universal social programs. No one bothered to point out that, compared with many other countries in the Western world, Canada does not have much to be proud of in the sacred trust department. No one bothered to recall that, decades after most other industrialized societies had put broad social welfare programs in place, most Canadians, with their Calvinist work ethic and free-market sentiments flying high, were still convinced that even the most niggardly assistance schemes would serve only to encourage sloth, greed and indolence. No one mentioned that Canada's social welfare system *still* tolerates more than four million people, many of them elderly, living below the poverty line, however that line is defined. No one mentioned that, compared with many other societies, Canada spends a pittance on its "sacred trust."

Over the last hundred years, the components of Canada's old-age-security system have evolved in response to a bewildering variety of crises, political pressures and societal needs. Federal and provincial governments — invariably at odds with each other — have reluctantly stitched together a hodgepodge of remedies and incentives to cushion the lives of older people in a complex and rapidly changing society as business leaders railed about the need to induce Canadians to save for the future so that they would not become an intolerable drain on tax revenues when they grew old. This intricate structure has been patched and mended over and over again in response to political ideology, economic necessity and the pressures of powerful interest groups. Today a tangled web of provincial and federal legislation, much of it enacted in the name of fairness, binds it all together. Yet the system is still not fair — and after more than a decade of attempts to improve it, there is still a long, difficult way to go before its deeply-rooted inequities are remedied.

More than a century ago, social reformers in most of the Western world began the campaign for government-sponsored programs to alleviate the human suffering that accompanied rapid industrialization and urbanization, the forces that were transforming their societies so quickly that traditional support systems could not keep up with the pace of change. In many places they were successful. But, like social welfare programs today, the reform measures they won were not entirely the result of sweet compassion and simple altruism on the part of the governments that created and funded them. Rather they owed their existence to political power-broking and a growing realization that industrialized societies could no longer count on the institutions of church, community and family to deal with the problems of a highly mobile, urban populace. If governments wanted a fit and willing work force at the ready when times were good, there was a price to be paid, especially when times were bad.

Reformers' efforts to channel government assistance to the elderly were more problematical. Because older people had little political power — and a diminishing ability to compete with the young in an industrialized workplace — their claims to state support were more tenuous and far easier to ignore. As a result, attempts to make provision for their income security took two directions: younger workers would be enjoined to provide for their own future needs through government-sponsored contributory employment superannuation plans. And if they were too poor to do that, society would have to provide for them with charity, through means-tested old-age-pension schemes paid out of tax revenues.

More than a century ago, German chancellor Otto von Bismarck was experimenting with centrally-administered contributory pensions for lower-paid workers in newly-unified Germany. Austria, Luxembourg, Romania, France and Sweden all had contributory old-age-security plans in place before the First World War; Holland and Spain by 1919; and Italy, Bulgaria, Czechoslovakia, Belgium and Chile by 1925. Denmark introduced a means-tested old-age-security plan as early as 1891. New Zealand had followed in 1898, Australia and the United Kingdom in 1908.

Canada was not in the vanguard of reform. Early efforts to introduce similar programs reflected and fostered a liberal social philosophy which many Canadians and their political leaders were loath to accept. With its vast expanse and rural frontier traditions, Canada was a place where men were men. Self-reliant and proud, they looked after themselves and their own families. While other societies began to come to grips with the enormous human cost of industrialization, Canadians, by and large, continued to view their neighbours' impoverishment as the result of moral turpitude, perversity or strong drink. In Canada, it seemed, people, especially old people, were poor because they deserved to be.

For decades, Canadian politicians shied away from the contributory old-age-security schemes that were becoming commonplace elsewhere as one means of distributing the burdens of retirement security fairly between employees, employers and government. Incredibly, it was 1965 before Canadians mustered the political will to set up the wage-related Canada Pension Plan that would oblige employers to contribute to the retirement security of their employees. In the meantime, provincial and federal governments squabbled over what should be done about the human suffering that they could neither ignore nor lock away in squalid institutions.

These deeply-ingrained traditions of individualism, self-sufficiency and the sanctity of the free marketplace seriously impeded the development of a rational old-age-security policy in Canada, just as they impede significant pension reform today. But there was a constitutional impediment to social welfare reform in Canada as well. The British North America Act, insofar as it addressed health and welfare matters at all, defined social welfare as a provincial, not a federal responsibility. The provinces were to oversee all public welfare through "the establishment, maintenance and management of hospitals, asylums, charities and charitable institutions." As a result, for decades regional politicians, fearful that their own constituents would be called upon to bear a disproportionate share of the burden and blame them for it, seized upon the Act's provisions to slow the pace of social legislation.

Trade unions and reformers began to agitate for public old age pensions in Canada well before the turn of the twentieth century. They met with little success, although in 1889, the report of the Royal Commission on the Relations of Capital and Labour called for a government-sponsored annuity system that would enable working people to "make provision for old age by periodical or occasional payment of small sums" to a federal program. That initiative failed. But by 1908, the Liberal government had authorized the sale of annuities to Canadian residents "to the end that habits of thrift be promoted." That scheme foundered too, in part because many employees simply didn't earn enough money to contribute to it. Then, in 1911, hard on the heels of defeat at the polls, the Liberal party stepped up its efforts to formulate a better system. Those deliberations, however, were interrupted by the outbreak of the First World War and by 1915 old age pensions seemed to be a dead issue in Canada.

Ironically, though, it was the war which finally forced the federal government to get involved in public pensions. For many years, opponents of federal pensions had needed only to point to the United States to bolster their case against government-sponsored pension schemes. From the turn of the century onwards, historian Desmond Morton points out, U.S. military pensions, routinely awarded as a blatant form of political patronage, had gobbled up a *fifth* of all U.S. federal revenues each year. Not only did the U.S. experience prove that pensions caused people to become lazy and unproductive, it was said, but it also demonstrated that such plans were bound to lead to dreadful abuses which could well bankrupt the country.

Then thousands of sick and disabled Canadian soldiers began to straggle home from the battlefields of Europe, and it quickly became apparent that the country was facing a crisis that far exceeded the limited capacities of local authorities. Ottawa had little choice but to make some financial provision for these men and their families. Furthermore, because the crisis involved veterans, there was no constitutional impediment for the opponents of federal intervention to hide behind. The British North America Act specifically gave the Dominion government jurisdiction over health and welfare services for

"Indians, prisoners in penitentiaries, sailors, passengers arriving from foreign ports" — and war veterans.

Ever mindful of the fiscally dangerous and corrupt state of affairs in the United States, federal officials set about designing a pension policy that could not be abused. They succeeded, but only by creating a Draconian system which, although it briefly had higher compensation rates than any other military pension scheme in the world, was arbitrary, highly bureaucratized and degrading to the claimants who had to "prove" to medical authorities that their disabilities qualified them for a pension. The result was a nightmare for any veteran whose malady was not visible, well-documented and totally incapacitating. Morton notes that

> Pension policy depended on medical knowledge and on doctors' attitudes. Ex-medical officers might know the effects of mustard gas or the limits of army record-keeping but, as [contemporary war historian] Sir Andrew Macphail complained, army life turned doctors into autocrats. The deference due to fee-paying patients curdled into a suspicion of "lead-swingers" and "malingerers." Macphail's own conviction that "shell-shock" could be dismissed as "a manifestation of childishness and femininity" was widely shared. If such "functional cases" were self-generated, denying a pension was part of the cure.

In an early instance of a pattern which was to repeat itself over and over again, the doctors and the bureaucrats who administered Canada's first pension act managed to exclude or seriously shortchange most of the people the legislation was designed to help. Morton points out, for example, that although 60,000 pensions were awarded annually — there were 183,166 Canadian battle casualties — fewer than five percent of the disabled veterans ever qualified as one hundred percent disabled and "the great majority" were rated as less than twenty-five percent disabled. Still, flawed as it was in the execution of its essentially liberal provisions, the Pension Bill of 1919 was a tentative step on the long road to Canada's "sacred trust": a societal commitment that, in the midst of plenty, no Canadian would be forced to live and die in abject poverty.

The First World War has often been described as a turning point for modern Western societies, the crucible of agony and upheaval which shattered any remaining illusions about the enormity of the social changes wrought by industrialization. Canadians shared that sense of dislocation. As wave upon wave of immigrants arrived on Canadian shores, as towns and cities grew rapidly and chaotically, as factories lured young people away from family farms, Canada began its own long and often painful transformation from a decentralized, rural society to an essentially urban and industrial economy. With these changes came enormous social challenges, not the least of which was the plight of older people who had lost not only their family supports, but their livelihoods as well. Yet it was a political oddity and not a broad-based commitment to alleviating the grinding poverty of the elderly that brought Canada its first federal old-age-pension scheme in 1927.

Even before the war, the opposition Liberal party under Wilfrid Laurier had identified and debated the need for a broad social security program that would include an old age pension. By 1919, the introduction of such a scheme had become party policy. At about the same time, a federal committee looking into the causes of the great Winnipeg General Strike of May and June 1919 recommended an "immediate inquiry" into "state insurance against unemployment, sickness, invalidity and old age." Shortly thereafter, a Royal Commission including federal and provincial politicians and representatives from both labour and business met in Ottawa to consider the report's findings. The commission recommended that the government begin immediate studies with a view to instituting unemployment insurance and old age pensions. By 1921, the studies were under way and it seemed that the tide was about to turn, particularly when, later that year, the Liberals returned to power under Mackenzie King.

The new prime minister had been deeply involved in

developing Liberal social welfare policy; in 1918 he had published *Industry and Humanity*, a 529-page volume detailing his own views on social conditions and social reform; and he was personally committed to the creation of an old-age-pension scheme. But, sensitive to anti-pension sentiment in the business community and mindful that 65 of 116 Liberal seats were held by social conservatives from Quebec who had little sympathy for old age pensions, he backed off. As economist Kenneth Bryden put it plainly in his influential 1974 book, *Old Age Pensions and Policy Making in Canada*, "King's main preoccupation was simply with staying in office," — a preoccupation that has afflicted politicians contemplating rational old-age-security policies in Canada ever since.

But in 1924, in response to pressure from trade unionists and strong urging from two Labour members — J. S. Woodsworth, the tireless Winnipeg social crusader and, a decade later, the first leader of the CCF, and his fellow reformer, William Irvine — a committee was struck to examine how the federal government and the provinces could co-operate on old age pensions. The House accepted the committee's unanimous report, which recommended pensions for the "deserving" indigent elderly "at the earliest possible moment." Still, King, with an eye as always to his political support, gave no indication that he intended to act on the recommendations. Then, in the general election of 1925, the Liberals suffered a setback. King lost his seat and the party's majority was trimmed to three. "Looking on gloomily from the sidelines," writes historian Kenneth McNaught, "King observed that the balance of power...was actually held by two men — Woodsworth and A.A. Heaps. It was not surprising, then, that he should seek means to assure the continued support of these two in crucial votes." That support had a price: a promise that, among other reforms, the government would move ahead swiftly on old age pensions. Woodsworth and Irvine had managed to force old age pensions onto the country's political agenda.

King complied, but the Old Age Pension Act that the House of Commons passed in 1926 was vetoed by the Conservative-controlled Senate. "The old arguments were revived," writes

Bryden. "The bill would penalize thrift, it would militate against family responsibility and private charity, it did not differentiate between the deserving and undeserving, and there was no public demand for it." Above all, it was clear, the legislation was viewed as a totally unacceptable intrusion by the federal government upon provincial turf. But another general election in September increased the Liberal majority and raised public consciousness of the pension issue. The bill was reintroduced in the House of Commons in February 1927 and passed the following month.

This time, the Senate, which King had pointedly suggested was badly in need of reform, grudgingly acquiesced. "Finding malicious satisfaction in the thought that failure of the provinces to cooperate would make the bill a nullity," Bryden writes, "they professed willingness to let the people see what a 'delusion and hollow mockery' it was. Most of the senators," he adds, "championed provincial rights not so much out of a desire to protect the freedom of the provinces to act in this field as in the belief that the provinces in fact would do nothing."

King himself envisioned the Act as a stopgap measure that would soon need to be replaced with a contributory scheme. And inevitably, given the attitude of the provinces, the bill fell far short of Woodsworth's hopes. Instead of the broad bill he had fought for, the Pension Act of 1927 was a compromise measure which authorized the government to do no more than reimburse the provinces for half of the cost of any old age support they provided to the "deserving" elderly up to a limit of $20 (about $145 in today's dollars) a month. Provincial control over public welfare, in effect, remained unchallenged.

It was not an easy matter in Canada in 1929 to demonstrate to the government authorities that one was truly "deserving" of such financial assistance. In the first place, only British subjects who had lived in Canada for twenty years and had reached age seventy, or the widows of "aliens" who had been British subjects before they married, qualified, and then only if they could pass a stringent and punitive means test that disqualified anyone with an income of more than a dollar a day. On top of that, even if a claimant's income was less than $365 a year, any amount over

$125 was subtracted from the pension. Worse, there was a provincial residency requirement of five years. If a claimant met this condition, the province would pay the pension, but it also retained the right to claim reimbursement from any other province in which the pensioner had resided in the previous twenty years.

The means test also took into account the value of pensioners' property and excluded anyone who transferred that property, say to a son or a daughter, in order to qualify for the pension. Native people were not eligible at all, despite the BNA Act's pronouncement that the federal government was responsible for the welfare of Indians, prisoners in penitentiaries, sailors and passengers arriving from overseas. Indeed, passengers arriving from overseas would *never* be eligible under the Act unless they had the good sense to be British.

Worse, the provinces were empowered to recover the total amount of the pension from the estates of deceased pensioners — together with 5-percent interest compounded annually — unless the estate were willed to another pensioner, in which case it doubtless disqualified that poor soul from collecting his own pension. And finally, provincial governments were under no obligation to take advantage of the federal program; even if they did, it was possible for them to opt out on a year's notice simply by repealing the provincial legislation that provided for the pension.

The Old Age Pension Act with its niggardly and racist provisions little altered survived until 1951, and remains a dubious landmark in Canada's history. It took a decade for all the provinces to accept the plan. British Columbia, Alberta, Saskatchewan, Manitoba and Ontario reluctantly implemented its provisions within two years, although most of them managed to shift a portion of their costs onto the municipalities. In 1931, the federal government assumed 75 percent of the cost of the pension. Still, Prince Edward Island waited until 1933 to put its plan into operation — and at the same time slashed the maximum pension by 25 percent to fifteen dollars a month. Nova Scotia implemented the plan in 1934; New Brunswick and Quebec followed in 1936. And just as sporadically as the pension was implemented by the provinces, so it was unevenly administered across the country, despite half-hearted federal efforts to ensure that a measure of uniformity would prevail.

During the Depression, the federal government was compelled to turn its attention to unemployment relief. As a result, old age pensions slid towards the bottom of the public agenda and stayed there for a decade, although near the end of his term in 1935, Tory prime minister R. B. Bennett proclaimed that it was time for a new economic system that would include unemployment and health insurance and new old-age-pension laws. In 1941, the maximum pension still stood at $240 a year, although the four western provinces, Ontario and Nova Scotia all provided meagre income supplements to the poorest of the poor. In 1943, with the unemployment problem temporarily solved by the war, the federal government increased the maximum pension temporarily to $300 a year under the War Measures Act; a year later the $365 total income limit was raised to $425. In 1947, the maximum annual pension rose to $360, and in 1949 — just prior to a general election — to $480.

But although the pension entitlement crept upwards, the eligibility restrictions remained intact. It was 1947 before the word "British" disappeared from the Act (although "Indians" were still excluded), before the pension authorities lost their claim to a pensioner's property and before the five-year provincial residency requirement was dropped. And, as always, the provinces were under no obligation to accept even modest improvements in the plan. As long as they met the requirements of the original Act, they could do as they pleased. More than half a century after the pressure for a fair and humane old age pension began to build, Canada's universal "sacred trust" for its older citizens had not yet been established.

Still, public dissatisfaction with the 1927 Act had been growing for a decade. The constant need for pensioners to prove their destitution was demoralizing and humiliating, just as thirty years earlier it had been deeply humiliating for veterans who were denied a pension solely because their wounds were emotional, not physical. Moreover, many critics of the Act believed that it was counterproductive as well. Any savings Canadians managed to accumulate as they approached retirement only had the effect of reducing their pensions. There was no incentive for them to save, even if they could afford to do so.

As early as 1938, a confidential brief had been prepared by the Finance Department for the Rowell-Sirois Commission, the body established by the federal government in 1937 to examine the "economic and financial basis of Confederation" and the "distribution of legislative powers in the light of the economic and social developments of the last seventy years." It argued that the means-tested pension was not a viable long-term solution to the problem of poverty among the elderly. Not only was it impossible to ensure that pensions were administered fairly, but clearly the future costs of the program were going to be much too high for the country to bear. Canada would pay a crippling price for its failure to introduce a contributory pension scheme.

Indeed, throughout the 1940s, as Canada plotted its future in the context of the war and of the international push to integrate and expand social welfare programs, the virtues of a contributory plan as part of a complete overhaul of the system seemed obvious to many Canadians, including Mackenzie King. In 1943, his government published Leonard Marsh's *Report on Social Security for Canada*, a wide-reaching blueprint for social security reform which caught the imagination of Canadians and attracted enormous public interest and support. Marsh's recommendations — for universal health care, family allowances and a contributory pension plan — fell upon the public consciousness with a force that politicians could not ignore.

As we have seen, King had assumed that a contributory scheme would soon replace or supplement the 1927 Act. Sixteen years later, in his 1943 Speech from the Throne, he once again raised the question of social insurance — and a contributory plan — as an urgent priority. A "comprehensive national scheme of social insurance should be worked out at once, which will constitute a charter of social security for the whole of Canada," King said. A year later, his Throne Speech again stressed the need for "a national scheme of contributory old age pensions on a more generous basis than at present in operation."

By this time, there was widespread agreement that the means-tested pension was both inadequate and inequitable. But, as usual, the perpetual constitutional struggle between Ottawa and the provinces stood in the way of genuine, sensible reform. Reluctant to jeopardize his overall objectives by engaging in a constitutional dust-up with the provinces over the right of the federal government to set up a contributory scheme, King and his advisors concocted a compromise two-tiered program in 1945. A version of that compromise was eventually enacted six years later under Louis St. Laurent in the form of the Old Age Security and Old Age Assistance Acts of 1951.

During those six years, Canadians had engaged in a spirited public debate on old age pensions. Editorial pages reflected the sense of urgency and optimism surrounding the pension issue and politicians scurried to hop on the pension bandwagon. The Canadian Congress of Labour distributed more than a million postcards to unions, and church and political groups, whose members bombarded Ottawa with demands for an immediate end to means testing. A joint committee of the Senate and House of Commons, which included MP Jean Lesage, a rising star in Quebec politics, as well as Liberal David Croll and the CCF's Stanley Knowles, both tireless crusaders for enlightened pension policies throughout their long political careers, launched an exhaustive inquiry into the matter.

Setting a precedent for deliberations on pension reform in the future, the committee conducted thirty-eight public hearings and fourteen private sessions on reform, and the Department of Health and Welfare analyzed the Canadian plan and compared it with plans in eight other countries. Opinions were sought from all quarters in an attempt to reconcile and reassure competing interests. As always, however, the voice of the corporate community was the loudest. Throughout the deliberations, business leaders complained, as they have been complaining ever since, that significant pension reform would threaten corporate profits, thus threatening the future economic well-being of the country. The Canadian Chamber of Commerce and the Canadian Life Insurance Officers Association argued, as the corporate lobby has argued ever since, that old age pensions should be kept to a bare minimum and that the government must take responsibility for making taxpayers conscious of their cost to the country so that they would not be forever demanding higher benefits.

Virtually everyone agreed by now that old-age pensions ought to be a federal responsibility and most wanted a contributory plan. But by the time the air had cleared, changes in tax regulations had encouraged more private employers to set up pension plans, meeting part of the need for a government-sponsored contributory plan. So the concept of a federal occupational plan, which by definition would not cover those who did not contribute to it, lost out to another priority: getting rid of the means test by replacing the 1927 legislation with a universal pension scheme. After six years of vigorous public debate, Ottawa, in effect, retreated to the compromise position arrived at in 1945.

Under the terms of the 1951 Old Age Security Act, all Canadians who passed a residency test became eligible for a small old-age security pension — still $40 a month (about $200 in 1989 dollars) — when they reached age seventy, regardless of how much money they had managed to save through company pensions or on their own. In addition, under the Old Age Assistance Act, those who were at least sixty-five but less than seventy years old and could demonstrate destitution — the means-test was still very much alive — were eligible for additional support, up to a maximum of a further $40 monthly, half of which would be paid by the federal government and half by the provinces.

The new programs were to be paid for by taxes — a fixed percentage of a general sales tax and of personal and corporate income taxes — especially earmarked for that purpose in an old-age-security fund. In fact, to all intents and purposes, the money was simply general tax revenue. But, politicians agreed, the public needed to *believe* that there was a limited amount of money available in a discrete fund in order to prevent old folks from making unreasonable demands for higher benefits —

shades of the old age pensions-as-moral-corruptors argument which many Canadians find so difficult to abandon even today.

In 1951, 308,825 Canadians received pensions under the terms of the 1927 Act. Under the new legislation introduced that year, the number receiving old age assistance more than doubled to nearly 700,000 — an indication of how restrictive the old legislation had been. Universality of the old age pension had finally arrived, nearly a half century after reformers had first called for it, cloaked in the great Canadian tradition of complex and inequitable compromise. The plan was politically popular, but in less than five years, inflation — the spectre that haunts Canada's pension system — had eroded the value of the old age benefit so seriously that pressure began to mount for an increase in the monthly payment. Despite the government's best efforts to hoodwink them into fiscal responsibility, pensioners had the temerity to insist that their pension benefits were too low.*

As the 1957 election approached, St. Laurent's Liberal government bowed to the growing clamour for higher benefits and raised the $40 benefit by fifteen percent, or $6 a month. That proved to be a political miscalculation: $6 a month seemed ridiculously low, even to voters to whom it meant nothing, and the Liberals were ridiculed by the opposition Tories who dubbed them the "six-buck boys." When Canadians went to the polls, they tossed out enough Liberals to install a minority Conservative government in Ottawa, making John Diefenbaker Canada's first Tory prime minister since King's Liberals had roundly defeated the Conservatives under Bennett in 1935.

The new government quickly honoured its election promises. Both the universal pension and the means-tested pension were increased — a further $9 was added to the monthly benefit — and the residence requirement was cut in half — from twenty years to ten — in part to attract political support among the country's growing immigrant population. No change was

*In 1987, 2,748,504 Canadians received the universal OAS benefit at a total cost of $9.5 billion. The average payment for the year was $3,514.95. In addition, 1,345,391, or about half of all Canadians over age sixty-five, qualified for additional government support averaging $2,614.56 for the year at a cost of $3.5 billion to the federal government.

made to the tax formula which paid for the plan. That came in 1959, after the Tories had won a massive victory in the 1958 election and after it had become even clearer that the old-age-pension "fund" was accumulating a large and politically troublesome "deficit."

The Diefenbaker government initiated sweeping studies of the adequacy of everything from the tax system to health care, including a detailed examination of old age security by University of Toronto economist Robert Clark. He concluded that the country desperately needed a contributory plan which would enable all Canadians to earn pension benefits that they could carry with them throughout their working lives. But, as always, the institution of such a plan would involve Ottawa in a head-to-head battle with the provinces. That was a confrontation Diefenbaker chose to avoid. Instead, the government settled for changes in tax rules which would encourage Canadians to save for their own retirement through Registered Retirement Savings Plans and induce trust companies and the insurance industry to expand the pension schemes available to employers.

By the time Lester Pearson became prime minister in 1963, the problem of financing the universal program in the face of demands for higher benefits had become even more urgent. As a holding device, the government turned to indexation — linking pensions automatically to increases in the cost of living — in the mistaken expectation that if benefits kept up with inflation, there would be no further political pressure to increase the real value of the pension. As had always been the case with old-age-security schemes in Canada, the benefits under the plan were too meagre to make a real difference in the quality of life for those who depended upon them. If the value of the pension was too low to begin with, indexation was a Band-Aid, not a cure.

Even so, the notion that the old age pension ought to rise with inflation was profoundly alarming to many of those familiar with its mounting costs. Even with no adjustment for inflation, critics argued, the government had committed itself to shelling out more money in the future than it could possibly afford. What was needed was not more government handouts but a contributory scheme that would improve the adequacy of old 'age pensions without depleting tax revenues. As we shall see in chapter two, such a scheme was finally introduced in 1966 in the form of the Canada Pension Plan. But while the CPP — and the equivalent Quebec Pension Plan — covered virtually the entire labour force, it did nothing to improve the often desperate situation of those older Canadians who were already retired.

In an attempt to help them, the federal government introduced the Guaranteed Income Supplement program in 1967. The GIS provided an income-tested supplement to pensioners who had no other source of income than the universal pension and was meant to be a temporary measure. Once Canadians began to collect their CPP pensions, policy makers predicted, there would be no further need to provide support for older Canadians through welfare. (It was a forlorn hope. The GIS, with its overtones of grudging charity to the destitute, is still with us.) At the same time, the extent of the poverty in which many pensioners lived shamed provincial governments into providing them with income supplements. In a pattern which by the 1970s was sadly familiar, the "universal" program that was designed to restore a measure of dignity to the elderly poor had driven them onto the welfare rolls instead.

In truth, Canada's "sacred trust" for its older citizens was both mean-spirited and opportunistic. Yet the myth that society provided adequately for its older citizens was enshrined. The principle of universal benefits for the elderly, however inadequate they might be for those who truly needed them, had become a powerful weapon in the hands of politicians.

Brian Mulroney learned a thing or two about the political potency of universality after the Tories swept into power on September 4, 1984. By then, the preservation of the sacred trust — an issue which surfaced almost accidentally in a campaign focused on jobs, jobs, jobs — had become a political albatross. As prime minister, Mulroney stuck to his guns as his critics continued to insist that the Tories secretly planned to launch an attack on universality despite their rhetoric to the contrary. In the House of Commons on December 19, 1984, three months after he took office, Mulroney angrily denied suggestions from both opposition parties that his government intended to fire an opening volley at the concept by levying a special tax on upper-income Canadians receiving Old Age Security pensions. Repeating his "sacred trust" promise, Mulroney accused the Liberals of distorting his words and the New Democrats of hypocrisy. If the NDP had their way, he charged, their own party policies would have "the effect of destroying the principle of universality, which we want to maintain." And, he added, "Any time you try to take that away from the elderly we'll put up the biggest fight you've ever seen."

Later that afternoon, outside the House of Commons, reporters pressed Michael Wilson, Mulroney's dour and determined finance minister, to clarify the government's position. Only a month earlier Wilson had told a Vancouver audience that it was entirely possible that Canada could no longer afford its universal social programs. Once again he appeared to flatly contradict the prime minister. The government, Wilson declared, intended to keep all of its options open, including the option of taxing back Old Age Security pensions from the elderly. "We've made it quite clear we want to shift some resources from the upper-income brackets, from the wealthier people in this country to the needy in this country," Wilson said, adding that this objective could well mean targeting wealthy pensioners. The government, he added, was now ready to initiate a public discussion on just how its goals could be achieved.

In the House of Commons two days later, federal Health Minister Jake Epp lambasted the opposition parties for attempting to create a "false image of our party as the enemy of the poor and the disadvantaged." Then he took a run at reconciling Mulroney's and Wilson's seemingly contradictory positions on universality. There was to be no special tax on old age pensions, he said. The goverment simply wanted to examine *all* social benefits for families and the elderly. In any event, any money freed up by changes to the system would be spent on other social programs. "The real fear of the opposition parties is not that we will dismantle these social programs, but that we will make them more rational and equitable," Epp declared. And, he added testily, "Our families also grow old. They also get ill. We also have compassion."

In January Epp announced that the government had concluded that no changes to old-age-security programs were necessary. But the suspicion that the Tories had a hidden agenda raged unabated, a suspicion fuelled by the growing emphasis both Mulroney and Wilson were placing on deficit-reduction. It was an issue which both had eschewed in the election campaign of the previous summer. But by the time Wilson brought down his budget on May 23, 1985, the government had decided to take a different tack on pensions — and on universality. In the budget, which he predicted would "sell by itself," Wilson declared that he intended to reduce OAS costs, not by levying a special tax on high-income recipients, but by limiting the inflation protection built into the plan. Senior citizens would understand, Wilson said, because they were not fools. They knew that the money was needed in the campaign to lower the deficit.

Wilson's plan to index old age pensions only when the annual inflation rate exceeded three percent did not sell by itself. Senior citizens whose private pensions had already been decimated by inflation did not understand. Instead they banded together in protest across the country. As support for their campaign mounted, it became clear that Wilson and Mulroney had miscalculated. A move which struck indiscriminately at the most vulnerable group in society was not going to fly — deficit or no deficit. The Great De-Indexation Fight was on.

What was all the excitement about? In part, certainly, it was about Brian Mulroney's credibility. The prime minister appeared to have said one thing — that he had no intention of reducing the financial support available to older Canadians — and to have allowed his advisors to do quite another. Furthermore, the Tories had said that they intended to tax the well-to-do. Now, it seemed, they wanted to penalize the poor as well. But it was also about the long-term social consequences of the limited de-indexation called for in the budget: for more than a decade many pensioners had watched as inflation ravaged the real value of their private pensions. Now the government wanted to ravage the real value of their OAS benefits as well.

After a brief, stunned silence, the protest against the government's plans rumbled across the country. The Canadian Council on Social Development estimated that the proposal to de-index would mean that 200,000 more Canadians — an increase of more than 20 percent — would slip below the poverty line by 1990. The Advisory Council on Aging said that 1.1 million Canadians could be forced to delay their retirement in order to survive and that many older people already retired would be forced into publicly-financed health-care institutions, because they would no longer be able to afford to live in their own homes. Usually polite and restrained organizations became suddenly militant. The New Brunswick Senior Citizens' Federation, for one, announced that it would launch a national campaign to fight the budget's provisions, which the organization's executive director, Bernard Richard, labelled "immoral, indecent and dishonest." The budget, he told a Liberal task force, "stinks and it sucks."

By mid-June, the stream of protest had become a flood and the government was running out of friends. Three major business lobbies on which Mulroney and Wilson had counted for support, the Canadian Chamber of Commerce, the Business Council on National Issues and the Canadian Organization of Small Business, scrambled to dissociate themselves from de-indexation. Even Tory backbenchers broke ranks to criticize the budget's provisions. Not for the last time, Mulroney's credibility was squarely on the line. The headline in the *Globe and Mail* on June 20, 1985, summed it up: "PM faces politician's nightmare over Canadian pension furor."

Once underway, the protest was unstoppable. Hundreds of pensioners packed their bags and headed for Ottawa to protest the scheme. At the same time, the opposition parties kept up a relentless attack on the budget. Turner, addressing a Liberal meeting in Fredericton, thundered, somewhat illogically, that Wilson's assertion that the budget was "tough but fair" would "go down in Canadian history, along with some other famous sayings: 'Let them eat cake,' and 'a chicken in every pot.'" In the House of Commons Ed Broadbent waved a telegram from the National Pensioners' and Senior Citizens' Federation at the government benches and shouted, "That's 400,000 Canadian pensioners who think that the government is wrong. Did you get that? They're saying that you're wrong."

Mulroney and Wilson did get it. After a brief attempt to hold the line, a grim Michael Wilson announced in the House on June 28 that he had abandoned his plans to partially de-index pensions. Instead, the $15 million the government had expected to save that year and the $245 million it had expected to save the next would be raised by an increase in corporate and gasoline taxes. A chastened Brian Mulroney even delivered an apology of sorts: "We never contended that we were perfect."

The seniors' revolt was directed specifically against the de-indexation of the Old Age Security pension. But it carried a broader message as well: that many Canadians were not prepared to tolerate a government which threatened to divert yet more of the severely limited financial resources of many older Canadians to the government, deficit or no deficit. It was also a warning to politicians in this country, whatever their political stripe. The rapidly growing army of older Canadians now has the numbers to make its wishes count. Age is becoming an ever more powerful political influence in Canada, even more powerful than such traditionally potent forces as race, class and sex. The growing numbers of older people — and the rapidly shrinking numbers of the young — in the rich industrialized societies of the West have implications for the future that Canadians are only beginning to comprehend. As Brian Mulroney discovered to his extreme discomfort, we will ignore them at our peril.

2

THE CANADA PENSION PLAN

WHERE HAS ALL THE MONEY GONE?

::

"It is already almost impossible, barely a generation later, to appreciate what strong emotions, interest, and political pressures in 1963-4 clashed around the idea of a comprehensive pension plan. It was denounced as a fraud and as certain to bring the ruin of the nation. It was caught so much in the tensions of changing federal-provincial relations that no sensible man should have been prepared to wager, in late 1963 or early 1964, that it would be achieved in foreseeable time."

Tom Kent, advisor to Prime Minister Lester Pearson,
A Public Purpose, 1988

"Whatever the ethics of this kind of an operation may be, it is what banks do, but they seem to have a better reputation for being trustworthy in the handling of other people's money than politicians."

Judy LaMarsh,
Memoirs of a Bird in a Gilded Cage, 1968

..

In December 1985, just six months after his retreat from the ill-fated assault on the OAS pension, Finance Minister Michael Wilson told Canadians that they would soon be paying more into the Canada Pension Plan each month. Benefits would be improved for some plan members, Wilson said, and the increased contribution rates would guarantee the financial health of the Plan for "decades to come." The higher rates would ensure that each generation of working Canadians would contribute fairly to the cost of the pension benefits they will eventually receive. The increase was both necessary and inevitable, Wilson added, because if contributions to the CPP did not increase, the Plan would be "totally depleted" by the year 2003.

The increase in CPP rates received little media attention, in part because few people disagreed with Wilson's basic assessment. The Canada Pension Plan was, in fact, about to go broke. Yet the need for the increase in contribution rates was not quite so straightforward as Wilson would have had us believe. The majority of Canadians don't have the foggiest idea how the Canada Pension Plan works. How could they make a judgement about the level of contribution rates and when — or if — they needed to rise?

There is a reason for this befuddlement. For twenty years Canadians had been led to believe that a "contribution" of 3.6 percent of their pensionable earnings to the Plan would secure them a modest inflation-protected pension on retirement day. Now they had been told that it was not enough; they would have to pay more for their pensions. But if the choice was between higher contribution rates and a bankrupt plan, what choice did they have? Obviously the rates would have to go up.

And so they did. On January 1, 1987, the contribution rate to the Quebec and Canada Pension Plans increased for the first time since the plans were introduced in 1966. The rate increased again on January 1, 1988, just as it will increase each year for twenty-three years more until the year 2011. By then, unless Ottawa and the provinces agree to raise it even further, the rate at which Canadians and their employers pay into the plan will rise to 7.6 percent of pensionable earnings — almost four times the rate the architects of the plan believed would be enough to provide a fair measure of retirement security to Canadians until at least the end of the century.

Not only that, the rates were going up despite the fact that, like Old Age Security, the Canada Pension Plan — and its Quebec counterpart, the Quebec Pension Plan (Régime des Rentes du Québec) — have never delivered adequate levels of income security to older Canadians. On January 1, 1989, the combined Old Age Security and maximum QPP/CPP benefits added up to just $879.53 a month, or an annual income of $10,554.36. And that figure, inadequate as it is, assumes that the recipient was entitled to a full pension, which the great majority of retirees, including most women, are not. Canada's public pension system, designed to guarantee basic income security in retirement for *all* Canadians, has in fact forced hundreds of thousands of older Canadians onto welfare.

What was going on here anyway? What had gone wrong with the Canada Pension Plan?

The answers to those questions lie in the troubled history of Canada's first contributory pension plan and in Canadians' traditional ambivalence about income support for the elderly. As country after country introduced broad social welfare programs in the 1940s, optimism ran high in the Western world that with careful and enlightened management the most blatant inequities of modern industrial society could be relieved. In Canada, a dramatic post-war economic boom had led to a rapid improvement in living standards for most people. The average household income at the time was growing at an annual rate of about three and a half percent. And with prosperity came a brave new commitment to guaranteed social security for every Canadian, young or old, rich or poor.

But although the country was better able than ever before to seek fair and effective ways to redistribute its wealth, the inevitable struggle over revenues and authority between Ottawa and the provinces had once again stood in the way of co-ordinated planning and comprehesive reform. As a result, Canada's new social welfare programs arrived piecemeal: the Unemployment Insurance Act in 1940; the Family Allowance Act in 1944; the universal Old Age Pension in 1951 — or not at all, as was the case with a proposal for a joint federal-provincial medical and hospital insurance plan in 1945.

It was hardly surprising that the programs satisfied no one. On the one hand, welfare specialists argued that the piecemeal approach was both inadequate and unfair. Politicians who cynically courted votes with promises of improved old-age pensions, they insisted, were effectively standing in the way of reform to other parts of the welfare system. On the other hand, older Canadians, especially in the large urban centres, who were trying to make do on their monthly pension cheques complained bitterly that it was impossible to live on the amount they were allotted each month. The business lobby and many government planners, for their part, were increasingly alarmed by rapidly escalating expenditures on the social programs, including old age pensions. The schemes, they warned, were dangerously close to becoming a fatal drag on economic development and had already become a threat to the country's long-term fiscal well-being. How could the politicians who so blithely promised higher pensions today be certain that the country could afford to pay for them tomorrow?

At the same time, it was impossible to ignore the fact that, in the midst of the best times most Canadians had ever known, thousands of older people were living in miserable poverty. Journalists regularly documented the desperate lives of single men and women starving in squalid lodgings which, dreadful as they were, gobbled up the greater part of their monthly pension allotments. "In a dark and cheerless room in downtown Toronto Miss Phoebe Grant, a tiny, wrinkled woman of 76, lives alone and almost friendless," began a 1949 *Maclean's* magazine article headlined "Pension Poverty." "She subsists on an old-age pension of $40 month and her life is a prolonged nightmare of scrimping and cheap buying.... All her bargain-hunting is devoted to food because she pays $24 of her pension for rent."

The dreary litany of suffering and hardship which followed showed that Miss Phoebe Grant was by no means unique. For although single elderly women have always been the prime victims of the pension system in Canada, the situation for many older men after the war was little better. Canada had entered the Depression still as a mainly agricultural society, but it emerged from the Second World War heavily urbanized and industrialized — and with dramatically altered notions of what constituted family, work and retirement. As the exodus from rural Canada to the cities and towns continued unabated, older men found it steadily more difficult to find work. In 1921, for example, nearly two-thirds of all Canadian men over age sixty-five were employed. By 1941 that number had dropped to 47.9 percent and by 1951 fewer than two in five were working. Despite the booming economy, the factories and industries of the cities had little use for aging employees, who, it was said, were difficult to train, were prone to accidents, and were too weak to withstand the rigours of heavy industrial work.

Not only was it harder for aging men and women to find work, but many older Canadians, who had endured the privations of the Depression in their prime working years, had accumulated virtually no retirement savings. At the same time, life expectancies, particularly among women, were increasing. In 1960, a man of sixty-five could expect to live for another thirteen years, a woman of sixty-five for another sixteen. So while many older Canadians had little or nothing in the way of savings, through absolutely no fault of their own, what little they had managed to save was also going to have to last them longer.

Even after the introduction of the universal pension in 1951, thousands of Canadians had suffered a sharp and humiliating decline in their living standards when they ceased to work — and thousands more would face the same prospect in the future unless something was done. And while politicians and business-men could argue endlessly over whether the government or the private sector was better able to look after Canadians' retirement needs in the future, the reality of the present could no longer be ignored: the needs of older people were not being adequately met.

As a result, the widening gap between the elderly poor and the prosperous middle classes was becoming a potent political issue, pushing the OAS benefit upwards with every election. By 1959 it had risen to $65 a month — nearly double in real dollars the value of the original means-tested pension introduced in 1927. These increases helped to alleviate the dire circumstances in which many elderly Canadians found themselves, but they also prompted a vigorous backlash: if benefits rose any higher, critics argued, many older people would receive more money when they retired than they had ever earned when they were working. With the implications of high inflation for retirement income still largely unrecognized, most people seem not to have considered that, as inflation climbed from zero in 1955 to 3.1 percent in 1957, perhaps it made some sense that benefits should take note of inflation.

By the early 1960s, with OAS benefits at $75 a month, pension authorities were pointing out that 2.5 million working Canadians earned less each month than the $150 a retired man and his wife together would receive from Old Age Security each month. That argument, of course, ignored not only inflation, but the fact that more than half of all Canadian women over age seventy and 40 percent of elderly men were widowed or had never married. It swayed public opinion nonetheless. At the same time, somewhat paradoxically, government experts continued to insist that most of Canada's pensioners lived comfortably with their children, despite the fact, as the 1961 census confirmed, that fewer than one in five Canadians over age sixty-five lived with relatives.

Predictably, the upward movement of the universal pension came under heavy attack from the business community too. Pensioners' constant demands for higher benefits, it was said, amounted to little more than a boondoggle that would inevitably lead the country along a slippery path to economic ruin. And there was a broader indictment of the social programs from the business establishment as well: *all* Canadians, it seemed, had come to expect far too much from their governments and their employers. In July 1957 William Mercer, president of Canada's largest firm of actuaries and pension consultants wrote:

> Mass production and advertising have created an insatiable demand for material things. It becomes important for us to have a car with vertical tail fins. When the stylists replace vertical tail fins with horizontal fins, we shall feel compelled to go along. To keep up with the Joneses we are not only unable to save for the future, we actually mortgage our future to get what we think we need today. We feel we must look to our employer or the government to take care of our future.

Mercer blamed this sorry state of affairs not just on rampant materialism, but on the weakening of family loyalties, on the disappearance of craftsmanship and above all on a "change in religious outlook." The world's great religions, he pointed out sternly, taught people to "seek spiritual security and not to be anxious about tomorrow." Wasn't it odd, he wondered, that "we go to church as much as we ever did but we seem to want security for this world as well as the next."

Well, perhaps it *was* inexplicable that poorer Canadians wanted to live out their days knowing where their next meal would come from. That was bad enough. But what really alarmed many people in the early sixties was that there appeared to be no way to prevent even greater demands on the public purse in the future. By 1964, a million Canadians were drawing OAS benefits and two and a half million Canadians had no income or incomes so low that they paid no personal income tax at all. Taken together, these two groups added up to nearly half of the entire electorate. Not only did these voters have the numbers to demand increases in OAS benefits at absolutely no cost to themselves, but their votes added up to a powerful incentive for politicians to up the pension ante every time an election loomed.

These various and sometimes contradictory objections to Canada's old-age-pension arrangements soon coalesced in a general consensus that the time had finally come to force all Canadians — and their employers — to contribute a substantial portion of their own retirement security. Having settled on a universal pension as the best remedy for poverty among the elderly only ten years earlier, many people accepted as a tenet of faith that if the OAS actually provided enough income for a pensioner to get by on, the country would soon be beggared.

In the 1958 election campaign, the Liberals under Lester Pearson had included a commitment to a national occupational pension scheme in their platform. By 1961, that general commitment had become a firm promise, a manifestation, as Pearson's confidant and advisor Tom Kent puts it in his 1988 autobiography, *A Public Purpose*, of Pearson's sense as a liberal historian of "the movement of human affairs, of change generally for the better." The Diefenbaker Tories had acknowledged the need for such a plan too, although they had done nothing to speed it along. The CCF — which became the New Democratic Party in August of that year — had long supported the concept. So as Canada headed into another general election in 1963, all three federal parties were publicly committed to measures which would shift at least some of the responsibility for old age security more directly onto the shoulders of individual Canadians and their employers. More than three-quarters of a century after Bismarck's early experiments with government-sponsored employment-based pensions, Canada was at last ready for a contributory pension plan.

When Pearson's Liberals squeaked into power with a minority government in March 1963, they were determined to move quickly on the pension issue. Pearson handed the daunting task of overseeing the plan and shepherding it through Parliament to Niagara Falls MP Judy LaMarsh. LaMarsh was astonished by the assignment, she admitted later in her outspoken 1968 autobiography, *Memoirs of a Bird in a Gilded Cage*. The feisty MP was painfully aware that she knew next to nothing about the design of pension plans. Indeed, her own top priority was the creation of a national health scheme. But as Pearson's minister of health and welfare, she plunged into the complexities of setting up the new plan with characteristic verve — and with the considerable expertise of an influential interdepartmental team which included deputy minister of welfare Joe Willard, and Pearson's own chief advisor, Tom Kent, behind her.

Although much work had already been done on the Liberals' pension proposal by Pearson's new finance minister, Walter Gordon, among others, LaMarsh and her experts faced a Herculean task: Pearson wanted draft legislation ready to present to Parliament in time for the upcoming session. So with the pressure on, the beleaguered team quickly settled on the two main problems which needed to be addressed: first, the new plan must provide an adequate minimum income for all Canadians who were able to contribute to their own future savings, whether or not they belonged to a private pension plan; and, second, the benefits of both the new plan *and the private plans* should be made portable: employees should not lose their accumulated pension benefits simply because they moved on to a new job. If Canadians were to be obliged to put aside the greater part of their own retirement income throughout their working lives, the rules should at the very least ensure that they would receive what they had earned.

Defining the goals was the easy part. Realizing them was another matter.* The plan, LaMarsh quickly realized, was enormously intricate and fraught with political peril. Decisions had to be made on difficult matters: vesting (How long did employees need to contribute to the scheme before they "earned" a pension?); universality (Would the plan include all workers or only those who earned above a specified amount? Would it apply to every industry?); coverage (Would the plan provide other benefits, such as disability pensions? Would it cover dependents?); age of eligibility (What should "normal" retirement age be? Should employees be allowed to continue to contribute to the plan after they had passed that age?). But more difficult was the fact that the plan had to be sold to the provinces. Without their agreement, there would be no federal plan at all.

LaMarsh was confident that a scheme could be devised which would both pay for itself for the foreseeable future with a contribution rate of 2 percent of pensionable earnings shared between employees and their employers, and finance an immediate increase in the universal pension to boot. Underlying that confidence was one fundamental assumption: that, as LaMarsh put it, there would be a "steadily increasing number of workers entering the labour field, to balance those leaving it, until at least the end of this century." The plan would be unfunded: benefits would be paid out of incoming contributions, so there would be no "pension fund" per se, and, if necessary,

*

---

*Private pensions, which fall under provincial, not federal, jurisdiction are *still* not fully portable across the country. As for the goal of providing an "adequate" minimum income: the current combined CPP and OAS benefit speaks for itself.

contribution rates could be gradually raised in the future as the plan matured.

In setting up the federal plan, though, the Liberals had to contend not only with the provinces, but with the insurance companies who saw the scheme as an intrusion on their turf — which, of course, it was. The industry mounted a massive campaign against the plan, incurring the wrath of everyone involved in its conception. The industry could claim expertise about private plans, recalls Kent, but "about a public plan they lacked understanding as thoroughly as they exuded self-interest." LaMarsh, as usual, minced no words when she wrote about the insurance lobby later: "The opposition of the insurance companies is a shameful chapter in the history of Canadian business, and I hope no industry ever tries so blatant an attack upon a duly elected Government again. In any event, despite its expense, it failed, in the long run. But it was cussedly troublesome to me."*

The greatest provincial stumbling block was Quebec. As the Quiet Revolution swept through the province after Maurice Duplessis's death in 1959, the Liberals who soared into power on the wings of reform were devising a bold and far-reaching agenda that would spell trouble for the federal plan. Fuelled by the economic vision of Jacques Parizeau and the charismatic leadership of Premier Jean Lesage, the province's new mood of cultural nationalism translated into an urgent push for social and economic change. But the last thing Lesage and Parizeau wanted was a revolution orchestrated in Ottawa, with its anglophone preoccupations and traditions. Quebec intended to conduct its revolution with as little federal interference as possible.

Parizeau and Lesage were convinced that if Quebec could gain control over all of the province's contributions to the new plan, it would acquire a powerful economic and political weapon. Not only did social welfare programs comprise an

---

*There are those who would argue, with justification, that the insurance industry is cussedly troublesome to this day in its attempts to block long-overdue pension reform out of sheer self-interest.

integral part of Quebec culture, but a provincially-operated scheme offered a golden opportunity to amass the investment capital needed to undertake the sweeping economic reforms Parizeau envisioned. If Quebec and not Ottawa were to administer the contributory plan for Quebeckers, the province would have free use of the money until it was needed, down the line, to meet provincial pension obligations. Furthermore, if there were to be a twenty-year transition period before contributors became eligible for the maximum pension, "down the line" seemed a long time away — long enough, certainly, for Quebec to launch its bold leap into the twentieth century.

Quebec's intentions constituted a major setback for Ottawa, as both LaMarsh and Kent later made clear in their accounts of the province's hurried attempts to devise its own plan in time to pre-empt the federal scheme. Quebec wanted the money in the fund to fill "the desperate need of the Lesage Government for ever-greater sources of finances," LaMarsh fumed, adding that "whatever the ethics of this kind of an operation may be, it is what banks do, but they seem to have a better reputation for being trustworthy in the handling of other people's money than politicians."

The Liberals' problem was twofold and it was serious. Not only did Quebec want its own plan, but the province could scupper the scheme for the rest of the country by withholding its consent to the federal plan. So it came as a relief to the Liberals when, at a federal-provincial conference in July 1963, Lesage announced that Quebec intended to implement a separate plan, but that he would not stand in the way of a federal plan for the rest of the country. Even so, Quebec's determination to have its own plan meant that Ottawa's plans for an unfunded scheme were, as Kent put it, "dead in the water." His own solution at that point was to abandon the plan altogether in favour of a significant increase in the OAS, leaving employment pensions to the provinces. Kent knew, however, that such a course was not politically practicable for it would require a large and immediate increase in federal taxes. It was a pity, he notes wistfully, because it "would have saved the Pearson government a great deal of stress."

Indeed it would have. When Quebec did unveil its own plan in 1964 — Pearson's timetable had by now been abandoned — its contents came as something of an embarrassment to the federal planners. From some points of view, and certainly in the view of the provinces, it was a superior plan to the one devised by Ottawa. Not only was it better funded through higher contribution rates; it also provided higher maximum benefits and included survivor, disability and death benefits as well. And Lesage's insistence that contributions from Quebec should remain in Quebec gave the other provinces a good idea. Perhaps they ought to insist on a piece of the action too.

Following Quebec's lead, the provinces pushed for and eventually won a formula that would allow them to get their hands on sizeable chunks of investment money too. Ottawa's dream of an unfunded pay-as-you-go plan that would in the long run more or less balance contributions coming in with benefits going out was finished. With Quebec adamant and Ontario premier John Robarts threatening to set up a separate provincial plan too, it was time for Ottawa to compromise once again.

Behind LaMarsh's back, as she angrily pointed out later, an agreement was worked out which in effect transformed the plan from a pay-as-you-go scheme to a partially funded one. Quebec would have its own plan, a scheme providing benefits virtually identical to those guaranteed by the federal plan but managed exclusively by the province. At the same time, Pearson offered the rest of the provinces two choices: they could either administer the CPP themselves or they could borrow "surplus" money from a federally-administered "fund" at advantageous interest rates.

The compromise plan set the retirement benefit at 25 percent of a specified upper limit on contributions — "maximum pensionable earnings" — and, borrowing from the Quebec proposal, made provision for survivor, death and disability benefits. The agreed-upon 3.6 percent annual contribution rate was lower than the 4 percent rate Quebec had wanted, but higher than the 2 percent rate Ottawa had originally proposed. Self-employed workers would pay both employer and employee shares themselves. With annual inflation running at between 1 and 2 percent, benefits were to be partially indexed through a cost of living adjustment up to a maximum of 2 percent, as Quebec wanted. And in line with Ottawa's proposals, low-earning years would be excluded from the formula that determined the pension benefit.

In an effort to ensure that the plan would help older Canadians in the near future — even if they had contributed very little to the plan by the time they retired — Ottawa nailed down a ten-year transition period, despite Quebec's preference for the longer twenty-year delay before full benefits would kick in. Quebec, Ontario, the Tory opposition and the business lobby had all argued strenuously in favour of a longer transition period, partly on the grounds that in a contributory plan employees should earn their pensions before they receive them. But Ottawa prevailed, arguing that it was not going to solve any problems to exclude all Canadians then over age forty-five from full benefits when they retired, even if that meant, as it did, that their contributions would not cover the full cost of their benefits.

As for funding, the provinces settled upon option two: Ottawa would administer the plan; the provinces would be entitled to borrow from any surplus in direct proportion to the contributions originating in their own jurisdictions. The partial funding arrangement was actually a compromise between those who wanted the Quebec and Canada plans to be fully funded to order to avoid massive intergenerational transfers from taxpayers to the elderly and those who wanted a plan that would be funded on a pay-as-you-go basis.

So the Canada Pension Plan became a hybrid beast with funding arrangements which can best be described as bizarre. From one point of view, the Plan functions as the unfunded, pay-as-you-go plan that Ottawa wanted in the first place. Under the terms of the compromise, all CPP contributions would be, in effect, allocated to general revenues. In return, the federal government promised to meet its pension obligations as they came due from the money it would collect from taxpayers in the future. This approach treats contributions to the plan as a tax as was originally envisioned, and not as an investment which accumulates in a pension "fund," is invested prudently, earns interest and is returned to plan members in the form of a monthly pension cheque when they retire. In fact, there is no fund. The money contributors receive as a pension is not the same money they paid into the plan. *That* money has been used to pay current pensions — or for other purposes which we shall discuss shortly.

This was an arrangement that was widely misunderstood at the time, even by the prime minister himself, Tom Kent points out. The attraction of the plan for Pearson, Kent notes, was not only that it would enable Canadians to retire "in security and with dignity," but that people "put money in when they earned it and took it out later." Pearson, Kent recalls, finally did come to understand, and welcome, the fact that a public pension plan with a short maturity period — paying full pensions only ten years after its inception — was in fact a considerable redistribution in favour of older workers who had not been able to build up retirement savings during the Depression and the war. But the prime minister, he adds, "never did get his mind round the fact that compulsory pension contributions from employers and employees are a payroll tax."

Pearson's confusion is a confusion that most Canadians share to this day. It is not hard to understand why. Because from another point of view there is indeed a "fund." There must be. The provinces, as is their right under the founding legislation, have been borrowing from it for years. Indeed, they have been borrowing from it at advantageous interest rates on a pro rata basis relative to provincial contributions, and they have also been borrowing the interest owing on what they have borrowed. And it is not clear that they ever can or will pay it back.

Outside Quebec, Revenue Canada collects all CPP contributions and places them in an account from which expenses and plan benefits are paid. Any "surplus" assets are deposited in a CPP "Investment Fund." The "surplus" assets in the plan may be borrowed by the provinces at a rate equal to the average yield on long-term Government of Canada bonds, a lower rate than most provinces could arrange on their own. All of these "loans" are for a twenty-year term, although the federal government has an option to call for repayment on six months' notice. This option has never been exercised and it never will be.

For the provinces don't have the money either. They have long since spent it on highways and bridges and community halls, on schools and universities, on megaprojects and bail-outs and loans to private industry. Many of these investments were necessary and beneficial, many were not. But either way, the money is gone. As a result, the "pension fund" that most Canadians believed would provide them with guaranteed retirement security has disappeared. And the only way governments can get it back is to raise our taxes. Under the circumstances, it is no wonder that Michael Wilson needed our money and that the provincial governments agreed that he should have it.

The success of the quintessentially Canadian compromise on an employment-based contributory plan was short-lived, even by Canadian standards. In 1975, Geoffrey Calvert, a distinguished New Zealand-born actuary who had, among other things, created a pioneering statistical data bank for the World Bank in Washington, D.C., published *Pensions and Survival*, an apocalyptic treatise that sent shock waves through the highly politicized world of pensions. Drawing on his statistical tools, Calvert warned that the Canada Pension Plan was a disaster waiting to happen. One of the remarkable things about Canada's public pension systems, Calvert pointed out, was that no one had ever measured the extent of their commitments — commitments that would have to be honoured by future taxpayers — or where those commitments would lead.

No one seemed to know or care, he said, what happened to the money the provinces borrowed from the CPP. In the four years to March 31, 1974, the Plan had furnished the provinces with $4.67 billion — 38 percent of all provincial borrowing — at favourable rates of interest. As a result, the Canada Pension Plan was going to run out of money. For more than a decade, the CPP had taken in more money in contributions than it had paid out in benefits. But that balance was about to shift. Unless something was done, Calvert predicted, the plan would be bankrupt before the end of the century. "The party," he warned, "will soon be over."

An enormous mistake had been made, Calvert said, when Ottawa agreed to the provinces' demands for a "funded" plan. Canadians would be far better off with a plan that really was "funded" in the usual sense of the word. Then surplus contributions could be channelled into private markets, instead of into the sinkhole of provincial election promises. The Quebec plan made far more sense, he added, because at least a portion of the fund was invested at market rates. And indeed, the Quebec plan *has* consistently outperformed its federal counterpart, averaging an annual rate of return between two and three percent higher than the CPP over most of its history. In addition, Quebec has led the way in improving benefits and widening coverage for plan members. Most of the changes introduced into the CPP in 1987 — including the division of pension credits between spouses, a drop-out provision for parents with young children and a flexible retirement age — were pioneered and introduced first in the Quebec plan.

By 1984, the giant Caisse de Dépôt et Placement du Québec, the investment agency which administers the provincial pension fund, controlled assets of $9.2 billion, nearly eighty percent of which belonged to the Quebec Pension Plan. Its stock portfolio alone that year was worth $3.2 billion, the largest pool of equity in Canada. Two years later, the agency's assets had grown to $25.2 billion, making it the country's eighth-largest financial institution and the largest player in Canadian markets. And, indeed, the fund had fulfilled the great expectations Lesage and Parizeau had for it, providing the capital essential for Quebec's economic transformation.

However, in recent years the Caisse has come under increasing fire for its inefficiency, its susceptibility to political interference and its sheer size and enormous powers. Its preferential borrowing rates to the Quebec Government have led to many of the same problems encountered by the CPP. Like other Canadians, Quebeckers have not received maximum returns on their investment in the fund, and they now face the same increases in contribution rates. Nonetheless, it seems clear that that loss has been more than compensated through economic development.

Calvert's book has been enormously influential in all subsequent attempts to set the pension system right, but his solution to the "ghastly" situation he described in *Pensions and Survival* — that Ottawa cut the provinces off and start funding the plan immediately — fell mainly upon deaf ears. His remedy did not go entirely unnoticed, however. Opposition parties have been using it to club provincial governments ever since. In 1981, for example, Ontario MPP David Peterson, speaking as Liberal finance critic, told a provincial committee on pensions that Ontario's $9-billion debt to the plan was "a great theft" from the beneficiaries of the CPP: "It is beyond my logic that the provinces owe $17 billion to the CPP and they don't plan to pay it back. Just how do you justify that?"

Then-treasurer Frank Miller, who as William Davis's successor as premier was soon to lead the Ontario Tories into obscurity, responded: "I find it hard to understand that you say I should pay off the pension debt and you complain bitterly when I raise taxes to balance the budget." He added that Peterson should know that if the provinces had not borrowed from the CPP, they would simply have borrowed the money privately at even greater expense to the taxpayer.

Perhaps so. Perhaps not. What is certain is that if the money were available, the provinces were going to borrow it, even if the CPP *were* going broke. The vast surpluses in the CPP fund — which existed simply because every working Canadian was paying into the fund while few pensions were being paid out — were an irresistible temptation for provincial politicians who could borrow the money without accounting for it to anyone. By 1983, CPP loans to the provinces and the federal government itself had risen to $24.6 billion and change. Ontario alone was in hock to the tune of $13.1 billion, British Columbia for $3.7 billion. As the system matured — that is, as more pensions began to be paid out — these loans left the federal government with an unfunded liability of growing proportions. By March 31, 1985, outstanding loans had risen to $27.6 billion. Either they would have to be recalled, or contribution rates would have to rise.

Few provinces have even attempted to analyze where the money has gone. Ontario, which has borrowed about 46 percent of the fund since it began in 1966, is an exception to that rule. *In Whose Interest?*, a report released in 1988 by an Ontario task force on the investment of public-sector pension funds, concluded that the money should have been better spent and better controlled. It also recommended that CPP money borrowed in the future should be deposited in a new investment fund "at arm's length from the Government" and channelled into market investments. By investing the assets of three of the provinces' own vast public employer pension plans — the Teachers Superannuation Fund (TSS), the Public Service Superannuation Fund (PSSF) and the Superannuation Adjustment Funds (SAF) — in the free market, the report estimated, the plans could earn, on average, at least 1 percent a year more than in the past. Over a ten-year period, that 1 percent would translate into at least $1.2 billion and could range as high as $2.2 billion or more.

The CPP, clearly, could also earn a higher rate of return than it does. But while improved returns would be a help, they would not solve all of the Canada Pension Plan's accumulated problems. In the two and a half decades since the Quebec and Canada Pension Plans were introduced, politicians have been less than candid with Canadians about the problems which beset the CPP. They have allowed us to believe that we will get what we have paid for, that our savings in the Canada Pension Plan are as "safe" as they would be in the bank. They have avoided using the word "taxation" and they have justified abuses of the fund in terms of all the good things those favourable-interest provincial loans have provided for society. There is doubtless truth to these arguments; but it is impossible to measure how much truth. Nobody really knows how well the provinces have spent the money or even where it has been spent.

Your own views on the uses that have been made of your money will probably have a lot to do with your political convictions, with the province in which you happen to live and with whether or not you believe Michael Wilson when he assures Canadians that the increases to the QPP/CPP contribution rates were inevitable now for the reasons he said they were. For in pushing for the rate increases, Wilson ignored the advice of his own CPP advisory committee, a body of outside pension experts working with the most recent actuarial report on the Plan by the federal Department of Insurance. The rate hikes were not needed at all until 1994, according to the committee's report. After that, a decade of modest increases would have been appropriate, to be followed by steeper increases "if necessary" when the time comes.

When he announced the rate increases, Wilson said that he had two options: to increase premium rates gradually or to wait until the fund was "bankrupt" and then double them. The first option, which he chose, is perhaps less painful — the increase amounted to a "mere" forty-six cents a week for most contributors in 1987. But, like a used-car salesman who assures you that the price of the car is "just a pack of cigarettes a day," there was little talk of how that forty-six cents — and all of the increases to come — will compound over the course of the twenty-five-year period. What cost you a "mere" $24.10 extra in 1987 will cost you $457.90 extra in 1987 dollars in 2012.

The rate increase slid through with virtually no political opposition and very little fuss from plan members, whose contribution rates had just been doubled with no significant improvement in their retirement benefits. Ottawa, in concert with the provinces, had managed to raise Canadians' taxes without so much as breathing the dreaded phrase "tax increase." Moreover, because low-income earners pay a higher proportion of their total earnings into the plan than upper-income earners, their taxes had been raised disproportionately at precisely the time when the Tory government was publicly committed to easing the tax burden for low-income Canadians.

And ironically, even though his scheme ensured that the provinces would be able to continue borrowing massive amounts of money from the plans, provincial finance ministers were unhappy with Michael Wilson, because he proposed a decrease in the level of transfer payments to the provinces in the future. The cash flow of the CPP Investment Fund can only decline as benefit payments rise faster than contributions to the plan. Yet the provinces, which must approve all changes to the CPP rules, still stubbornly resist all attempts to reduce the amount they can borrow from the fund, although in 1984 they did agree, reluctantly, to start coughing up some of the interest owing on the loans. It now remains to be seen whether Wilson or his successor can fulfil promises to slow the growth of the transfers by $2 billion a year by 1990. It won't be easy. In 1985, as David Peterson was settling in as Ontario premier, he reminded Brian Mulroney that the cutbacks would mean "a real beating" for his province's ability to pay for its health-care and university systems. So much for theft from the taxpayers.

Today after years of dark rumblings that the CPP would "go broke" before the turn of the century, the good news is that our chances of receiving the pension we were promised are excellent. The bad news is that, although for twenty-five years we will have paid an ever-increasing percentage of our income to the plan, the amount of our CPP retirement pension in real dollars is not likely to be affected by the higher contribution rates. Under current rules, even when the CPP benefit is combined with the Old Age Security pension, it will still not be enough to sustain us adequately when we retire.

It is hardly surprising that Wilson opted for a bird in the hand. After all, his aim was to reduce the deficit, not to expand the inadequate benefits of the CPP or to keep the contribution rate down. And, although his timing is going to cost Canadians a great deal of money without significantly improving their pensions, he was absolutely correct when he pointed out that there are reasons other than provincial borrowing that the CPP ran into trouble so soon after it was established.

Less than three decades ago Judy LaMarsh believed that it was possible to design a pension plan with relatively low contribution rates which would "pay" for itself for decades to come and still provide a decent income for older Canadians. It was not to be. Once the provinces gained control of the money, LaMarsh realized, the game was over: it would be next to impossible to wrest it back when it was needed. And, suspicious as she was of provincial prerogatives, she might have guessed that they wouldn't even pay the interest owing. But the situation was even worse than she could know. How on earth could she have predicted double-digit inflation? And how could she have known, in the midst of the great baby boom, that Canadian women would decide to stop having babies?

3

THE GREYING OF CANADA

WHO WILL PAY THE PRICE?

::

"We speak of contributions, and tell today's employee to write down his earnings up to the Yearly Maximum Pensionable Earnings, deduct the Yearly Basic Exemption, multiply by nine, double (or quadruple) it, cross off the last figure and divide by 100. He does this arithmetic and pays his contribution and thinks he is accumulating something real. . . . We do not tell him that this is not so, and that in the end, after he has paid a lifetime of these contributions, there will be nothing more to support his benefits than his children's and some other children's willingness and ability to pay taxes."

Geoffrey Calvert, *Pensions and Survival,* 1975

"It is very difficult to keep in mind that pension reform is primarily a women's issue when the most knowledgeable people in the field are actuaries and economists (almost all male) who speak a language that is unintelligible to all but the most faithful readers of financial pages."

Louise Dulude, *Pension Reform With Women in Mind,* 1981

. .

MP Judy LaMarsh's confident prediction that contributions flowing into the Canada Pension Plan would more than offset the benefits flowing out until well into the twenty-first century was a promise that would prove impossible to keep. Even as Ottawa and the provinces were putting the final touches on the compromise CPP plan in 1965, economic and social forces were gathering the momentum which, within a decade, would make a mockery of the assumptions on which the CPP was based. After all the hard work, all the hard feelings, all the hard compromises, a headline in the *The Toronto Star* on August 18, 1979, less than fifteen years later, would declare: "Canada Pension Plan going broke, economists say."

In fact, the ink on the final formulation of the CPP had hardly dried before the scheme ran into difficulty.

The architects of the Canada Pension Plan had one particularly compelling reason for linking pension benefits to increases in the cost of living: they believed that by indexing the pension, they would put an end to the by-now familiar clamour for higher benefits every time an election rolled around. With indexation, all increases in both the Old Age Security and the Canada Pension plans would be predictable, orderly and shielded from political abuse. Self-serving politicians would no longer be tempted to compromise the country's fiscal health with unrealistic promises of higher pension benefits.

The indexation formula itself was as safe as houses: the increase in benefit levels was restricted to a maximum of 2 percent a year. Thus, even if the inflation rate rose above 2 percent, costs would be kept under control. The possibility of runaway inflation seemed remote anyway. The inflation rate in the preceding decade had been remarkably stable: in 1955 there had been no inflation at all; in 1956 the rate had stood at 1.5 percent and in 1957 it had risen to 3.1 percent. But a year later it had dropped back to 2.5 percent, and for the next six years the rate never exceeded 2 percent, averaging just 1.5 percent for the entire ten-year period. In the late 1950s and early 1960s, the prospects for continued economic stability seemed bright indeed.

Yet, even then, some astute economic observers were worried about the possibility of rampant inflation in the future. In 1957, actuary William Mercer, for one, warned that it could happen, precisely because of the full-employment policies and costly welfare measures undertaken since the war. Some economists, he cautioned, even believed that increased — and ill-advised — government spending could soon cause inflation in Canada to rise to five or even ten percent a year. "Let us hope they're wrong," Mercer wrote.

But suppose they were not. If the rate of inflation in the future turned out to be five percent a year or, worse still, ten percent, Mercer mused, a young man could look forward to paying $2.50 for a pack of cigarettes, or $15 at ten-percent inflation. A low-priced car would cost $20,000 (or $135,000). A bottle of whisky might sell for $45 (or $275). The possibility clearly horrified Mercer, as it surely must have horrified everyone who took his words to heart. A low-priced car for $20,000? Was such a thing possible? Mercer hedged his bets. "Please remember," he reassured his readers, "I'm not forecasting this kind of inflation. I just want to illustrate the terrific *long*-term effect of various rates of inflation."

In fact, Mercer's predictions were not far off the mark. Although the low inflation rates of the next few years belied his words, in 1965, the very year the Canada Pension Plan was introduced, inflation, the great nemesis of pension schemes, moved sharply upwards in the first in the string of misfortunes that would beset the plan in its first decade. That year, the inflation rate rose to 2.4 percent. In 1966 it rose again to 3.7 percent and in 1968 to 4.0 percent. By 1969 with inflation at 4.5 percent, the corresponding increases in the cost of living had so far outstripped the automatic increases in pension benefits that the demands for higher annual benefits — and inflation protection over and above the two-percent limit — began all over again. And with good reason.

Retirees who depended upon their monthly OAS and CPP benefits to survive soon realized that the real value of their pensions was declining precipitously — despite the two-percent-indexation provision. As they retired with partial CPP benefits under the ten-year transition provision — the maximum CPP pension would not kick in until 1976 — many older Canadians were being forced to apply for the Guaranteed Income Supplement, the means-tested supplementary payment which had been envisioned as a temporary welfare measure to assist those who were already too old to qualify for CPP benefits.

The CPP, which was designed to eliminate the dependency of older Canadians on welfare programs, had been severely tested by inflation. Not only were the monthly benefits minimal to begin with, but they were steadily losing their purchasing power. Many Canadians who had enjoyed comfortable lifestyles when they were working — and believed that their retirement income was adequate and secure — suddenly found themselves staring poverty in the face.

From Ottawa's point of view, the outlook was equally grim. A chronic political headache which seemed to have been solved — the constant demand for improved benefits — had not been solved at all. Not only would the indexation formula have to be changed, at added cost to the plan, but the Guaranteed Income Supplement would have to be retained as well. The pension ante was about to go up again. And because few Canadians understood how the plan worked, a corresponding rise in contribution rates was out of the question politically. After all, the plan boasted a huge "surplus." Why should contribution rates go up?

In 1973, after the usual tortured negotiations with the provinces, the Trudeau government rejigged the plan. New legislation removed the two percent cap on benefit increases, retroactively increased benefits to contributors who had already retired, liberalized the formula governing the Year's Maximum Pensionable Earnings and repealed the retirement- and earnings-tests so that pensions would be payable at age sixty-five, even if their recipients continued to work full-time. By January 1974, all three pensions — the QPP/CPP, OAS and the Guaranteed Income Supplement — were fully indexed to the Consumer Price Index.

These changes were expensive — and they were grist to Geoffrey Calvert's mill. Assuming normal life expectancy and a retirement age of sixty-five, the internationally known actuary pointed out, full indexation would add at least 48 percent to pension values and the long-term costs of the Canada Pension

Plan. But because the 3.6-percent contribution rate remained unchanged, no contributor, no matter how old or young, would pay for anything like the actuarial value of the benefits he was promised. "This is intoxicating stuff for any politician or social worker," Calvert fumed. "Here is a system that seems to have a magic capacity to get more and more benefits out of the hat with nothing more at all going into it." Calvert's warnings were borne out by the statistics. By 1979, the Economic Council of Canada estimated that contribution rates to the QPP/CPP would have to rise by two and a half times to cover the full cost of future benefits promised to current contributors to the plans.

The cost implications of ensuring that benefits would maintain their purchasing power in periods of high inflation were bad enough. But inflation was by no means the only unpleasant surprise in store for the guardians of the Canada Pension Plan. There was worse to come.

When Judy LaMarsh and her experts consulted 1961 census figures, they could see plainly that Canada boasted one of the industrialized world's youngest populations. Indeed, in the years between 1952 and 1965, when the QPP/CPP took its final shape, Canadians had produced babies at a truly amazing clip — more than 400,000 of them, on average, each year. And not only were more babies born, but thanks to life-saving advances in medicine, hygiene and nutrition, more of them survived infancy, enhancing the impact of the higher birth rates.

This was Canada's great baby boom, the population explosion writer John Kettle analyzed in his 1980 book, *The Big Generation*. And it was a dramatic phenomenon indeed. By Kettle's reckoning, which took into account not only the birth rate but immigration statistics as well, Canada's Big Generation numbered 6,591,700 souls on Census Day 1966. And that, he noted, was thirty-three percent of the country's total population. One out of every three people in Canada had been born in the preceding fifteen years!

The baby-boomers were the bedrock of the Canada Pension Plan. As this seemingly ever-expanding army of young people entered the work force, their contributions to the Plan would more than cover the cost of pensions for those leaving the system at the other end. Never mind that the heady post-war economic revival had already begun to level off. Canada's capacity for human and economic growth in the future appeared to be limitless. And as long as there were more contributors coming into the plan than retirees leaving it, the CPP's solvency would be assured.

In 1965, that seemed a reasonable proposition. The baby-boomers were growing up in families whose real income had risen higher and faster than ever before. They were better educated, better nourished and healthier — and their expectations of life would be immeasurably higher than those of their parents who had endured first the hardships of the Great Depression and then the disruptions and anxieties of the war years. And, with the economy going gangbusters, there would be plenty of jobs for them to fill when the time came. Indeed, the economic good times which followed hard upon the heels of the Korean War were unprecedented in Canada's history. Productivity was high, inflation was low and liberalized immigration policies reflected the country's urgent need for a larger labour force.

But with little warning, another dark cloud appeared on the horizon. In the midst of unprecedented economic prosperity and high employment, the seeds of inflation had been sown. The growing concentration of power in corporate hands — together with a largely unregulated market and the rapid growth of foreign ownership in Canada's economy — pushed the inflation rate up. And as inflation rates rose, the economy began to cool, in part because the post-war boom had placed severe and little understood constraints on national economic development. As a result, when the members of the first wave of baby-boomers born immediately after the war began to enter the work force, they arrived in greater numbers than the economy could easily absorb. As unemployment rates began to rise, both in absolute numbers and as a percentage of the total labour force, the post-war dream of full employment and ever-expanding economic growth began to fade.

Even more ominous in its long-term implications for the CPP was a sudden and totally unexpected decline in the country's birth rate. The great Canadian baby boom had dramatically reversed a century-old demographic trend in Canada: for more than a hundred years the birth rate had been gradually dropping. Statistics on these matters were not collected in Canada until 1921. But demographers working with early census figures estimate that in the decade between 1851 and 1861, there were about 45 live births each year for every 1,000 Canadians. By 1921, that number had dropped to 29.3. It continued to decline sharply during the difficult Depression years and by 1937 had dropped even further, to only 20.1 births per 1,000 population.

But although the general trend in fertility was downwards, upswings in the economy had led to periodic upward turns in the birth rate. In general, when Canadians felt optimistic about the future, they married earlier and on average produced more children. Thus it was no surprise that the birth rate had started to edge upwards in 1937 as the high unemployment of the Depression years began to ease. By 1946, it had risen to 27.2, matching the levels of the early 1920s. It rose even higher to 28.9 in 1947, levelled off briefly, and then began to edge upwards again. In the course of the next decade, Canada's average annual birth rate would exceed that of the United States and every major European country.

Thus, when Judy LaMarsh surveyed Canada's demographic and economic landscape in the early 1960s, one of its most striking features would have been this vast country's seemingly boundless capacity for population growth. Times were good, jobs were plentiful — and Canadians were confident enough to want large families again. But, in the mid-1960s, with virtually no warning at all, Canadian women, like women in Western societies everywhere, tossed a spanner in the works. The great baby boom came to a screeching halt. It seemed that in the brave new post-war world with its sweet suburban fantasies, its station wagons for hauling all those children about, its labour-saving gizmos and life-enhancing gadgets, women had been quietly plotting their escape.

When U.S. feminist Betty Friedan articulated their frustrations in her 1963 book, *The Feminine Mystique*, she tapped a sensitive nerve, a nerve which had been jangling at least since the war, when thousands of women had moved into the work force, often into positions of power and responsibility. In 1945, for example, more than one in three Canadian women held a job. Friedan had also identified a current of deep discontent at the precise moment when new contraceptive methods enabled women who wanted something more than a clutch of babies, a house in the suburbs and a new Hoover to do something about it.

Contraception was a criminal offence in Canada until 1969, although birth-control techniques had long been practised to limit the size of families, especially in times of economic uncertainty. But more reliable contraceptive devices — the newly developed birth-control pill, the IUD, the diaphragm, which by the mid-1960s were widely available to any woman prepared to ignore the law — were different. Not only were they more effective than the old methods, but a woman who wanted to minimize her chances of an unwanted pregnancy now had little difficulty in doing so, with or without the co-operation of her partner.

As plummeting birth rates and rising abortion statistics soon showed, many women, given the opportunity, simply didn't want as many children as the architects of the Canada Pension Plan had assumed they would. The great population explosion which the planners had taken as the beginning of a new demographic trend in Canada turned out to be simply a blip in the old one. Against all expectations, the country's birth rate began to decline precipitously in the mid-1960s. And even more surprisingly, it just kept on dropping, impervious to the upwards fluctuations in the economy which had always caused it to rise in the past. Canada's post-war baby boom was well and truly over.

It took some time for this unexpected turn of events to sink in. Politicians and planners, understandably, were preoccupied with meeting the considerable needs of the baby-boomers as they moved through the education system, as Kettle put it, "like a pig swallowed by a boa constrictor." In 1961, 14.7 percent of all Canadians were below school age. A decade later, a whopping 21.3 percent of all Canadians were in school, creating an unprecedented and costly demand, first, for new elementary schools, then for new high schools, then for new universities. In the midst of all the excitement, few people stopped to ponder the implications of Canada's youthful population profile and falling birth rates for the future of the CPP. Canadians had their hands full just keeping up with the immediate and urgent needs of the young. The question of what would happen when they grew old hardly seemed worth asking. That problem, if it was to be a problem at all, was a good fifty years down the line. Anything could happen in the meantime.

By the mid-1970s, though, the alarm bells began to go off. Calvert, for one, pointed out that one critical barrier for public pension plans had already been breached: Canadians were no longer having enough children to *sustain* the size of the population — much less to increase it. That seemed impossible, but it was true. And it meant that the Canada Pension Plan had been based on a fundamental, but totally mistaken, assumption: that the total fertility rate (the total number of births per 1,000 females throughout their lives) would never fall below 2,159.

In 1959 that rate had stood at 3,935. By 1966, it had dipped to 2,812, but was still well over the breakpoint. By 1970, though, the rate had plummeted to 2,331 and by 1974, the last figure available to Calvert when he wrote *Pensions and Survival*, it had declined to 1,875 — a staggering thirteen-percent drop from the CPP's worst-case scenario. Had the rate stabilized at that level, Calvert pointed out, the result, "in due course," would have been a thirteen-percent shrinkage in the work force available to support the pensioner population.

The trend, we now know, was far more relentless than that. The rate did *not* stabilize at 1,875. By 1978, it had dropped to 1,757, by 1982 to 1,694, and by 1985 to 1,669. The trend was even more marked in Quebec, traditionally the province with the highest birth rates in Canada. In 1960 that balance shifted. For the first time, Quebec's annual birth rate fell below the national average, where it has remained ever since. The traditional economic predictors of fertility, it was now clear, were no longer as reliable as the policy makers had thought.

Today, demographers see few signs that Canadian fertility rates will begin to rise significantly in the near future, despite the media attention focused on biological time-clocks and Yuppie motherhood. Indeed, 1986 census figures showed that in the previous five years Canada had experienced its lowest population growth rate ever. From a high in the average annual rate of growth of about 3.29 percent in 1956-57, the long downward plunge — to 2 percent in the 1960s, 1.3 percent in the 1970s and 0.84 percent in the first half of the 1980s — is still a free-fall. The implications of this stubborn demographic trend have only begun to emerge as critical factors in such social policy areas as daycare, pay equity and immigration — and unless there is a sudden and dramatic turnaround, they will play an increasingly dominant role in pension policies as well.

There is, inevitably, a high degree of uncertainty in predicting how Canadians, or anyone else for that matter, will decide to behave in the future. Despite dozens of studies and at least as many different theories — ranging from public concern about the worldwide population explosion to societal angst about nuclear war to the self-absorption and me-first-ism of the Woodstock era — it is still a mystery why the birth rate plunged as suddenly it did. The availability of the Pill and other highly effective contraceptives clearly had something to do with it. So, certainly, did the wave of feminism which swept middle-class women out of marriages and into the work force. So, too, did the rising expectations which many lower-income families soon discovered demanded two salaries — and fewer children — if they were to be realized.

And it is clear that an entire generation can change its mind almost overnight, even on a question as basic as how many children to have and when to have them. Demographers today are more wary about predicting the future than were some of their predecessors. Leroy Stone of the Population Studies Centre at the University of Western Ontario and Susan Fletcher of Health and Welfare Canada's Office of Aging, two Canadian demographers who have taken a special interest in pensions, for example, have gone to some trouble to warn pension planners that there are some things which can be predicted with certainty and some which can't. Fertility falls into the latter category. It is hard enough to predict the intentions of people who are already in their childbearing years, much less to forecast the fertility of people yet unborn.

Using ever more sophisticated tools and analytical techniques, demographers have learned to expect sudden change, or at least to allow for its possibility. One way they do this is by making several predictions, based on a range of behaviour patterns. But when they have applied these techniques to Canadian birth rates, even the projections designed to reflect assumptions on the "high" side suggest that there is little likelihood that birth rates in Canada will return even to 1971 levels by the turn of the century. The "low" assumptions suggest that they will continue to decline.

Birth rates in the future may be difficult to predict, but there is little guesswork involved in predicting one effect of the low birth rates for the past quarter century on Canada's demographic profile in the first quarter of the next: most members of the generation of Canadians who will provide the baby-boomers' pensions with their tax dollars have already been born. "It is a sobering thought that those who will be sixty-five years old or over in the year 2031 — roughly the point at which the coming shift in age composition will reach its peak — are already alive and that their future numbers will be affected only by migration or death," reported the Economic Council of Canada in its exhaustive 1979 study of the pension system, *One in Three: Pensions for Canadians to 2030.*

It is an even more sobering thought that since that report was written, the demographic projections on which they were based have been revised. Today, the members of Kettle's Big Generation are in their twenties and thirties, most of them still many years away from retirement. But the greying of Canadian society, which will shift an ever greater pension burden onto fewer and fewer shoulders, is already under way — and it is under way at a faster pace than anyone expected. This trend has many people very worried. "It is the number one national question of the time," Quebec premier Robert Bourassa said recently, acknowledging that it is an even greater problem for Quebec — which still has the lowest fertility rate in the country at 1.43 births per woman, compared with a rate of 1.7 for Canada as a whole.

In 1927, the year of Canada's first old-age-pension legislation, fewer than 6 Canadians out of every 100 were age sixty-five or older. Today that ratio stands at 12 in 100. By the first decade of the next century, when the baby-boom generation begins to move into the ranks of the senior population, the ratio is likely to be about 18 in 100. That means that, within twenty years at the most, *one-fifth* of the entire Canadian population will be age sixty-five or older. To look at it from another perspective, there were 2.7 million Canadians aged sixty-five or older in 1985, three times more than in 1927, a statistic which is quite meaningless on its own. What is significant is that while the over-sixty-five population tripled, the population as a whole did not. Its numbers slightly more than doubled in the same time period.

There have been many surprises for demographers in the last few years. The magnitude of Canada's baby boom was the first. The sudden and precipitous decline in the birth rate which began in the 1960s was the next. But perhaps the most surprising trend of all has been that of longevity: older people in Canada are living longer than anyone expected they would. In 1979 the Senate Committee on Retirement and Age Policies estimated that the number of Canadians receiving government pensions, then numbering 2.1 million, could reach 3.4 million by the year 2000, a prediction that was based on a "worst case" projection.

In fact, the prediction erred on the low side by more than half a million people.

Population projections usually involve general trends and gradual change, not dramatic revisions of very recent predictions. But to the astonishment of the experts, the death rate among "old" older people has declined dramatically, an eventuality even the prescient Geoffrey Calvert found so unlikely that he dismissed the possibility with the curt comment that "death rates and expectations of life change very slowly." Perhaps it is just as well that Calvert didn't see this one coming. If he had, he might have been too depressed to write his book at all. The pension situation was dire enough as it was.

In the last five years, predictions about the future for older Canadians have undergone some startling revisions. "Surprise in the 1970s" is how Statistics Canada describes the phenomenon in an uncharacteristically perky subtitle in a 1987 report entitled *The Seniors Boom.* The report calls the marked decline in mortality rates at the oldest ages "the second most consequential development (after the baby boom) in the recent demographic history of developed countries." The upsurge of life expectancy among seniors is similar to the baby boom, the report adds, "in that both phenomena surprised most of the demographic forecasters."

Demographers Stone and Fletcher describe the contours of the most recent surprise. The story begins, they say, with older women back in the 1950s. In the thirty years since then, they have shown a remarkable series of substantial falls in mortality rates. For example, the death rate among women aged seventy years or more has declined by 6 percent or more over each of the six five-year periods between 1951 and 1981. The decline in the death rate among women between the ages of eighty and eighty-four has been even more startling. In the years between 1966 and 1971, it fell by an astonishing 11.8 percent. In short, in the years since the Canada Pension Plan was set up, the chances of older people growing even older have improved dramatically. An eighty-year-old woman in 1941 had one chance in ten of attaining the age of ninety-two. By 1971 those odds had improved greatly to one chance in five, and today they are even better. The highest declines of female mortality continue to occur among women over the age of eighty.

The trend has affected longevity predictions for men as well. It was not until the late 1970s that older men began to register similar patterns in mortality rates. But after years of "poor and sporadic" declines, they too experienced a remarkable drop in death rates in the five-year period between 1976 and 1981, primarily as a result of a trend towards healthier lifestyles. Although the most dramatic decline — fourteen percent — was among men aged fifty to fifty-four, every older age group recorded a mortality decline of at least six percent.

What does it all mean? Barring war or epidemic, it means that in the next forty-five years, Canada's over-seventy-five population is expected to triple in size to about one million people — with the number of Canadians over age eighty-five increasing from 224,000 to nearly 750,000. These, as the authors of *The Seniors Boom* point out, are amazing statistics. Only five years ago, in a projection which was deliberately on the high side, Statistics Canada forecast a 58-percent growth rate for the population aged eighty years or more in the years between 1986 and 2001. In the most recent projections, that growth rate was revised upwards to 77 percent!

Taken together, these projections spell even more trouble for Canada's public pension programs. Not only will more and more Canadians collect their pension benefits in the coming decades as the system matures and the baby-boomers move into retirement, but they will collect them for many years more than anyone expected they would. Looking to the future, the Statistics Canada demographers predict that as Canada enters the twenty-first century, the population aged sixty-five or older will number about 4 million. In the second decade of the century, they estimate, that figure will grow to 6 million. By 2031 it will reach a peak of 7.5 million. If you are forty or younger today, you will be one of those 7.5 million. In 1984, the last year for which comprehensive figures are available, your QPP/CPP contributions — along with those of about 11.3 million other Canadians — helped to pay the pensions of 2,065,504 retirees. When you retire in 2031, it seems likely that fewer than 23 or

24 million contributors will be available to pay for your pension — and for the pensions of 7,499,999 other Canadians. In 1979, there were six taxpayers available to support each pensioner. By the year 2025, there will be fewer than three.

As Geoffrey Calvert made clear more than a decade ago, if Canadians in the future were to have the public pensions they had been led to believe they had "earned," something had to give. Even if economic growth were strong, if the population imbalance between old and young could not be checked through a turn-around in the birth rate or through massive immigration, there were only two choices. Either Canadians must expect less from the public programs in the future and save more in order to provide a more substantial portion of their own retirement needs themselves — or more of them would have to remain in the workplace longer.

But Calvert was whistling in the wind. The trend in Canada since then has been towards earlier, not later, retirement. Private-sector employers have seized upon early retirement as a way of solving temporary problems, offering older employees attractive retirement packages in order to downsize or streamline their operations. Many unions, too, have stressed early retirement as a means of ensuring jobs for their younger members. As a result, for the last ten years, labour-force participation rates among Canadians aged fifty-five to sixty-four have been dropping steadily, from 80 percent in 1979 to 71 percent in 1984. Indeed, the revisions to the Canada Pension Plan which Michael Wilson introduced in 1987 make it possible for Canadians to collect their CPP pensions at reduced rates at age sixty if they so desire. How does this square with the problems confronting the Canada Pension Plan? Why are Canadians being encouraged to retire early, when their continued presence in the work force would seem to be necessary to the long-term health of the CPP?

The answers to these questions are complex. Not only do they vary from industry to industry and from region to region, they also depend upon fluctuations in the economy. But, underlying those factors is another: the ever-expanding presence of women in the workplace. Between 1976 and 1981, as Canadians began to panic about the implications of declining birth rates for the QPP/CPP, the participation rate of women between the ages of twenty-five and thirty-four in the Canadian work force was increasing by a staggering forty percent. It is largely their presence that has helped to alleviate many of the problems which beset the plan.

Yet these two trends — early retirement and the feminization of the workplace — have had an effect on the Canada Pension Plan which many policy makers — and politicians — are only beginning to comprehend: that the main beneficiaries of the Canada Pension Plan today are primarily the men who retire on full pensions, just as the main beneficiaries of the trend towards early retirement are primarily men who can *afford* to retire early. And while they are collecting their pensions, it is the ever-increasing numbers of women entering the workplace who are paying for their pensions.

At the same time, because most women have spent less time in the work force and earn less, on average, than their male counterparts, most of them are destined to pay a higher percentage of their salaries into the plan throughout their working lives. As a result, many women will be forced to remain at work long after their male colleagues have retired, simply because they cannot afford to do otherwise. The plan which was intended to transfer wealth from current contributors to the elderly is now transferring wealth from women to men as well.

In its brief history, the Canada Pension Plan, which was designed to solve the problem of basic retirement security for all but the very poor and the unemployed, has encountered more than its share of unanticipated problems — from runaway inflation to high unemployment to plummeting birth rates to a nonsensical funding mechanism guaranteed to cause trouble down the line. To these woes must now be added another: as women fill the void created by the low birth rates of the last quarter century, they have become, ironically, both the saviours and the prime victims of the system. Unless their salary levels rise, they will pay more, on average, for their own pension benefits, just as they will provide a disproportionate amount of the pension benefits of the men who retire before them.

It was not until the early 1980s, when Louise Dulude, among others, began to document the glaring inequities of the pension system as a whole, that the full extent of the "women's" problem began to be recognized. Yet, as we shall see in the next chapter, the failure of the public pension system to meet the needs of women was only one aspect of a far greater problem. If the Canada Pension Plan, which treats men and women equally in its rules, if not in its results, managed to discriminate so deeply against women, the private pension system and the legislation under which it operates were much, much worse.

· 4 ·

PENSION REFORM

HERE TODAY, GONE TOMORROW

::

"Surprising as it may seem, the traditional family ... where the man is the breadwinner and the wife stays home, has already passed into history."

Monica Townson, *Pension Reform for Women*, 1983

"Only the law of the sea has shown greater durability, intractability and ability to remain the subject of endless study, debate, commissions, reviews, post-doctoral theses and newspaper columns without anything tangible getting done."

Donald G. Coxe, Daly Gordon Securities, in an address to the Association of Canadian Pension Management, May 1984

..

By the late 1970s, politicians could no longer ignore the plain fact that Canada's old-age-security policies were not working. Employer-sponsored pension plans, which the powerful insurance lobby had long insisted would quickly expand to cover most of the labour force, still accounted for less than ten percent of the total income of Canadians over age sixty-five. And despite decades of well-meant attempts to devise income-security programs to protect all Canadians in their later years, thousands of people still embarked upon retirement each year with little or nothing in the way of personal savings. In 1978, for example, more than half of all single Canadians over age sixty-five depended upon their government pensions to survive because they had no investment income at all.

Theoretically, this should not have been a problem. The combined OAS and QPP/CPP benefits were meant to guarantee a barebones — but adequate — retirement income to the majority of older people, while the GIS was meant to relieve the distress of the truly destitute. But the support these programs provided was simply not enough. All Canadians received Old Age Security, but with an average monthly benefit of $148.60 in 1978 it was not nearly enough to live on. At the same time, only about ten percent of the contributors to the QPP/CPP qualified for the full pension benefit on retirement.* And even those few who did qualify received only twenty-five percent of an average pre-retirement salary [YMPE] — a totally inadequate replacement level, even when combined with OAS. Taking all these factors into account, it had become painfully obvious to critics of the system, as reform advocate Louise Dulude noted ironically, that many Canadians became poor only when they got old.

Only a decade after the QPP/CPP was supposed to have solved the problem of providing Canadians with basic old-age-income security, the need to reform the system had become urgent. QPP/CPP benefit levels were too low while the plans were slowly going broke. The private sector had not delivered on its promise to expand pension coverage, yet its spokesmen adamantly opposed expansion of the public plans. Occupational pension plans excluded part-time, mobile and occasional workers, yet employers said they could not afford to provide coverage for them. Pension coverage was wildly uneven: public-sector employees, with their benefits indexed to inflation, had much better pension plans than employees in the private sector who were not protected against inflation at all.

These fundamental weaknesses in the system had already penalized great numbers of older Canadians who had been led to believe that their retirement income was secure. Unless something

*In 1978, the average monthly OAS benefit was $149, the average monthly Canada Pension Plan benefit was $94 and the average monthly Quebec Pension Plan benefit was $98.

was done quickly, those same flaws would continue to undermine the retirement security of Canadians in the future.

The prime victims of these shortcomings, as they always had been, would be women. The vast majority of older women in the 1970s could look forward to little or nothing from the QPP/CPP, primarily because most of them had not held paid full-time jobs for extended periods in their lives, if they had worked outside the home at all. The plans provided survivor benefits, but even a full widow's pension amounted to little more than a pittance. And the plight of unmarried women was even worse. For most of them, the pension system was a very fast track into penury. In 1978, of all Canadians living in poverty, nearly three-quarters were women — most of them over age sixty-five and on their own.

The root of the problem was the system's stubborn resistance to change. Pension schemes, both public and private, had been developed by men with men in mind. Their actuarial assumptions, the legislation governing them, even the language in the plans themselves were tailored to meet the needs of a "typical" Canadian employee: a male who embarked on his working life at age eighteen, worked full-time for the next forty-seven years, and for only one employer after about age thirty-five, received salary increases and pension entitlements which reflected his years of experience and retired on a full pension on the day he turned sixty-five.

As recently as thirty years ago, the notion that pension plans should also be tailored to meet the special needs of women would have been dismissed as absurd. Men, after all, were the breadwinners and the guarantors of security for their families. And because it was their work and their savings that would provide retirement security not only for themselves but for their wives as well, the pension system had been deliberately fashioned for them and, not surprisingly, few people questioned that it should be so.

In 1957, for example, when William Mercer warned against the dangers of entrenching mandatory retirement at age sixty-five, he called the practice an affront to all Canadians. But "all Canadians" apparently did not include women. Pension plans, he said, should give "a man" the right to retire at a specified age, but should not force him to do so. Retirement at age sixty-five, Mercer added, was based on several naive assumptions, including the idea that it is more economical to pension off "healthy men" who still want to work than to disturb the tradition that "a man's" old age suddenly starts on his sixty-fifth birthday. It was a fantastic assumption that "all men" become unproductive at about the same age and an outrageous assumption that "an older man" can suddenly change his way of life while he is still healthy.

Mercer was making a perfectly legitimate point and making it rather well. Yet, in the process, like virtually everyone else who was concerned with pension policy, he managed to ignore more than half of the entire population. Who would have guessed from his words that, even in 1957 when he wrote them, women made up more than twenty-five percent of the Canadian work force? Mercer's views were not unusual and they were not thoughtless. Indeed, they probably reflected the sentiments of most Canadians in 1957, including those of the many working women who also saw their own long-term security inextricably tied to their husbands' careers. But the fact was that a pension system designed to meet the needs of men — especially of men who worked for one or two employers all their lives — ignored the realities of Canadian life even then.

Working women, including mothers, were becoming the norm rather than the exception, and the number of single-parent families headed by women was rising sharply. The vast majority of working women — and most men too — did not stay in one full-time job in one place for their entire careers, as the private pension system assumed they would. Many women spent their working lives in part-time jobs, and not in the full-time employment that both the private plans and the Canada Pension Plan required for full pension entitlement. These were the facts. Yet so deeply was an outmoded world view entrenched that these wide-reaching societal changes had virtually no impact at all on the pension system in the 1950s when many occupational pension plans were set up.

Two decades later, the problem would be vastly greater. As women flocked into the workplace in even greater numbers in the 1960s and '70s, they encountered a pension system which pretended they did not exist, and then made them pay for benefits they would never receive — a system which refused to acknowledge that marriage and family and employment patterns had changed and which ignored the fact that it was no longer a given, if it ever was, that most women would have a husband to support them in their old age.

In the mid-seventies — at about the same time that it became so clear that the Quebec and Canada Pension Plans were headed for trouble — the penny finally dropped: unless the pension system was overhauled to reflect Canadian society as it actually was, more than half of the country's population would continue to be at very great financial risk in their later years through absolutely no fault of their own.

Recognition of the problem, however, was not sufficient to solve it. Despite its obvious weaknesses, the system still proved extraordinarily resistant to significant change. As Louise Dulude, pension expert for the Canadian Advisory Council on the Status of Women, put it in 1983: "Every report on pensions issued in the last few years — and there have been many — starts off by declaring that women are the prime victims of the present system. Having said this, nearly all of them go on to recommend 'reforms' that would benefit typical male workers and ignore women's needs almost entirely."

Canada's pension system, Dulude pointed out, was a disaster for women not just because it was intrinsically unfair, but because it managed to reproduce all of the other economic injustices women suffered throughout their lives. Because occupational pensions, both public and private, are a function of both years of service and salary, women had been doubly penalized. Not only did they receive lower salaries than men in similar jobs, those low salaries also ensured that they would receive lower pensions when they retired. Moreover, the system had also punished women for moving in and out of the work force to care for the children that only they could have and it made no allowances at all for the fact that married women still performed the lion's share of household duties in addition to their workplace responsibilities.

Why was it so very difficult to introduce change into a system which was so demonstrably inadequate? A large part of the problem, reformer Monica Townson noted, was that most of those involved in the debate had a "rather limited view" of pension reform for women, an assessment which may well have been the understatement of the decade. In fact, the extent to which politicians, employers and the pension industry banished women from their sight is the single most striking feature of the long-running tug-of-war, waged largely by men, over the appropriate role of public and private pension plans in Canada. As politicians, unions, employers and the private-sector pension lobby tussled over power and money, it was primarily Canadian women who paid the price of their posturing, their indecision and, in some cases, their greed.

In the last decade, more ink has been spilled on the subject of pension reform than any sane person (present company excepted, of course) would want to read. Between 1976 and 1986, no fewer than a dozen major committees were convened to examine Canada's old-age-security arrangements (see Bibliography). The members of these committees — from politicians to corporate movers and shakers, from union leaders to retirees, from pension-industry experts to civil servants — worked hard. They commissioned hundreds of studies and they interviewed thousands of Canadians. In the course of ten years of relentless inquiry, they identified and dissected dozens of problems with the system, beginning with the main one: that the country's jerrybuilt pension system was not getting the job done — and because of inflation, the situation was getting worse, not better.

One overriding impediment to change in the decade-long reform exercise was utterly predictable: the old battle lines had not changed. Even with the system in crisis, pensions were still, above all else, a *political* issue. No matter how bad things got, employers and the pension industry would continue to resist significant government intervention into the private pension system, the provinces would resist any reform which threatened to slow the rate of CPP transfer payments from Ottawa and employers would continue to insist that reform was just fine — as long as it didn't cost them anything.

Still, by the early 1980s most of the participants in the debate realized that, despite the political opportunists, the footdraggers, the obfuscators and the hard-core ideologues, the system had to change. For economic as well as compassionate reasons, the country could no longer tolerate a pension system which didn't work. And above all, it could not, and would not, tolerate another generation of older women plunged brutally into poverty.

Throughout the late 1970s and early 1980s, women's groups grew much more insistent in their demands for change, and better organized too. They made their message very clear: Canadian women were up against the wall of a pension system which was patently unfair to them. Not only were OAS benefits too low, they also assumed that most older women were part of a couple sharing two OAS pensions and the husband's occupational pension as well. Single, divorced or widowed women were left to make do as best they could.* And despite the efforts of many provincial governments to provide additional support through welfare supplements, their poverty was acute, their distress relieved only by the fact that at least their medical expenses would be met by the universal medicare program introduced, like the CPP, by Judy LaMarsh and the Liberals in the mid-1960s.

Moreover, women who *had* worked outside the home for most of their adult lives had also been penalized by the system. Because so many of them worked part-time and in service-sector and retail jobs where employer-sponsored plans were uncommon, most women had no private occupational coverage at all. Not only did their low incomes and family responsibilities ensure them inferior pensions from the QPP/CPP, they were

*The situation was even more difficult for most immigrant women. In 1977 a change to OAS rules actually worsened the pension situation for them. The change required immigrants to live in Canada for forty years before they qualified for a full OAS pension. (See also Appendix B).

also penalized by a private pension system which punished them for moving in and out of the work force and for leaving jobs before they had met the vesting requirements that would protect their pensions — usually age forty-five and ten years continuous full-time service.

Under the chaotic legislation governing occupational plans across the country, it was even possible for a woman who changed jobs every few years to be a full-fledged member of a pension plan for thirty-five or forty years and to earn no pension entitlement at all. Each time she left a job before completing ten years of continuous service, her employer's responsibility to her simply vanished. And to add insult to injury, even if she rolled her pension refunds into an RRSP, the annuity that the RRSP would purchase at age sixty-five would provide a monthly benefit actuarially reduced to reflect the fact that women live longer than men on average.

The system even managed to discriminate against women whose employment histories exactly mirrored those of men. In the past, for example, it was not uncommon for employers to allow male employees to join the company pension plan earlier than women on the grounds that a woman would be likely to leave for family reasons and probably wouldn't need a pension plan anyway. On top of that, many pension plans specified different normal retirement ages for men and women, effectively preventing female employees from earning a full pension by forcing them out of the workplace earlier.

At every turn, it seemed, women were the victims of a system that was out to get them. And still the politicians dithered. In spite of the magnitude of the problem, many of them appeared to be more interested in tinkering with the system than in overhauling it, lest they offend their corporate friends and supporters. For its part, the private sector appeared to be moving resolutely in the wrong direction. Not only was coverage not expanding — the majority of private-sector employees still had no access to an occupational pension plan — but recession had caused many employers to lay off younger employees (effectively cancelling the pension coverage they had already earned) or to phase out their defined-benefit plans altogether.

The National Pension Conference, which convened in Ottawa on April 1, 1981, was the culmination of more than five years of constant debate on the pension system. At the massive gathering to get the reform ball rolling on a national scale at last, pensioners' groups, labour representatives and an increasingly vocal and well-prepared lobby orchestrated by the National Action Committee on the Status of Women launched an attack on the $14-billion private-pension industry, lambasting employers for their failure to expand the system and improve benefits. More than fifty-three percent of all retired Canadians, they pointed out, lived below the poverty line; only fourteen percent of retirees' income derived from the private plans; and because the plans were not indexed retirees were losing most of the real value of their pensions to inflation, which was also decimating the real value of pensions deferred until retirement when plan members changed jobs.

Most of the critics argued for an immediate expansion of the QPP/CPP, dismissing the pension industry's preference for mandated occupational coverage as self-serving, ineffective and unfair. The CPP, they pointed out, was simpler, easier to understand and far more efficient than the private plans could ever be. Furthermore, the industry's insistence that Canada couldn't afford an expanded CPP was nonsense. Even with an aging population, keynote speaker Shirley Carr, then executive vice-president of the Canadian Labour Congress, told the 357 assembled delegates, Canada's long-term rate of economic growth would more than cover the costs of providing better pensions. "I do not share this pessimistic view of the future," she said.

Liberal Health Minister Monique Bégin agreed. Most European countries, she told the delegates, had already experienced without great difficulty the population shifts that Canada could look forward to in the future. And, she added, if the business community was worried about too much pension money accumulating in the hands of the federal government at the expense of capital markets, as clearly it was, there was no reason at all that CPP contributions couldn't be channelled into the private sector for investment. And, if that still wasn't enough to satisfy corporate Canada, private employers could be allowed to opt out of the public system — provided their plans were equally good or better.

Private-sector spokesmen made little effort to contain their antagonism to the reforms their critics were demanding. While the corporate community paid lip service to ending the unfairness, their representatives, with the pension industry squarely onside, objected to most of their proposals. The reason was always the same: it would cost them too much. Besides, what was all the fuss about, anyway? Women didn't need pension protection because they were well provided for by Old Age Security, by spousal provisions in pension plans and by welfare; women didn't really need very much money to live on when they got older; women could rely on their families to support them; women needed more social-support systems, not more money.

By the time the conference ended three days later, the political groundwork had been laid for the necessary discussions between federal and provincial governments — and most delegates had even managed to agree on a few basic reform measures: some form of pension for homemakers under the QPP/CPP, better coverage for spouses under both the private and public plans, improved vesting, locking in and portability rules for private pensions — and inflation protection to be paid for from the excess earnings of the plans themselves.*

Nine months later, in December 1982, the Trudeau government unveiled several modest proposals for reform — and turned the larger questions over to a parliamentary task force for a year of study. The proposals, presented in a federal Green Paper, called for a quick increase in CPP coverage up to the level of the average industrial wage — a statistical indicator that tracks inflation better than the Consumer Price Index. The document also called for improved coverage and portability — and for mandatory inflation protection. Pension reform, said Bégin when she introduced the proposals, would be the "most important dossier on social policy in the 1980s."

The members of the task force, chaired by Douglas Frith, a

*Since 1974, the Canadian Association of Pension Supervisory Authorities (CAPSA), made up of senior federal and provincial pension authorities, had been trying to find ways to attack the greatest structural impediment to private pension reform: the lack of uniformity in provincial pension rules across the country. Their 1982 report, *A Consensus for Pension Reform*, formed the basis for the federal-provincial negotiations.

young Liberal member from Sudbury, Ontario, began their work with this stark assessment of the pension situation on their minds: "Women now over the age of sixty-five and who are alone because they are widowed, divorced or single, are likely to be poor." Women's groups have insisted that the problem of pensions is largely a women's problem, the committee's report noted, adding that "the Task Force accepts this claim." Indeed, the 1983 report, which committee members fervently hoped would be the final word on pension reform for the foreseeable future, singled out no fewer than nineteen measures that would have to be implemented to make the system fair for women.

Some of them — including an immediate increase in the Guaranteed Income Supplement and a mechanism to ensure that the OAS benefit would be protected from political interference in the future — were designed specifically to make certain that the fragile safety net protecting older women would be raised a notch or two. It was essential, the task force said, to keep the universal benefits safe from the intervention of politicians intent upon reducing their governments' deficits at the expense of the elderly.

Another set of recommendations aimed to protect women, especially women who had chosen to remain at home under the QPP/CPP. They called for mandatory QPP/CPP credit-splitting between spouses on retirement or in the event that a marriage broke down, improved post-retirement survivor benefits, an expansion of the general drop-out provision to twenty-five percent of the years with lowest earnings — and a pension for homemakers.*

The homemakers' pension was a contentious concept, as it still is today, and the problems surrounding it were related directly to the dual nature of the Quebec and Canada Pension Plans. On the one hand, the plans are occupational schemes, designed for those who contribute to them. On the other, they

---

*Splitting CPP credits between spouses upon divorce or separation had become possible in 1978, but only about three percent of divorcing couples opted to split the credits, often because women did not fully understand the long-term implications of giving up their rights to their husbands' pension benefits at the time of divorce. Credit splitting is *still* not mandatory and automatic.

are an integral part of the retirement-income system, in some cases providing greater benefits than individual contributors have paid for themselves. So while it might seem obvious that women without income cannot have an occupational pension plan, it is less obvious that they should be totally excluded from the broader benefits provided under the CPP.

The disagreements over a homemakers' pension reflect major differences in perspective on women's role in society among women themselves. While everyone can agree that women who did not work in the past should not be impoverished in their old age simply because their husbands have died, there is considerably less agreement on what to do about women who do not hold paid jobs today. For the government to provide them with CPP benefits even though they have not contributed to the plan would seem to be unfair to all those women who look after their families and work as well. Yet, if homemakers are not permitted to "earn" a pension, they are at risk of repeating the cycle of poverty experienced by women in the past.

A federal report released in December 1983 recommended that CPP credits accumulated by spouses during their marriage be shared equally when the younger spouse reaches sixty-five, in effect creating a homemakers' pension by dividing a husband's pension in two parts and giving half of it to his wife. It also recommended that an additional CPP benefit be given to couples with only one spouse in the work force, with the benefit to be shared between husband and wife. Under the scheme, a husband could contribute to the CPP on his wife's behalf, using a hypothetical salary defined as half of the Year's Maximum Pensionable Earnings. All women who stayed home to look after a relative, a spouse or children under eighteen, the report said, should be eligible for the pension under these terms.

But as critics of the scheme quickly pointed out, that meant that a woman who earned a minimal income in an underpaid and difficult job would not be eligible for the pension because she was working, while a wealthy woman who chose to stay home to look after her children would qualify. In addition, a two-income couple could end up with a lower pension than a single-income family. Further, the scheme did nothing to improve the lot of single women. Indeed, it could end up providing the most support to high-income families in which the wife does not work at all, but still hires a housekeeper to perform household duties.*

These difficulties underline the difficulty of designing a plan which would satisfy — and be fair — to all women, but they do not necessarily constitute a reason for abandoning the concept. The point of such a pension is not only to place a value on work done in the home, but to ensure that older women receive whatever support the government is prepared to guarantee them anyway in the form of a pension, not as welfare. During the 1984 election campaign, Brian Mulroney made a pension for homemakers one of his major campaign promises after women's groups pinned him down in a televised debate on women's issues. In December 1985, Jake Epp, minister of health, promised legislation before the next election. The women are still waiting to hear back from Mr. Mulroney.

The homemakers' pension is designed to help women who do not work outside the home, and it will continue to be a divisive issue. But the Frith Task Force recommendations which would most improve pension coverage for the majority of women were straightforward. Instead of viewing women primarily as homemakers whose pensions would depend in large part on the earnings of their husbands, they aimed to make sure that occupational pension plans did not penalize working women whose employment patterns were, for whatever reason, different from men's — but who nevertheless were full participants in the work force.

When the committee issued its report in 1983, workplace

*Saskatchewan's Progressive Conservative government introduced a voluntary, tax-deductible, funded homemakers' pension plan in 1986 with a maximum yearly contribution of $600. The government matched the contributions of low-income earners, up to a limit of $300. Although the plan was instantly popular, its critics charged that it was tailored to benefit the spouses of middle- and upper-income earners and that it had added to the province's deficit without helping those who truly needed it.

participation rates for women in their prime childbearing years had reached 72 percent across Canada, more than 79 percent of employed women between the ages of twenty-five and forty-four held full-time jobs and 45 percent of mothers with children under the age of three were working — an increase of about 40 percent since 1976. Yet fewer than one working woman in four had any private-pension coverage at all. What these women needed most of all was exactly what men needed too: an occupational pension system that treated them fairly. The problem was that what was fair for a man was not necessarily fair for a woman, given the reality of Canadians' lives.

Society "is just beginning to recognize the implications of the observation that women's work and the patterns of their working lives are not the same as those of men," the report observed. Although the role of women as homemakers would continue to "impose constraints on the ability of many women to enter the paid labour force and to earn the wage of someone who is not also a homemaker," there were many ways in which the system could be improved to better serve their needs.

Coverage under the occupational plans, the report said, must be extended to part-time employees, pensions must be vested after two years and they must be portable from employer to employer. Wives should be entitled to complete information about their husbands' pension plans and vice versa and sex-differentiated mortality tables should be prohibited. In addition, there must be more flexible limits on tax assistance for retirement savings and a tax credit to replace the current tax deduction for retirement savings.

And that was just for starters. The report admitted that even these measures would not be enough to solve women's pension problems, although they were all that could be accomplished through the pension system itself. "As necessary and as beneficial as these recommendations are," the report noted, "we acknowledge the obvious: that those with low pay will be those with small pensions." The solution to that problem would come only when Canadian society found ways to ensure that women received equal pay for work of equal value. Otherwise pension reform could be expected to do no more for women in the paid labour force than to relieve their poverty.

By the time the Frith Task Force got down to business, the critics of the system had long since coalesced into three broad camps: those committed to a significant expansion of the Canada and Quebec Pension Plans, those who argued that pension improvements should be left in private-sector hands and those who wanted a mixture of legislated public and private reforms. Yet most of them agreed that, without inflation protection, the beneficial effects of the other reform measures aimed at private pensions would be seriously undermined. If pensions failed to maintain their real value after retirement, reform would be largely an empty exercise.

Spokesmen for the corporate lobby, on the other hand, made it clear that they would fight any attempt to index pensions to inflation tooth-and-nail. The powerful Business Committee on Pension Policy which represented thirteen business groups, including the Canadian Manufacturers' Association, the Canadian Bankers' Association, the Canadian Federation of Independent Business — as well as the insurance industry — told the task force that its members opposed any form of mandatory inflation protection, although they did deign to agree that portability ought to be improved. The best way to protect pensioners from inflation, the Committee's brief said, was to fight inflation itself, a goal which could not be achieved if employers had to pay more to improve and expand pension benefits. Besides, looking after pensioners should be "the joint responsibility of employers, employees and society as a whole."

In the end, the task force accepted this proposition — conditionally. Under heavy pressure, most committee members backed away from recommendations which would have wrested occupational pension coverage away from employers and transferred it to the federal government, just as they stopped short of forcing all private employers to provide pension plans for their employees. But at the same time, they made it plain that the majority of the task force members believed that the private sector should be put on notice. "It is important for them to believe that this time we have got to have a proper pension system for Canadians through the private sector," said Nova Scotia Liberal Russell McLellan. "This is the last opportunity." If employers could not find ways to expand coverage within three years, the task force urged, governments should seriously consider mandating a fairer solution.

The report, as it was intended to do, provided a focal point for the critical federal/provincial deliberations on pension reform which had taken place sporadically since 1981. Without agreement in that forum, most of the reforms would never be implemented. Yet, despite an agreement in principle that speedy reform was necessary, the only real consensus so far seemed to be that it was going to be virtually impossible to deal with the reforms women wanted in both the public and the private plans. With the country in the grips of recession, what realistically could be done?

That was a view which the business community and the pension industry continued to endorse whole-heartedly. As they had in so many of the earlier inquiries into the pension system, the spokesmen for corporate Canada threw up their hands in despair when confronted with the extensive changes the women's groups wanted. Because women were, well, *different*, they insisted, it would be next to impossible to do much for them without giving employers time, say a hundred years or so, to fully adjust their thinking and their plans. And indexing? No way.

Although the foot-dragging was widespread, much of the blame for the slow pace of reform must be laid squarely at the door of the pension industry. Older Canadians were now paying the price of the insurance companies' largely successful lobby in the 1960s to keep CPP benefits at a minimum, in order to protect their own interests in providing retirement security to Canadians through private occupational pension plans. As a result of their success, any member of a private pension plan who changed employers after earning a pension suffered from the vesting and portability rules which made it impossible to carry pension benefits from job to job. And as hundreds of thousands of Canadians whose pensions from former employers had been "deferred" discovered when they retired, these deferred pensions — which had been locked in, usually until age sixty-five — ended up benefiting mainly the insurance companies who sold their former employers an annuity on their behalf at the time of the job change.

Moreover, the corporate community had stepped up its noisy attacks on the vast public-service pension plans — virtually the only occupational plans which provided their members with automatic protection against inflation — in a transparent effort to defuse criticism of their own pension schemes. The public-sector plans — those covering civil servants, municipal employees and teachers among others — had always been better than their private counterparts, in part because the governments which established them wished to set an example for private employers to follow. And by the late 1970s, mainly because most of the plans were subject to collective bargaining, most of them had been further improved with guarantees that benefits would keep pace, at least in part, with inflation. In 1973, for example, federal civil servants — and MPs — had been granted automatic inflation adjustments by an Act of Parliament, protection enjoyed by fewer than one percent of all employees covered by the private sector plans. These improvements, which were a direct result of the collective bargaining process, had begun to make the pension industry very nervous indeed — precisely because, with inflation soaring, they made the private plans look bad.

The civil service plans became a popular target — and a handy diversionary tactic — for conservative politicians, for the insurance industry and for the business community in general. In 1978 the National Citizens Coalition, a well-funded lobby of about 30,000 anonymous free enterprisers headed by insurance executive Colin Brown of London, Ontario, had taken out advertisements in newspapers across the country to attack what it called the "rip-off" public service plans. If Prime Minister Pierre Trudeau, who was then fifty-eight, were to retire at age sixty-five, one ad pointed out, he would receive an annual pension of $180,800 by the time he turned eighty-five. That was bad enough, the ad suggested, but the broader implications of the public plans were even worse. If every public servant received an indexed pension provided by federal and provincial governments, the public coffers would soon be depleted. And why, the NCC wanted to know, should the taxpayers pay one nickel for public servants' pensions anyway?

The Public Service Alliance of Canada, the union representing most federal civil servants, fought back. Its members, the union noted in its own full-page ads, had more than paid for their own pensions in the past: since 1924 they had channelled more than $1.98 billion into the plan. In return they had received $1.86 billion from the government.* Not only were union members still waiting to see the government's first nickel, they were also wondering what had happened to the interest on their money. Since 1970 the interest paid by Ottawa when it borrowed from the plan had crept up from 4 to 7.2 percent. But at the same time, bank interest rates had risen to 12-to-14 percent. If anybody was getting "ripped off," it certainly wasn't the government.

The NCC, the union said, had it backwards. The solution was not to *de*-index public pensions, but to force private employers to *index* their own schemes — and the sooner the better. After all, when Pierre Trudeau received his pension, it would be worth in real dollars more or less exactly what it was meant to be worth in 1978. That certainly would not be the case for members of the private plans whose pensions were constantly losing their value to inflation.

Yet the public sector plans *would* be cause for alarm in the future, for many of the same reasons that the CPP had run into difficulty. Because of the low interest rates paid by

---

*When the Trudeau government introduced a bill to bring public pension benefits under its newly-introduced 6-and-5 anti-inflation program in 1982, about thirty Liberal backbenchers joined the chorus of opposition protest. Civil servants had *paid* for their indexation through increased contributions, they said, and they deserved to collect it. A compromise agreement — 6.5- and 5.5-percent increases for the next two years — ended the revolt. That two-year limitation, of course, meant that civil servants would never recover the full value of the pensions they had paid for.

governments — federal and provincial — when they borrowed from the funds, some plans were unable to keep up with inflation. Others appeared to be headed for trouble in the future. A 1988 report by respected actuary Laurence Coward, for example, concluded that Ontario public servants should pay two percent more — on top of their current seven-percent contribution — into their plan to retain their existing indexed pensions. Union president James Clancy responded angrily to the report, pointing out that if the billions of dollars in the fund had been invested at a decent rate of return in the past, it would have had a very comfortable surplus today.

The National Citizens Coalition's ferocious ten-year attack on the civil service plans was a virulent strain of the same insurance lobby propaganda which had driven Judy LaMarsh to distraction in the industry's dogged campaign against the Canada Pension Plan. But it was certainly not the only below-the-belt attack on the reform effort. More credible lobby groups conducted their campaign against reform with enormous insensitivity too. Their stock response to growing concern about the high levels of poverty among the elderly — that the extent of their difficulties had been deliberately overstated for political purposes — was designed to impede a fair solution to such basic problems as indexation, not to find one.

By the time the Frith Task Force convened, their rhetoric had become very hard to swallow indeed. Industry spokesmen insisted that employers could not afford to improve their plans. But to many thoughtful observers, it seemed more likely that the pension industry's antagonism to reform was based entirely on self-interest — and that its members' philosophical preference for a free-market solution to all pension problems was more than slightly tinged with greed. So far, the only thing that philosophical preference had succeeded in ensuring was that QPP/CPP benefits would be too low — and that the majority of Canadians would be frozen out of private occupational pension coverage altogether.

Over the objections of the private sector lobby, the government soldiered on. In February 1984, Finance Minister Marc Lalonde announced that all federally regulated employer-sponsored plans would be subject to new rules. As of January 1, 1987, he said, all future pension entitlements regulated by the federal government must be indexed to sixty percent of the Consumer Price Index, up to a maximum annual adjustment of eight percent. Employers would be free to use a different formula, but only if it equalled or bettered those minimum requirements.

Lalonde's proposals were a step in the right direction — and they reflected the widespread consensus among critics of the private-pension industry that some form of inflation protection was absolutely necessary to protect plan members in the future. Still, because they did nothing to improve benefits earned prior to 1987, employees approaching retirement would have little to gain from the changes. Nor would the proposed rules do anything to improve the pensions of employees who had already retired. But most serious of all, the new rules never came into effect. When the Liberals were voted out in September, 1984, Lalonde's proposals departed with them.

The new Conservative government paid lip service to the general thrust of pension reform and vowed to speed the process along. And the provinces at last settled down to serious negotiations in their ongoing deliberations with federal authorities. In the course of the winter of 1984-85, an unofficial consensus position took shape, the precise terms of which were never announced. They could be inferred, however, from the contents of the Pension Benefits Standards Act, 1985, the federal legislation governing federally-regulated employment pension plans.* Theoretically, the federal legislation, while it would not directly affect most Canadians, would serve as a model for new provincial legislation across the country.

Under the terms of Ottawa's new rules, pension benefits earned after January 1, 1987 would be vested and locked in after two years of membership in an occupational plan, a provision which clearly would have helped thousands of women had it been in

*The legislation covers less than ten percent of the work force under federal jurisdiction, primarily in banks, airlines and other transportation industries and in some communications firms.

effect earlier. Furthermore, employees who moved on to another job could choose to transfer their pensions to their new employers' plans — if the new employer agreed to accept them — or to a locked-in RRSP. This provision, too, was a potential improvement for women — and for many men as well. In addition, employers must allow full-time employees to join the company pension plan after two years in the job, another provision which would help many people — if the pension plan were worth joining.

Part-time employees must also have access to a pension plan, or to a similar plan, to that provided for full-time employees, a step forward for women who work part-time while their children are young — unless, of course, the plan is a bad one. In that case, it is likely that no one, particularly women earning minimal salaries, would benefit from participating in it. Nor · could the sex of pension-plan members be taken into account in calculating contributions or benefits — a provision clearly in women's interest as long as employers did not then discriminate against them in their hiring practices as a result of the change.

The legislation also stated that spouses of pension plan members must be given access to pension information — an improvement as long as the rules governing disclosures are strong ones. And in changes designed to help older women immediately, plan sponsors must provide survivor benefits of sixty percent of a plan member's retirement pension for surviving spouses and these benefits must be continued, even after remarriage. Although the amount of the benefit was low, the change was an improvement. Finally, under the terms of a provision which has been widely misunderstood — and which will be discussed at some length in Part II — employers would be required to contribute at least fifty percent of the cost of any vested pension earned after the effective date of the legislation.*

---

*The fifty percent rule provides that employees must contribute no more than fifty percent of the cost of their own pensions. The rule does not mean that the employer's contribution must at all times match or exceed the employee's contribution. The federal legislation excuses employers from the rule if they index their plans by at least seventy-five percent of increases to the Consumer Price Index beyond the first one percent annually ([75% of CPI]−1) — a timid nod towards the principle of inflation protection.

There can be no question that these reform measures would help to correct many of the most egregious structural problems which had plagued occupational pensions for so long and that they would improve the position of women — and many men — who had access to an employer-sponsored plan. But they did nothing to ensure that coverage would expand into workplaces where it did not already exist, leaving more than half of all working women with still no access to an employment plan. Employers who had no pension plan for full-time employees, for example, were not required to set one up for part-time workers. And because more than eighty percent of women who work part-time are employed at low salaries in jobs which offer no private pension coverage, much of the legislation was irrelevant to the very people most victimized by the system in the past.

On top of that, the legislation required that part-time workers earn thirty-five percent of the Year's Maximum Pensionable Earnings — $9,695.00 in 1989 — a cutoff which would exclude the majority of part-time workers. Moreover, the bill did nothing to ensure that basic pension *benefits* would improve. Nor would the new survivor-benefits provisions help women whose husbands did not belong to an occupational pension plan, as nearly half of all Canadian men did not.

It would be nice to be able to say that, apart from all that, everything was fine. But everything was not fine. The terms of the compromise were a serious disappointment to everyone who had fought so hard to persuade the politicians, private employers and the pension industry that only a complete overhaul of the system could even begin to make up for past injustices, especially for past injustices to women. In fact, the model legislation did virtually nothing to improve the lives of thousands of Canadians who had already reached retirement age. And because it applied only to pensions earned after January 1, 1987, it did little for those who would retire in the next decade or so. And, incredibly, the legislation managed to sidestep the most important question of all for members of private pension plans: it failed to mandate inflation protection, the reform measure on which most of the other measures depended if they were to be effective.

In a companion piece to its legislation covering the occupational plans, Ottawa overhauled the rules governing Registered Retirement Savings Plans. Ottawa, as we have seen, introduced RRSPs in 1957 to guarantee individual Canadians who had no occupational-pension-coverage tax advantages similar to those granted to members of employer-sponsored pension plans. Over the years, however, RRSPs assumed another function as well: they allowed employees who *did* have occupational coverage to shelter additional retirement savings, over and above those locked into their pension plan.

The point of the program was (and is) to encourage Canadians to save for their own futures, and to give them a tax break when they did. Not only did contributions to an RRSP result in immediate savings in income tax because they are deductible from earned income, they also provided a tax shelter for interest earned on contributions and for any capital gains generated by the fund, allowing money to accumulate at a more rapid rate than it otherwise would. Tax owing on the money, of course, could only be deferred as long as the money remains in the RRSP. But because retirees have lower tax rates because they have no employment income, less of their money would wind up in the taxman's pocket.

But the taxman intended to get most of that money back. The idea was that when people cashed in their RRSPs they would turn the money over to the federal government which would, in turn, give them a lifetime annuity which would provide a monthly pension cheque until they died. Ottawa got the money, the retiree got the monthly cheques. But it didn't quite work out that way. By the late 1950s, the insurance companies — the only other institutions allowed to sell annuities — were selling most of the RRSPs. The industry was practised at selling life insurance policies which, it persuaded the public, were similar to RRSPs. So when an insurance salesman said that the best way to avoid paying tax on the full amount of the RRSP was to buy an annuity from his company, Canadians tended to believe it. And when they did, the funds in their RRSPs wound up not in the government's pocket, but in the ledgers of the insurance company.

Since then, the RRSP bandwagon has been rolling merrily along, with more and more institutions offering more and more variations on the original theme. But somewhere along the way, the purpose of the program — to provide Canadians with both an inducement to save and an orderly and safe way of saving — got lost. Today, the RRSP scene is wild and woolly and, as those who had the bulk of their retirement savings tied up in the market discovered after Black Monday, not necessarily safe. That will almost certainly change. As governments become increasingly concerned about the security of taxpayers' retirement savings, they will seek ways to regulate the industry and to channel more of the billions of dollars in pension industry hands back into government coffers.

In the meantime, the emphasis has been on giving everyone a fair kick at the can. The new rules governing RRSPs are a credible inducement for all Canadians who can afford to do so to save more for their own retirement and they are certainly fairer than the old ones, which primarily benefited high-income earners (see Appendix B). In the future, Canadians not covered by the private plans would be allowed to triple their contributions to deferred-profit-sharing plans or RRSPs, a change which would allow them the same tax breaks already enjoyed by plan members. For anyone who could afford to salt $18,000 away in an RRSP each year, the changes were good news. For most women — and many men too — they were irrelevant: their salaries were far too low. For them it meant that their employer would be forced to contribute on their behalf only to the CPP. They would be obliged to provide their private pensions themselves.

The Pension Benefits Standards Act, in itself and as a model for provincial legislation, represented a small step on the road to genuine reform of an inadequate system. But the push towards reform began to lose momentum as provincial governments — under great pressure from the private sector — reached their own levels of tolerance for change. What had briefly looked like consensus swiftly began to unravel. And when pension reform at last reached the legislative stage in many provinces across the country, the uniformity which was absolutely necessary to make it work began to fragment, as even *The Mercer Bulletin*, the influential monthly newsletter published monthly by the prestigious firm founded by William Mercer, admitted in January 1988. "Pension reform along the lines of the consensus developed since the 1981 National Pension Conference is now becoming a reality," said *The Bulletin*, but "sadly the ideal of uniformity in pension legislation amongst the jurisdictions has not been achieved, even in the essentials such as the period of service required for vesting."

Yet that failure didn't prevent corporate Canada and the pension industry from presenting the consensus to Canadians as a radical and thorough reform of the system, when in fact it was nothing of the kind. Two critical issues raised so compellingly in the Frith report — the expansion of occupational pension coverage and the mandatory indexation of private pensions to protect retirees from the horrendous effects of inflation — remained as contentious as they had ever been. After all the hard work, from the moment the great Canadian consensus on pension reform was secured, it began to fall apart.

The complex ten-year effort to reform the pension system was not entirely in vain. It made the public and some private plans fairer for working women and many working men as well and in its emphasis on survivor benefits, it improved the prospects for older women who depend on their husbands for their security in retirement. But it left many issues, including a pension for homemakers, unresolved. And, as we shall see in Part II, the consensus, such as it was, largely ignored the issues which will dominate the debate over pensions in the future: employees' rights, pension fund ownership, controls on pension fund investment and the ethics of pension fund policies. That battle is just getting underway.

··

PART TWO

IN SEARCH OF CORPORATE SUCCOUR

::

5

THE BATTLE FOR THE
DOMINION STORES PENSION PLAN

::

*"It is not necessarily desirable for employees to know. If I say
company ABC is taking out of its pension plan, it can cause a
lot of labour unrest. They wonder: 'Is the company stripping
me, ripping me off?'"*

Ontario Superintendent of Pensions
Gemma Salamat, February 1986

*"Who is more interested in the solvency of a pension plan than
its members, who are either depending upon it as a source of
income in their retirement years, or looking forward to the day
when they will, or must?"*

Mr. Justice Robert Reid, Supreme Court of Ontario,
August 1986

..

It looked like the mismatch of the decade: a belligerent and
determined Conrad Black in one corner, six underdogs in the
other. But when the gloves came off in the fight for the surplus
funds in the Dominion Stores pension plan, the ensuing
dust-up shifted an escalating dispute over who owns — or
should own — the assets in private pension plans out of the
shadows and into front-page headlines across the country.
Canadians accustomed to feeling their eyes glaze over at the
mere mention of the word "pension" were intrigued: if Conrad
Black, the country's best-known free marketer, or his hired

hands, were thinking creatively about the company's pension plan, something interesting must be up. And when the air finally cleared, politicians more practised in talking about pension reform than in effecting it had resolved at last to intervene in the cosy world of private pensions. Union leaders, traditionally wary of pushing too hard on pension issues for fear of alienating their young constituents, began to rethink their priorities. And many members of private plans began to wonder if what had happened to the Dominion Stores employees could also happen to them. All this because, it seemed, Conrad Black had finally gone too far.

Brad Gaull, Alan Dixon, Harold Pym, Dorothy Ritchie, Joe Calderone, and Bill Batchelor don't look like giant-killers. Nor did they ever expect to *be* giant-killers. Just a few years ago all six of them worked for Dominion Stores in and around Toronto. Ritchie was a bookkeeper, an employee of the once-mighty supermarket chain for twenty-six years. By 1985, at age sixty-two, she was looking forward to retirement. Pym, a manager in the produce department in Dominion's Kingston Road store in Scarborough, had been with the company since 1952. Gaull and Calderone, both grocery clerks and both twenty-year veterans with the company, worked at the Kingston Road store too. They had all hoped to see out their careers with the company quietly. Dixon and Batchelor, though, had been laid off in the upheavals that wracked the company after it changed hands in 1978.

All six were, or had been, members of the Retail, Wholesale and Department Store Union. And all six were as mad as hell. Repeated attempts to get straight answers from the company about store closings had ended in frustration. There was great and continuing confusion about severance entitlements. And disturbing rumours about the pension plan had begun to circulate. What, they all wanted to know, was going on at Dominion Stores?

Once, the Toronto-based supermarket chain had seemed invincible — mainly, as pert housewives in hokey TV ads told us brightly, because of the meat. For years Dominion operated more supermarkets across Canada, from Nova Scotia to

Saskatchewan, than any of its rivals, and the company regularly reported the highest return on sales of any Canadian supermarket chain. But by 1978, when Toronto financiers Conrad and Montegu Black bought the giant food retailer, the chain had begun to lose ground to its rivals and many of its 376 stores were aging money-losers. The Blacks did little to reverse the slide. By 1982, thirty-eight percent of the Dominion outlets were losing money and analysts estimated that the company was losing about $1 million each week. Customers in search of bright new stores, creative marketing and trendy delicacies were drifting off to Loblaws to buy their scallopini.

In 1981, the Blacks had sold eighty-six Quebec stores to Montreal's Provigo Inc. In 1982, Winnipeg-based Canada Safeway Ltd. bought six more, effectively removing Dominion's presence from Western Canada. In Ontario, about one hundred stores closed their doors, thirty-eight of them to become franchised, non-unionized Mr. Grocer operations. And as the familiar Dominion logo disappeared across the land, sales faded too. By the end of 1984, revenues had declined from an all-time high of $2.77 billion in 1981 to $2.21 billion and the company had reported after-tax losses of more than $12 million in the six-month period which ended on September 30 that year.

As the once proud and profitable chain disintegrated before their eyes, Dominion's remaining employees waited nervously for the inevitable to strike them as it had struck so many of their friends and colleagues. What else could they do? No more stores meant no more jobs. Dorothy Ritchie knew that all too well. She had watched the process unfold at first hand. In just four years, she had been assigned to four different Dominion stores in Toronto. Each in turn had shut its doors, to be sold to a franchisee or demolished. The Danforth Avenue store where she worked now, Ritchie was convinced, could well be next. And this time, it could be the end of the line for her after nearly a quarter century with the company.

It had been Ritchie's responsibility to close the books at each of those four stores and it was not a task she relished. She had listened closely to the concerns and complaints of colleagues who had lost their jobs and what they had told her was not reassuring. Many of them were unsure about the exact amount of their pension benefits, the details of how and when they would receive a pension, and their entitlement to early retirement. Others were having difficulty understanding their severance entitlements. Still, like Ritchie, they took some comfort from the knowledge that the pension plan contained a sizeable amount of money — money which they believed belonged to them. At least that would provide some relief from the continuing layoffs in the form of generous severance payments.

But as Ritchie and her co-workers pondered their uncertain futures, the rumours proliferated. There were tales of long-time union employees suddenly and inexplicably promoted into management positions, only to be laid off soon afterwards with far less compensation than they would have received had they remained in their union jobs. There were rumours of more store closings and predictions of even more massive layoffs to come. Then, in late December 1985, Ritchie was shocked to hear from a colleague that Dominion Stores had applied to the Ontario Pension Commission to *remove* money from the pension plan. Could it be true — in spite of all the assurances that the plan belonged to the employees — that company executives intended to use the money in the pension fund to cover the costs of winding down company operations? And if it were true, what could be done about it? If it was difficult for employees to find out what was really going on, it seemed virtually impossible for them to do anything about it. And pensions, after all, are difficult and complex matters.

Brad Gaull and Bill Batchelor had heard the rumours too and they were sufficiently worried about the pension plan to approach the union with their concerns. They didn't get very far; union officials remained silent on the issue. But Gaull and Batchelor weren't about to give up. They believed that the money in the pension fund belonged to the members of the plan and should be used to improve severance pay for laid-off employees, not to enrich the company as it phased out operations.

They had reason to believe that. Over the years, Dominion

Stores had issued brochures and letters to employees at least once a year, announcing improvements in the pension plan and spelling out the benefits employees could expect on retirement. And most of the documents had stated, apparently unequivocally, that all contributions to the plan would be used "for the exclusive benefit of members, retired members or their beneficiaries and could not, under any circumstances, revert to the company."

These communications seemed so elementary that many employees hadn't even bothered to keep them. Employee Harold Pym was different; although at fifty-three he was still years away from retirement, he had kept all the brochures and the letters and the statements, some of them dating back more than thirty years. Not that he was worried. Everything seemed to be just fine and, anyway, what were unions for if not to protect his rights, if they needed to be protected at all? There had been no complaint about the plan as far as he knew. Yet perhaps it was time to take another look.

When Pym dug the material out in 1985, he discovered a brochure he had received in 1952 when he joined the compulsory scheme as a new employee. The brochure described the pension plan Dominion sponsored for its unionized employees and pointed out that it represented "a very real advance in bringing to you financial security for your years of retirement." It also offered this guarantee: "Should the Plan be discontinued, no further increase in the amounts of pensions of the employees will take place, but all contributions made by the company will remain in the Plan for the benefit of employees."

Pym found similar brochures from later years and even one or two letters from Dominion executives about the plan. In 1972, for example, he had received a letter from T.G. McCormack, then Dominion's president, which described the company's new, improved plan.

> The first pension plan of Dominion Stores Limited was inaugurated in 1944. The Plan was revised and improved upon in 1951, 1963, and again in 1966....[The company] is never satisfied with things as they are. Times change. With the assistance of a leading firm of consulting

actuaries, the company has made an exhaustive study of modern pension planning. As a result of this study, a new Retirement Income Plan was introduced on January 1, 1972. The Plan is outlined in this booklet. You will find it a very real advance in bringing to you financial security for your years of retirement and also excellent protection for your dependents.

McCormack had urged Dominion employees to read the booklet carefully. And why not? As private plans go, the Dominion plan was a pretty good one. In 1979, for example, it provided an annual pension of $18 a month for each year of service up to a maximum of thirty-five years, or $12,221.40 for an employee retiring that year on a full pension. Furthermore, the company had gone out of its way to make it clear that the plan was operated solely for the benefit of its members and to underscore that its assets belonged to employees and retirees. Under the heading "Plan Administration," for example, was this statement: "All contributions whether by members or the company are used for the exclusive benefit of members, retired members or their beneficiaries. They cannot revert to the company."*

In June 1980, Pym had received another communication about the plan. It summarized the most recent, 1979, version of the plan and included a letter from the company's current president, Allan Jackson. "Your Company Pension is provided for your own use and benefit, and it is protected by law," Jackson wrote. "It cannot be assigned, or borrowed against." Indeed, the assurances just kept rolling in. The Annual Benefit Reports issued by Dominion in 1982 and 1983, for example, made this promise: "Your company plan is provided for your own use and benefit and is protected by law. The pension fund is invested by one of Canada's leading fund managers and cannot be used

---

*From 1977 on, pension coverage was subject to collective bargaining as part of the collective agreement between the Retail, Wholesale and Department Store Union and the company. Prior to January 1, 1979, all Dominion Stores employees were required to contribute 5 percent of their base salaries to the plan. As of January 1, 1979, employee contributions were reduced each year — from 3.5 percent of gross salary in 1980 to nil in 1984.

in any way by the Company except for the provision of pensions." The documents, Pym recalled later, seemed just fine to him. Given their clarity and precision, he could find no reason to doubt that the pension fund belonged to the employees, not to the company. Still, the rumours continued to circulate and Pym was uneasy.

As store after store was sold or shut down, many of the rumours which had circulated over the past few years had turned out to be true. Alan Dixon could testify to that. Dixon had taken a job at Dominion Stores as a warehouse employee in June 1978. But in January 1983, the company laid him off from the West Mall Distribution Centre in Etobicoke along with 36 other full-time employees. Those layoffs were just the tip of the iceberg. In the course of the next four years, about 250 employees would lose their jobs at the Etobicoke warehouse alone.

On May 16, 1984, Dixon wrote to Dominion Stores. He had several things on his mind, but mainly he wanted information about his own contributions to the pension plan. When he was laid off, Dixon had received a refund from the company of the contributions he had made to the plan while he worked for Dominion. He had also received interest on the money. But he was puzzled. Why had his contributions earned so little interest? The interest rate the company had applied to his contributions as of January 1, 1983 had been only 8 percent. On July 8, 1984, the rate had fallen to only 6.75 percent. These rates seemed very low. The bank rate on prime business loans at the time had been running between 12 and 13 percent. Why, he wondered, was the discrepancy so great?

Dixon was not satisfied with the reply he received from the company. "Interest rates are based on C.I.B.C. [Canadian Imperial Bank of Commerce] nonchequing savings accounts interest rates, quoted on January 1 of each year," said the letter from personnel manager Brian Burden, who left the matter at that. In Dixon's view, the explanation was not an explanation at all, other than that Dominion could pay whatever interest rates it liked. So he wrote to the Pension Commission of Ontario, the provincial regulatory body charged with protecting the interests of plan members, asking for copies of the documents relating to the plan: the last two Annual Information Returns, the two most recent actuarial certificates and a balance sheet setting out the liabilities of the plan, the value of the assets of the fund and any unfunded liabilities, deficiencies or surpluses in the plan. Dixon knew that Dominion was required, under Ontario law, to file these documents with the Pension Commission and to allow each plan member to review them on request.

On June 11, 1984, Dixon received a letter from the Commission informing him that a summary of his request had been sent to the company, along with a request for written permission to release the requested materials. To the company! This, it seemed to Dixon, did not constitute progress. The reason he had written to the Commission, after all, was because he believed that the company was giving him the run-around. And sure enough, Dominion did not reply to the Commission's request on his behalf either. On July 18, the Commission again wrote to Dominion on Dixon's behalf, pointing out that "the employer is required to make available certain information within thirty days" and that "Mr. Dixon is entitled to the information."

Again, Dixon received nothing from the company, but in early August, the Commission itself sent him the December 31, 1981, actuarial certificates — which indicated that the plan had a "funding excess" of $30,939,000 — and the two most recent information returns, which provide details of plan membership and employer/employee contributions to the plan. The first, for the period January 1 to December 31, 1982, showed that plan members had contributed $3,189,940.64 to the plan and that Dominion had contributed $1,650,000.00. The second, for the period January 1 to December 31, 1983, indicated that employees had contributed $2,628,263.46 and that Dominion had contributed nothing. The company, it appeared, had used the surplus in the plan to cover its own obligations to plan members, a legal and not uncommon practice.

In the meantime, the layoffs continued. Then, in early 1985, came the announcement that many employees had been expecting: ninety-three Dominion Stores in Ontario — 43 percent of the chain's remaining outlets — were to be sold to the Great Atlantic and Pacific Co. (A & P) for $115 million. All employees whose pensions were not vested, whether they were laid off or terminated, would receive the full amount of their contributions to the plan, plus any interest owing on their money.* The amount of interest would be determined by the company. But soon Dixon became preoccupied with an even more intriguing question than that of interest rates. Two months later, in December 1985, he learned that Hollinger Inc., Dominion's parent company, had recently mailed out an interim financial report to its shareholders. Dated November 22, the report announced that Dominion Stores had applied to the Pension Commission for permission to remove about $60 million from the "surplus" in the company's pension plans: "Dominion applied in November 1985 for regulatory approval for recovery of a portion of the surpluses in its pension plan resulting from overfunding by Dominion," stated the report, signed by the Hollinger chairman, president and chief executive officer, Conrad Black:

> The amount of such recovery is expected to be approximately $60 million but the actual recovery will be dependent upon the value of assets to be retained in the plans in respect of continuing employees. It is possible that the aggregate amount of surpluses eventually recovered could be somewhat greater, perhaps as much as a further $15 million, but this is dependent upon a number of factors, including eventual levels of continuing employment by Dominion which will be determined by the nature and extent of future rationalization and winding-down activities.

---

*Under Ontario laws governing defined-benefit pension plans, employees who had not reached age forty-five and worked for the company for at least ten years were not entitled to a pension. The pensions of those who met these criteria were "vested" and "locked" in until the employees reached age sixty-five, at which time they would receive the promised benefit, made up of their own contributions to the plan, their employer's contributions on their behalf and interest on the money.

The document also confirmed the employees' suspicions that Dominion intended to use some of the surplus money to cover the costs of dismantling the supermarket chain. The money would be used, Black wrote, to offset costs related to "the winding-down and rationalization of Dominion's ongoing activities, including non-recurring adjustments, employee termination costs, possible damage payments in respect of alleged violations of collective bargaining agreements and expenses of further store closures."* This confirmation really was the last straw for many longtime Dominion employees. Not only would their friends who had already lost their jobs miss out on the increased benefits the plan could easily provide, but the assets of the plan were to be used to eliminate even more jobs in the future, most likely including their own!

Dixon was irritated by the seeming indifference of the Pension Commission to his worries — and he was deeply concerned about his severance pay. It seemed clear that the company wanted to withdraw the surplus before the severance and termination issues — and their relationship to the pension plan, if any — had been resolved. His friends, Dixon knew, were receiving cheques that appeared to be final severance payments with a message stamped on the back that read: "Accepted in full satisfaction of any and all claims which the undersigned might have against Dominion Stores Limited and/or Willett Foods Limited arising out of my employment and/or the termination thereof." To get their severance pay, it seemed, they had had to sign away all claims on the company, including any claim they might have had to the surplus assets in the pension plan.

Above all, though, Dixon was puzzled that Dominion could lay claim to the surplus money in the plan at all. Every communication Dominion employees had received from the company about pensions for more than twenty years, he knew from conversations with his co-workers, had suggested that such a withdrawal was simply not possible under the terms of

---

*The value of the assets of the plan covering unionized employees as of November 1, 1985 was $58,370,000. The plan's liabilities were $15,306,000, leaving a "surplus" of $43,064,000.

the pension plan agreement. So once again he wrote to the Commission. The documents he received — excerpts from the plan relating to the termination of the plan itself — partly explained the mystery. To his astonishment, Dixon read that the language in the plan had been changed retroactively in a 1981 amendment which stated, in part:

> While it is the present intention of the Company to maintain the Plan in force indefinitely, the Company necessarily reserves the right to amend or discontinue the Plan at any time.... In the event that the Plan shall be terminated by the Company, the assets then remaining in the pension fund shall be applied in accordance with the terms of the Pension Benefits Act 1965 of Ontario (or other applicable legislation) as shall be determined in consultation with an actuary. Any assets remaining after the satisfaction of all benefit rights or contingent rights accrued under the Plan, *shall revert to the company* [italics added].

It was the first Dixon had heard of the change.

In the meantime, Brad Gaull had been having his own problems with Dominion and with the Commission. Since the previous May, he had been trying to find out how much money he had accumulated in the pension plan. After several false starts, Gaull finally learned in a telephone conversation that he had twelve thousand dollars in the plan as of the end of 1983. But he had been unable to discover how that figure had been calculated. When he heard that Dominion had applied to withdraw money from the plan, he phoned the chairman of the Pension Commission, J. C. Maynard, objecting strongly to the withdrawal. Gaull also told Maynard that if the company had amended the plan in a way which would allow such a withdrawal, he was unaware of such an amendment.

Joe Calderone, chief grocery clerk at the Dominion Store on Kingston Road, wanted to know what was going on, too. He initiated his inquiries in December with a call to the Pension Commission, asking to speak with Gemma Salamat, Ontario's superintendent of pensions. She was not available. He phoned again a week or two later. She was still not available. Undeterred, Calderone sent Salamat a registered letter. In it he described himself as a Dominion employee who had been a member of the pension plan for eighteen years. "Other members as well as myself," he wrote, "have been trying to contact you by telephone to get important information concerning our pension plan. Since we have been unsuccessful, I am taking the liberty of writing to you in this regard."

Calderone described his objections to any plans Dominion might have to remove money from the plan: "I would like to know," he wrote, "if the request made by Conrad Black (Nov. 11/85) for $60 million dollars of surplus funds from our pension plan was approved by the Pension Commission Board? If so, I would like to know when and for what amount. I would also appreciate knowing if this money has been released to Mr. Black and when." Calderone also asked for a copy of the current plan. He received no reply.

On December 16, Dixon and some of his friends had also fired off a letter to the Pension Commission expressing their dismay over the proposed withdrawal. "We are very concerned about the appropriateness of this move," he wrote. "When we joined Dominion, the Pension Fund was ours — now it appears that the Company has contrived (through a new plan filed after Mr. Black took control and without telling us about the change in the plan) to get rid of its employees and capture the funds which we thought were there to assure our retirement." Dixon asked the Commission to put off a decision on Dominion's request until continuing and former employees had a chance to make their views known. Three weeks later, he had received no reply to the letter.

The angry Dominion workers were learning a lot about the wonderful world of pensions. In many cases, surplus withdrawals were perfectly legal. But the planned Dominion withdrawal didn't seem to be one of those cases. For years the company's employees had been promised that all funds in their own plan were theirs and theirs alone. Could it be that the promise carried no weight at all? And there was still great confusion about the severance and termination pay forwarded to employees who had already been laid off or fired. Surely the Pension Commission would not allow the company to pocket the surplus in the plan before that issue was resolved.

Surplus withdrawals, in fact, were not a new phenomenon. Until the early 1980s when private pension funds began to overflow as returns on their investments skyrocketed — causing the assets of most defined-benefit plans to far exceed their liabilities — the practice had not been widespread. Nor was it particularly controversial. But by the time Alan Dixon wrote to the Pension Commission, that situation had changed. More and more employers were eyeing the surpluses that had accumulated in their plans, partly as the result of swollen investment returns on employees' money and aided by the rapid decline of the real value of pensions paid to company retirees. And if they weren't actually applying to the Commission for approval to withdraw money, many employers were using the surplus assets to reduce their own contributions to the plan. Such "contribution holidays" required no approval from anyone.

Canadian employees needed only to look to the situation in the United States, where the art of raiding the surplus was far more finely honed than in Canada, to see how tempting these surpluses could be to employers. For years, U.S. companies had felt bound by the Employee Retirement Income Security Act of 1974 which declares that money in ongoing pension funds must be used exclusively for the benefit of employees and retirees. But as the assets in the funds mushroomed, company lawyers looked for a loophole and soon found one. A firm did not need to go out of business to fold its pension plan. It could simply stop the plan, pay the benefits owing — and pocket whatever was left over. By prematurely folding the plan, unprincipled companies were able to seize money which should have paid for benefits in the future. In 1985 alone, U.S. companies terminated 8,674 pension plans, more than double the number of plans wound up in 1980.

This practice was a clear violation of the implicit promise made to employees that their pension plan would continue unless the company itself went bankrupt. But by 1985, according to statistics compiled by the U.S. Pension Rights Center, more than one thousand U.S. companies had skimmed off a total of $12 billion in pension assets. Worse, because U.S. courts found that the tactic was not illegal, it contributed to a wave of hostile takeover bids in which the target company's pension plan was the prime quarry. When these takeovers succeeded, employees were invariably the losers.

Such ethically reprehensible practices were not common in Canada. But the number of companies viewing their pension funds as a ready source of capital had increased rapidly as the "surplus" assets in the plans continued to grow throughout the early 1980s.*

It had also become clear that in most provinces there was very little if anything in the way of legislation to protect plan members from employers intent upon raiding the pension funds either through surplus withdrawals or contribution holidays. If they existed at all, the rules and regulations governing private pension plans across Canada, for the most part, had been put into place before the surplus "problem" developed. The Ontario Pension Benefits Act, which might have protected the Dominion employees, and was among the most detailed and specific anywhere in Canada, made no mention of surplus assets at all. The Ontario Regulations — the details governing implementation of the Act — on surplus withdrawals were little better. For one thing, they ignored the question of the surplus in ongoing plans, stating in Section 21.(2) only that "no funds shall be paid out of a pension plan to an employer unless consent of the Commission is obtained." In other words, the regulations left the question of the surplus in ongoing plans entirely to the discretion of the Pension Commission. If an employer wanted to take money

---

*In 1980, for example, the Ontario Pension Commission approved applications from twenty-two companies to withdraw a total of $2.7 million from the surpluses in their plans. By 1985, those statistics had changed dramatically. In the year which ended on March 31, 1986, the Commission allowed fifty companies to withdraw a total of $187.2 million from their plans. By the end of that year, estimates of the "surplus" assets in employer-based pension plans across Canada ranged as high as $40 billion on total assets of $140 billion.

out of the fund, it was the Commission's prerogative to approve or deny the transaction, with or without telling plan members what was going on.

And what if a company went out of business and wound up its pension plan? Until 1982, the regulations stated only that, if a plan was wound up, "no part of the assets of the plan shall revert to the benefit of the employer" unless "provision has been made for payment of all pension benefits and other benefits under the terms of the plan to employees, former employees, pensioners, dependents and estates." In 1982, a further proviso was added: employers would not be allowed to use the surplus in terminated plans for their own purposes, unless "the pension plan provides for such reversion."

In the absence of legislated rules, the Ontario Pension Commission had developed its own guidelines over the years. But it was not easy for employees to determine what they were and how they were applied. As the Dominion employees learned to their outrage, it was difficult even to get through to anyone with authority at the Commission. When correspondence was ignored and requests for information were redirected to the recalcitrant employer who had refused to produce the information in the first place, one fundamental question was inescapable: Whose interest was the Commission protecting, the employees' or the company's?

Dixon and his friends, united in adversity, decided that the answer to that question was pretty clear. They also decided that it was time to get some help. They made an appointment with Toronto lawyer David Moore, who heard their story with increasing disbelief. Moore was not primarily a labour lawyer and he admits he knew very little about pension plans. That was about to change.

The six Dominion employees believed that the Pension Commission had scheduled a meeting on January 14, 1986, to consider the withdrawal request. They raced the clock to gather documents and letters and prepare affidavits describing their Byzantine dealings with the company and with the Pension Commission itself in the hope of persuading commission officials that the withdrawal should not be approved. Then, on January 10, just four days before what he believed would be the critical meeting, Dixon received a reply of sorts to his inquiries. The letter, signed by Nurez Jiwani, a senior pension officer, contained a copy of the Commission's guidelines on pension surplus withdrawals, but offered no information at all about Dominion's application and ignored Dixon's request to appear at the meeting. Instead, it referred the matter right back to square one. "As discussed in the bulletin," Jiwani wrote, "in reviewing an application for refund of surplus, the Commission takes into consideration the solvency of the plan, provisions of the plan documents and the Act and Regulations. If the Commission guidelines are met, the application is approved. If you have concerns with respect to the provisions of the plan, *we advise you to contact the company* [italics added]."

On the morning of the meeting, lawyer David Moore dispatched a letter to the Commission by courier, once again explaining Dixon's concerns and requesting an opportunity for him to make a submission to the body. To Commission head Maynard, Moore wrote:

> Without having had access to Dominion's application, it is difficult to assess all of the issues that may have to be determined by the Commission in its adjudication of the request.... These matters are of the utmost importance to Mr. Dixon and others like him who are or were contributors and beneficiaries under the plan. It is respectfully suggested that persons in that position are entitled to a reasonable opportunity to respond to the application for any recovery of "surplus" prior to any determination by the Commission of that issue.

The letter was delivered, by the courier, to the Commission offices at 11:55 A.M., about the time Moore and his clients believed the meeting would take place. They received no reply.

But it really didn't matter. Although Dixon and his friends didn't know it until later, the Commission had already approved the withdrawal on December 17, nearly a month earlier. The January 14 meeting had only tied up loose ends —

that is, if granting Dominion Stores permission to retroactively amend the pension plan to allow surplus withdrawals from an ongoing plan can be called a loose end. On that day, the Dominion employees learned later, the Commission had approved this amendment:

> Effective January 1, 1986...subject to the approval of the Pension Commission of Ontario, if, at any time in the opinion of the Plan actuary the assets of the Pension Fund exceed the actuarial liabilities of the Pension Fund in respect of benefits specifically described under the Plan, *such assets or any portion thereof may be refunded to or used by the company in a manner to be determined solely by the company* [italics added].

A few days later Gaull made another attempt to persuade the Commission to block the withdrawal. He phoned Maynard to make absolutely certain that the officials dealing with Dominion's application had been aware of the fact that the employees had not been informed of the company's intentions. He got nowhere. Officials at the Commission refused even to confirm that the withdrawal had been approved. Finally, after several unsuccessful attempts, Dorothy Ritchie succeeded in contacting Gemma Salamat on January 21. Salamat told her that the withdrawal had been approved, but did not provide any details of the application, the date of the decision or the amount of money involved. She also said that the withdrawal had been possible because the union had agreed to it or had arranged the Plan in a manner which provided for it.

This latest rebuff was the turning point. Gaull, Dixon, and the rest of the group decided to take Dominion Stores and the Pension Commission to court. On February 18, Moore applied to the Ontario Supreme Court for orders which would oblige the Pension Commission to reveal the proceedings surrounding Dominion's application to remove the funds and quash the Commission's authorization of the withdrawal. The union, too, was finally prepared to move. On February 6, it had filed a separate but similar application to the Supreme Court, asking that $37,951,000 — the portion of the $60 million withdrawal deriving from the unionized employees' fund — be returned to the plan.*

On February 21, Supreme Court judge Allan Hollingworth heard an application from the union and the employee group. They wanted the court to order Dominion to return the money to the plan as "a matter of urgency" in order to protect the plan's assets until the court could rule on the withdrawal itself. And they wanted an immediate judicial review of the Pension Commission's decision to approve the withdrawal. The application was only partly successful. In a ruling handed down on March 10, Hollingworth said that he was satisfied that the "integrity" of the fund was protected until the court determined ownership at a later date. "On the first day I heard this matter," Hollingworth said, "this was a very real concern to me, particularly when [Dominion's lawyer] Mr. [Lorne] Morphy, in his always frank discussion to the court, admitted that the $38 million which had been drawn by Dominion Stores had already been spent." These concerns had been allayed, Hollingworth said, when Dominion Stores arranged for a $38 million letter of credit with its bankers to make up any deficiency in the fund.

Not content to leave the matter in the hands of the company lawyers and the courts, Conrad Black himself waded into the fray soon after the applications were filed. Commenting on provincial NDP leader Bob Rae's allegation in the Ontario Legislature that the withdrawal of pension surpluses was a form of "legalized theft," Black told a Toronto *Globe and Mail* reporter that Dominion employees had no right to complain. The employees were "slovenly," their union leaders were "corrupt" and, besides, the employees had been robbing the

---

*Despite Dominion's contention that the union had agreed to the withdrawal, officials of the Retail, Wholesale and Department Store Union had no knowledge of the withdrawal until they read about it in newspaper reports in January, according to national director Don Collins. At no time, Collins said in his affidavit to the court, had Dominion given notice to the union or to any of its members that the company intended to apply to withdraw the surplus assets from the plan, even though the pension plan formed a part of the union's collective agreement with the company. The union, Collins said, had not been informed by the company — or by the Pension Commission — that the Commission would consider such a request nor had they been notified that the withdrawal had been approved.

company blind. More than $30 million worth of inventory was disappearing from Dominion stores every year, Black said, and truckloads of goods had been stolen from the warehouse. Cashiers, he said, allowed their friends to waltz through the checkout counter without paying for their groceries. Under those circumstances, Black suggested, how could they complain about a surplus withdrawal that was entirely legal?

Liberal MPP Monte Kwinter, whose Ministry of Consumer and Commercial Relations was in charge of pensions, rose to Black's defence in Dominion Stores' handling of the surplus, calling the withdrawal itself "perfectly legal, perfectly moral, perfectly ethical." But Black's outburst was too much for Ontario Labour Minister William Wrye. "Mr. Black has tarred all the workers with totally unsupported allegations. This is totally unfair," he told Regina Hickl-Szabo of the *Globe.* "Most people will probably see through those allegations," Wrye added. "Mr. Black has provided no proof — probably because it doesn't exist. I think he really ought to give some thought to making a public apology." Wondering aloud why Black had not had his employees charged with theft if he knew such large-scale theft was taking place, Wrye concluded that Black's remarks were "demeaning to those workers and ultimately did nothing for Mr. Black."

Black's public outburst was also too much for Brad Gaull. Black seemed to be trying to further antagonize employees, Gaull told Hickl-Szabo: "Mr. Black should look himself in the mirror first before he calls others slovenly. I have worked in twenty-five Dominion stores and have been with the company twenty years and I have never seen that kind of theft happen — and if we have corrupt union leaders I want to know about it." The company later apologized for Black's remarks.

But Black was not finished yet. In his regular column in the May 1986 issue of the *Globe and Mail*'s *Report on Business*, he itemized his troubles with the ailing supermarket chain. Then he turned to the pension issue:

> A $62 million section of the pension fund surplus, which had arisen almost entirely as a result of investment instructions given by a committee of the board of

directors, was transferred to taxable corporate income after application of the exacting tests to prevent abuses rightly applied by the Pension Commission of Ontario. More than 125 percent of necessary coverage for all the plan's possible obligations was left in the fund. An extraordinarily fatuous controversy ensued.

On January 27 this year, Ontario NDP Leader Bob Rae asked Premier David Peterson if he was aware that Conrad Black, "the most symbolic representative of bloated capitalism at its worst," had skimmed $62 million out of Dominion Stores pension plan surplus while engaging in wholesale layoffs of employees. The inference was made and amplified by NDP questioners that Dominion had paid nothing to its laidoff workers, and that I, personally, had stripped the pension plan surplus and had left the plan in a parlous financial condition. The Labour Ministry summoned Dominion officials for a meeting that lasted almost all morning Jan. 28 and that afternoon the Premier rebutted the NDP's absurd allegations about improprieties in management of the pension plan and pointed out that surpluses and shortfalls in corporate pension funds were legally and historically to the account of the shareholders.

The pension issue, Black continued, had been well handled by the Toronto press, but the termination question had been "clumsily dealt with." And all three Toronto papers, he added,

especially the *Globe and Mail*, [had] played up a comment of mine that a felonious minority of employees had been in the habit of stealing $30 million a year from Dominion inventory, more than the company had ever reported as an annual net profit, though not abnormal by industry standards. Though the *Globe and Mail*'s foreseeable (and foreseen) headlining of this aside was somewhat irresponsible, it had the desired effect of abruptly ringing down the curtain on the NDP labor morality play about pensions and severances.

On that point, it turned out, Black could not have been more mistaken.

A panel of three Ontario Supreme Court judges heard the case in the last week of May 1986. Responding to allegations that the company had made no attempt to notify plan members that the plan had been amended to permit Dominion to withdraw money from the fund, Domgroup lawyer Lorne Morphy insisted that the complaints were totally unfounded. (As a result of corporate restructuring, Dominion Stores Ltd. had changed its name the previous month.) The union and the employees, Morphy claimed, could have objected to changes in the plan had they wanted to. At that point, the Honourable Robert Montgomery took Morphy to task. "I don't think they knew what was happening to them," he said. "It's pretty plain when you read it," Morphy countered. "With respect," Montgomery replied, "I think it's smoke and mirrors."

The judges also questioned Morphy's contention that the union had agreed to the amendment to the plan. Could he provide specific evidence?, Montgomery asked. "I can't point to a specific document, no," Morphy replied. But they seemed most bemused by Domgroup's argument that, if the company had the right to keep the money from a terminated pension plan once its obligations had been met, then it also had the right to take money from an ongoing plan. If that were so, said Mr. Justice Robert Reid, why had Dominion bothered to create the retroactive amendment of January 14?

But the wrath of the court fell hardest upon the Pension Commission which, Reid noted, appeared to have "misled" Gaull by suggesting that no decision in the Dominion application had been made when, in fact, the decision had been taken in mid-December.* The Commission "seems to take the view that employees and pensioners have no right to know anything," Reid told Commission lawyer Thomas Marshall. The company had given the employees many assurances over the years about

---

*The Commission's position on the withdrawal was laid out in documents it filed with the court. The Dominion pension plan, the submission said, appeared to give the firm "exclusive management responsibility" of the pension fund and "unilateral authority" to amend the plan at any time. Furthermore, the pension agreement did not require Dominion to give its employees any information about the pension plan. The Commission therefore had proceeded on the understanding that no prior notice of withdrawal was necessary and that the company was "under no obligation, although it might have attempted to notify the many beneficiaries, if appropriate."

the fund, Montgomery said. "Then they turn around and take it away. How does that wash?"

After deliberating over the summer, on August 18 the judges ordered Domgroup to repay $37,951,000 to the pension fund, the amount of the withdrawal the company had made from the union plan. In a forty-six-page decision, Mr. Justice Robert Reid wrote that the company's application to withdraw surplus from the plan was "the consequence of severe difficulties the company had begun to experience at least as far back as 1983. Stores were being sold, employees were being laid off or dismissed, and substantial losses were occurring." In these circumstances, Reid wrote, Dominion's managers "saw the pension funds as a source of succour." Notwithstanding Dominion's difficulties, however, the company "had no right, under the plan documents, to apply to remove the surplus." It had received the funds and continued to hold them "without authority." The ruling gave the company seven days to submit a proposal for the "expeditious return" of the funds.

As for the Pension Commission, it had "violated the rules of fairness" by not notifying the Dominion employees that the company had applied to remove the money from the fund. "Why, in the absence of any provision entitling Dominion to withdraw assets, the Commission did not require Dominion to give notice to plan members has not been explained," Reid wrote, adding that "the consent given by the Commission was given notwithstanding that on the documents before it, Dominion had no apparent right to receive the surplus." The Commission had failed in its duty to protect employees and had even misled them: "When in November 1985, Dominion applied to the Commission for consent to remove the surplus, the plan had not been terminated, and Dominion had no right under the plan documents to apply to remove the surplus." In ruling that the Commission's consent to the withdrawal be quashed, he added that the judges had found it "difficult to imagine why the Commission was established without accepting that its principal function was to protect the interests of plan members."

The day after the judgement was handed down, Domgroup

president Peter White, a close friend of Prime Minister Brian Mulroney since their law school days together at Laval, later his appointments secretary in Ottawa, then publisher of *Saturday Night* magazine, and now Mulroney's principal secretary, told reporters that the decision would not be appealed. He added that the company had no plans to reapply to the commission for permission to withdraw the funds, because it would now require a court order to get them. Noting that the court had not resolved the issue of who owned the surplus, White said that he still believed that the issue would be decided in the company's favour. The company, he pointed out, had brought an owner-ship case to court in March, but Domgroup had not decided "if we will definitely pursue it."

White announced that the company would return an addi-tional $24 million plus interest — money removed from Dominion's two non-union pension funds — to the plan. "It is difficult to justify not putting these funds back, in light of the court decision," White told the *Globe*. "There is no significant difference between these plans and the other one. We'd also like to show that it's not necessary to sue us to get us to do the right thing." On September 12, Domgroup applied for permission to pay the funds into the court rather than into the pension plan. They were concerned, company officials told the court, that the Ontario Legislature would soon enact laws to amend the Pension Benefits Act, making it impossible for Domgroup to withdraw the funds from the plan in the future.

Five days later White announced that the company had changed its mind about the appeal. Domgroup officials had learned that the Dominion employees, now calling themselves the SOS (Save Our Surplus) group, had launched yet another lawsuit.

And indeed they had. When the SOS had finally got their hands on the documents relating to their pension plan, there was another surprise in store for them. The documents indicated that Dominion had already withdrawn $16.5 million from the pension plan in early 1983, two years before the withdrawal they *did* know about. When their lawyer David Moore wrote to the company requesting that the money be returned to the plan because it had been removed in the same way as the later withdrawal, he received no reply. So the intrepid SOS decided to battle on.

Domgroup's appeal was never heard. In February 1987, the company, the union and Loblaws agreed on a resolution of the disputes which had been raging for so long. The agreement allowed Domgroup to keep $30 million of the pension surplus — half of the current value of the $38 million it had withdrawn from the unionized employees' plan — plus the $16.5 million it had withdrawn in 1983. The rest of the money would be shared by members of the pension plan. Secondly, Domgroup would post a $5-million deposit in a trust account to settle the long-simmering dispute over severance pay. Thirdly, Domgroup would give the union $7 million. Of that, $5 million would be used to compensate laid-off employees for the loss of their jobs.*

In the spring of 1989, the parties were ready to make an application to the court for approval of the settlement. The court would also be asked to consider a plan for distributing the money to the employees, a process which could take months or even years. In the meantime, none of the former Dominion workers has received a cent of the "surplus" funds to which they are entitled.

For Brad Gaull, Alan Dixon, Harold Pym, Dorothy Ritchie, Joe Calderone and Bill Batchelor, the battle for the surplus has been a bittersweet experience. The most important question — who owned the surplus in the Dominion Stores pension fund? — will never be resolved. But their outrage was not in vain. The battle,

---

*The agreement also stated that Loblaw Companies Ltd. would buy fifty-eight Mr. Grocer stores from Domgroup. The 1,500 employees involved would be covered by a union contract. Under the terms of the contract, however, Mr. Grocer stores would pay lower wages than Loblaws supermarkets. Employees who had been laid off when Dominion had franchised the stores to independent operators would be given first chance to be hired when vacancies occurred, but there were no guarantees that they would be rehired. Union officials insisted that the deal was the best way out of a complicated and potentially ruinous situation. Further court cases, said Collins, could well have dragged on for years, jeopardizing the sale of the Mr. Grocer stores and costing more jobs to union members.

frustrating and inconclusive as it was, finally forced many politicians to do what they should have done long ago: to take a hard and close look at the laws which govern private pension plans in this country and at the weak and ineffective regulatory bodies entrusted with ensuring that the plans operate fairly and openly.*
And, wonder of wonders, the controversy finally caused many Canadians who dutifully "contribute" to private pension plans each year to wake up and take notice. As the dispute over private pension plans heats up, it is now clear that the fight for the Dominion Stores pension fund was merely a crucial skirmish in a much larger war. The outcome of that war could ensure that in the years to come millions of Canadians will actually receive the retirement income they have earned — just as it could bring down the curtain on a pension system run amok.

*
*In many provinces across Canada, the Dominion Stores employees would have faced a truly impossible task; for, although the Ontario legislation and the Pension Commission itself were weak, at least they existed. In most jurisdictions, the machinations of the company would never have come to light at all. They very nearly did not in Ontario.

6

PRIVATE PENSIONS
B.C. AND A.D.

::

*"It's a matter of B.C. and A.D.: Before Conrad and After
Dominion Stores. Canadians looked at what that company
had done and they said, 'Hey, that's not right, that's not fair —
and what has that Pension Commission done about it?'
Dominion Stores, I'd say, was the Anno Domini of pensions."*

John Kruger, troubleshooter,
chairman of the Pension Commission of Ontario, (A.D.) January 1988

··

Ah, the irony of it all. When the SOS group and the company
union took Dominion Stores and the Ontario Pension Commission to court, Conrad Black complained that the media and the
politicians had got it all wrong. Inferences had been made,
Black pointed out, that he, personally, had "skimmed" the $62
million out of the Dominion Stores pension plan and that he,
personally, had left the plan in a "parlous financial condition."
It was mischievous and quite inaccurate, Black suggested in his
column in the *Globe and Mail's Report on Business* magazine,
to blame *him* for "normal business efficiencies" carried out by
company executives "after application of the exacting tests to
prevent abuses rightly applied by the Pension Commission of
Ontario."

Black had a point. Some journalists and politicians *had*
succumbed to the temptation to treat the Toronto financier and
Dominion Stores, a company he controlled through a network of

complex and oft-shifting corporate structures, as virtually synonymous. Such journalistic shorthand was a godsend to headline writers who otherwise might have had to waste their time confirming exactly what Black's company was called on that particular day. But he was right: it was rhetoric, it was dubious journalistic practice, it was a cheap shot, and it eventually led to provocative headlines such as "Black can keep $30 million pension cash in union deal" (*Toronto Star*, February 3, 1987), which were neither quite accurate nor quite fair.

But the gentleman did protest too much. His allegations that Dominion Stores employees were pilfering $30 million from the company each year served only to focus even more public attention on the disturbing drama unfolding in the courts. In the end, the Dominion Stores employees emerged as folk heroes, while Black ended up looking rather silly. And his outbursts played into the hands of the very people he wished to discredit: all those who had been saying for years that private-sector intransigence and corporate greed were the main stumbling blocks on the path to desperately-needed and long overdue reform of the country's pension system.

Once the Dominion Stores case hit the headlines, the "pension problem" was transformed almost overnight into a hot topic. Up to that point, it has been a problem which most Canadians had studiously ignored on the grounds that it was too boring, too complex or too depressing to think about. Politicians who had been dithering over pension reform for more than a decade suddenly saw an issue that they could sell in their own constituencies, if for no other reason than that Conrad Black was "involved" in it; journalists who had shied away from pensions, because they, personally, didn't expect to be in one job long enough to earn one, pricked up their ears. Unions long frustrated by legal and bureaucratic impediments to pension challenges took heart; middle managers wondered about their own pension plans; *managers* wondered about their pension plans. Overnight, thanks to Conrad Black, pensions — *pensions*, for heaven's sake! — had become a sexy issue.

For all those Canadians who had been angered by the inequities and hypocrisies rampant in Canada's private pension system — and there were many — this sudden blast of publicity was a mixed blessing. On the one hand, retirees, consumer advocates, women's groups and organized employees who had been trying to put an end to the shortcomings in the system for years clearly owed Conrad Black their thanks for focusing public attention on private pensions. On the other hand, by concentrating only on Black and the surplus issue, the burst of media attention tended to oversimplify the more complex problems which had bedevilled the pension system for so long. While it was true that there were good guys and bad guys, Robin Hoods and free-market privateers, it was also true that many of the problems with the system were considerably more complicated and difficult than that.

On balance, Black's intemperate allegations and the questionable ethics of the company he controlled marked a critical turning-point in the seemingly endless debate on pension reform in this country. Because of him, many of us who had paid no attention at all to our pensions began to wonder what was going on with private pension plans. Why did the Dominion Stores pension fund have such a large surplus in the first place? Why did the company think it had a right to claim the money? Why didn't the assets of every pension fund belong to the employees who had contributed their hard-earned money to it? Whose money was it, anyway?

Before Conrad, most of us who are members of occupational pension plans dutifully "contributed" two or three percent of our salaries, or even more, to the plans year after year, without complaint and without question. These "contributions" were rather like income tax deductions, a melancholy fact of life inexorably reflected in a tiny box on monthly paycheques. And as the slick brochures most of us received at one time or another explained, the deductions were for our own good: they would provide us with the best possible guarantee of financial security and independence on retirement day at no risk whatsoever. Indeed, the brochures made clear, the company pension plan was a perfect example of why the company was a fine place to work. The pension plan was proof of our employer's enlightened and benevolent corporate outlook.

Take Doodads Inc., for example, a typical if fictional Canadian corporation. If we bothered to read the glossy company brochures, we would have learned that Doodads Inc. introduced its trail-blazing pension scheme in 1952 in recognition of the hard work and devoted service of its employees. Since then the company's executive team had worked hard to provide the best plan possible. And the hype didn't end there. Over the years we were given glowing accounts of the benefits the plan guaranteed us on retirement and reminded why the plan was so wonderful. Doodads' plan, like many private-pension schemes, the brochures noted, was a contributory defined-benefit plan and it was top of the line. Employees who stayed with the company for ten years would eventually receive a pension based not only on their own "contributions," but also on the generous contributions the company had made on their behalf.

Moreover, each passing year brought more good news in the form of a statement of benefits earned to date, along with an upbeat explanation of how Doodads Inc. had recently improved the plan on our behalf. Those improvements usually involved a more advantageous formula to determine the size of the pension benefit we would receive on retirement. Perhaps a benefit based on 1.5 percent of salary for each year of service had been improved to a benefit based on 2 percent of salary — obviously a good thing. Or perhaps a pension based on an average of salary in the last five years of employment had been improved to an average of salary in the last three years of employment. Assuming that salaries increased in those years, a final three years' average would produce a higher pension benefit than one averaged over five years. And if salaries had kept pace with or exceeded inflation, so much the better. That would mean that we hadn't actually *lost* ground in those years. In short, however the variables had been rearranged, the end result was likely to be more money in our pockets on retirement day.

So what was wrong with that? What was wrong with that was what the brochures *didn't* tell us. Nowhere did they describe what happened to Doodads Inc. employees on the day *after* they retired.

The pension benefit they had been promised was entirely in order. If the monthly benefit was to be $600 a month, it *was* $600 a month. The catch was that, in real dollars, the benefit would never be worth that much again, ever. From retirement day on, the $600 would begin to wither away. The villain, of course, was inflation and the consequences were dire indeed.

Take Fred, for example. Fred retired at age sixty-five in 1972 with a pension of $300 a month from Doodads Inc. In addition, he received the Old Age Security benefit to which all Canadians over age sixty-five are entitled (then $80.72 a month) and the Canada Pension Plan benefit he had earned through his contributions to the compulsory government pension plan (then $27.25 a month). As a total pension package, it was not bad. The combined benefits seemed to guarantee that Fred would enjoy the lifestyle he expected and believed that he had earned, even though, at $407.97 a month, they amounted to not much more than half of his pre-retirement income. And indeed, for a while they would do just that.

But something happened on the road to Happy Valley. In the course of the next ten years, the cost of living increased in Canada by an average of about 9 percent each year. Fred's Old Age Security cheque and his Canada Pension Plan benefits increased, too, to about $168.00 a month and $68.00 a month respectively, because they were automatically adjusted each year to keep up with the cost of living. But Fred's company pension increased not a penny. Quite the contrary. In real terms, it declined by 57 percent. By 1982 it was worth only $129 a month in 1972 dollars, instead of the $300 Fred had counted on when he retired.*

Like many unsuspecting Canadians who believed that their

---

*As Fred gets older, of course, his financial situation will continue to deteriorate. An employee who retired from Doodads Inc. with a pension of $100 a month in 1965 received a pension worth only $26 a month in real dollars in 1985. But even an employee who retired as recently as 1980 with a $1,000 benefit saw its real value decline to $634 by 1985. Furthermore, even when inflation is relatively low, the gap between the cost of living and the purchasing power of a pension cheque continues to widen significantly. A 3-percent annual inflation rate will erode the value of a pension by 25.6 percent over ten years.

pensions would be sufficient to maintain their pre-retirement lifestyles, Fred had not fully grasped the dreadful impact inflation could have on a fixed benefit. He assumed that his pension was, and would continue to be, adequate — mainly because his employers had led him to assume it. In reality, the private pensions Fred and his colleagues had worked so hard to build simply vanished before their eyes.

It didn't take long for Fred to discover that he'd been had. He would be far better off today, he realized, if, all those years ago, he had told Doodads Inc. to forget it: he would take the company's "contribution" to the plan in the form of higher wages and look after the future himself. But, like most members of private pension plans, Fred never had that option. After he reached age thirty, his membership in Doodads Inc.'s pension plan was compulsory and he was trapped. If he left the company before he had worked there for ten years, he would have received his own contributions back at a rate of interest determined by the company. Nothing more. No tax breaks, no "contribution" from the firm. If he stayed with the company, he was in the plan whether he liked it or not — and whether or not the fund was performing well and was managed in his best interests.

Fred did stay with the firm and, all things considered, his pension when he retired was all right. Not wonderful, but all right. It was only *after* he retired that the trouble began. And big trouble it was, too. By 1988, Fred's $300 pension was worth less than $100 in 1972 dollars.

What had gone wrong? Nobody *wanted* Fred to have a lousy pension. The answer to that question, like the answer to many questions about pensions, depends largely on your point of view and your sense of fair play. From the vantage point of Mr. Manyshares, the company president, it was simply an act of God, an unforeseen and unforeseeable rise in inflation rates, that caused Fred's pension to lose most of its purchasing power within a few years. When the pension plan was established in 1952, nobody could have predicted that inflation rates would begin to spiral out of control in the early 1970s. Nobody could have anticipated that private pension plans would become mini gold mines for their sponsors. Nobody would have believed that, in 1988, employers like himself would be entranced and instructed by a book entitled *Pension Funds and the Bottom Line: Managing the Corporate Pension Fund as a Financial Business.** And nobody could have known that Fred's pension would rapidly disappear. After all, nobody *wanted* double digit inflation and nobody *wanted* Fred to suffer. Therefore, it must have been an act of God.

From Fred's vantage point, of course, the view was rather different. Fred assumed that he had earned — and indeed had paid for — a pension benefit which would maintain its value in real terms until the day he died. He thought that he had earned the right to share in the good fortune of Doodads Inc. when inflation and an over-heated stock market drove pension-fund-investment returns off the charts. He thought he would have a pretty comfortable retirement. Unfortunately, he thought wrong. While the economic climate of the last decade worked to the very great advantage of most employer-sponsored pension plans — and therefore to the very great advantage of most employers — it worked to the extreme *disadvantage* of the employees the plans are supposed to protect.

The critical question to ask here, though, is not whose fault it was that pension benefits declined in value so sharply over the last two decades. After all, inflation was not a uniquely Canadian problem with a uniquely Canadian solution. The real question was how governments, private employers and the pension industry reacted to such rapid, unexpected and unwelcome economic change. The answer, for the most part, has to be "very badly." When the assets of pension plans began to mushroom beyond all expectations in the early 1980s, it seemed obvious to many people that retirees should not be

---

*The influential 1986 book by Toronto pension consultant Keith Ambachtsheer is based on a proposition that would have astounded Mr. Manyshares as recently as a decade ago: that "pension plan assets and liabilities now rival in size those of the main-line businesses of the sponsor corporations" and should be managed accordingly — for the benefit of the corporation and its shareholders. Incredibly, if its pension plan were managed creatively and well, Doodads Inc. could make as much or more from the plan as they could from selling doodads.

victimized by inflation while their former employers were enjoying windfall gains on their money. Some employers saw it that way too, and they responded by voluntarily increasing pension benefits for their retirees. But most employers did little or nothing to ensure that benefits would retain their purchasing power — and politicians and policy makers, long on rhetoric but decidedly short on will, let them get away with it. They are still getting away with it.

And the odd thing is that for all those years, most younger Canadians with access to private pension coverage sat back and did nothing, secure in the misapprehension that it could never happen to them. This extraordinary indifference to a pension system which gobbles up a significant chunk of lifetime earnings and offers no guarantees at all that benefits will maintain their purchasing power after retirement seems inexplicable. But perhaps the explanation for it is not really very complicated. No one likes to think about retirement and old age and no one likes to tangle with an employer on an issue as complicated as pensions. To make matters even worse, most Canadians are deeply confused about what an occupational pension is or should be.

Nobody these days holds to the old-fashioned view that a private pension is simply a "gift" from a generous employer to his employees, despite all of the high-blown rhetoric to the contrary. That notion lost any plausibilty it might ever have had shortly after the Second World War when pension issues began to land on the table as part of the collective bargaining process.* Despite this, most Canadians continue to believe their employers when they promise them a "good" pension to

*

*A 1948 U.S. court case, *Inland Steel v. National Labor Relations Board*, determined that pensions were part of wages and were therefore subject to collective bargaining. Following that decision, many American unions launched a drive for non-contributory pensions. The drive soon spread to Canada. In 1950 the United Auto Workers won pension plans from the Ford Motor Company of Canada and General Motors and enshrined the principle that improvements to the plans would be an integral part of the negotiating process.

cushion their retirement years, while the experience of the last decade, culminating in massive and widespread employer contribution holidays and huge surplus withdrawals, has demonstrated how fragile those promises were. The only "good" pension is one which retains all or most of its purchasing power; yet in 1984, the last year for which comprehensive figures are available, 93.7 percent of all private sector pension plans in Canada had no form of automatic inflation protection whatsoever.

Moreover, although it still suits most employers to describe their pension plans as corporate largesse, the popular notion that private pensions were ever "gifts" has always been a myth. When private employers created pension plans, they invariably had pragmatic reasons for doing so — and those reasons rarely had much to do with corporate beneficence. Indeed, most private sector plans were created for a straightforward and unexceptionable reason: to keep the enterprise competitive. An attractive pension plan could induce valued employees to remain with the company and it could attract desirable new people to the firm as well. The pension plan could also serve as an effective way to regulate the size and the composition of the work force. By institutionalizing a rigid set of rules — most notably, mandatory retirement at age sixty-five — the pension system as a whole enabled employers to clear the decks for younger people without the cost, inconvenience and embarrassment of vetting older employees' performances in order to provide a justification for firing them. In short, the plans served many purposes, but most of them had more to do with corporate profits than with corporate generosity.

Canada's complex old-age-security system, as we have seen in chapter one, evolved as the result of attempts, some of them sadly misguided, to ensure that older people would not be obliged to work if they were physically unable to do so or if they were locked into soul-destroying jobs. But the cure — forced retirement at sixty-five — may have been as bad as the disease. Over the years, the "right" to retire inexorably turned into a compulsion to retire, in part because it made sense to have a definition of when "old age" begins, even if that definition was totally arbitrary.* Private pensions came to be seen as a reward to employees in honour of a lifetime of service that had drawn to its natural conclusion. And soon mandatory retirement at sixty-five had become so deeply entrenched in the Canadian mind that, until recently, few people even bothered to question the whys and wherefores of it.

Today Canadians are debating the merits and disadvantages of forced retirement at sixty-five. At the same time, the thrust of pension reform in the last decade has been to make it possible for employees to vest their pensions earlier, to carry pension entitlements with them from job to job and to drop out of the work force for indefinite periods of time without losing accumulated pension benefits. Indeed, several jurisdictions have already introduced legislation to permit employees to claim their pensions as early as age fifty-five or as late as age seventy if they wish to do so. The reform process, however, has failed miserably to produce the provincial uniformity necessary to guarantee all Canadians equal pension rights. At least the debate has had a clarifying effect on our notion of what a pension *is*. Clearly, a benefit which is vested, portable and may be claimed any time between the ages of fifty-five and seventy is not a *gift* from anyone. It is a deferred wage to which employees are entitled for a simple and straightforward reason: they have earned it.

As challenges to forced retirement make their way through the courts under the Charter of Rights and Freedoms, the rigidity of the pension system and its deadening effect on the creative policy-making necessary to meet future economic and social demands are becoming more and more apparent in the arguments mustered in support of the practice. Employers' first line of defence against such challenges is usually that their

*Forced retirement is a managerial tool in more ways than one. If employees join a pension plan at age thirty-five and retire at sixty-five, the task of the actuaries who must determine how much money is needed in the plan to provide their pensions is far less complicated than if employees retire at different ages. One unhappy result of this has been employer reluctance to hire older people because of the extra paperwork, and therefore costs, involved in calculating their benefits.

pension plans cannot accommodate flexible retirement because they were not designed to do so. Paradoxically, this argument has not stopped many employers from offering early retirement schemes when it suits their purposes, that is, when they want to downsize their work force to meet corporate goals.

The employers who created the first occupational pension plans more than a century ago had very specific goals in mind, goals not unlike those of employers today who sweeten the pension pot to get rid of aging, high-priced employees. One of the earliest plans, the Superannuation Act of 1870, was established with the motive, as historian Desmond Morton puts it, of "easing the departure of venerable officials inherited from the United Provinces and allowing the young Dominion government to make fresh appointments, particularly from the lower provinces." The minister of finance, Sir Francis Hincks, notes Morton, was "characteristically blunt" about the purpose of the legislation. It was "not for the benefit of employees, but for the protection and benefit of the public and to enable the Government to get rid of persons who had arrived at a time of life when they could no longer perform their work efficiently."

Large private companies, too, saw the advantages of pension plans in improving the efficiency of their operations. In 1874, for example, the Grand Trunk Railway of Canada set up a compulsory superannuation fund for its clerical staff in which employees contributed 2.5 percent of their salaries and the company matched the contribution to provide a benefit based on one-sixtieth of the employee's salary at retirement multiplied by the number of years he had contributed to the plan. By contrast, Canadian Pacific offered a plan fully paid by the company in which employees with at least ten years' service became eligible for a pension at sixty-five based on one percent of their average earnings the previous ten years multiplied by their total years of service.

In proclaiming the plan in 1903, Morton and historian Margaret McCallum note, "the CPR emphasized that the company's action was entirely voluntary, that employees derived no rights from its creation and that they could be discharged without pension or have their pensions cancelled for gross misconduct." And, indeed, they point out, in 1908 the railway *did* cancel the pension rights of employees who had struck the company, as did the Grand Trunk in 1910 in the course of a bitter strike. (The rights of the strikers were restored in 1923, after the railway had become part of the government-owned Canadian National Railways.)

By that time, there were about one hundred and seventy employer-sponsored pension plans across the country, many of them designed specifically to defuse labour unrest and stave off strikes — as well as to force older employees out of jobs. Or, as an Imperial Oil official put it in testimony to the Royal Commission on Industrial Relations in 1919, corporate welfare was "not philanthropy and it is not benevolence: it is a cold-blooded business proposition." Largely because of this philosophy, the plans spread rapidly from the civil service and the railways into factories, retail stores, and banks. By 1930 the number of plans in Canada had increased to more than seven hundred, covering between 10 and 15 percent of the labour force.

Not surprisingly, the expansion of the private plans came to a halt during the Depression when employers had no need to provide inducements other than a day's work to job-hungry Canadians. By 1937, no more than 8 percent of working Canadians had a pension plan. About 70 percent of Canadians had no old-age income protection at all. But when the unemployment rate plummeted to near zero during the Second World War, private pensions made a comeback, this time with a new twist. In 1942, the minister of National Revenue was empowered to approve pension plans as corporate tax deductions.*

As a result, the plans took on a new lustre in employers' eyes and by 1947 there were about 3,400 plans in existence across the country. Moreover, by 1950 unions had become the rule rather than the exception in most Canadian industries and, following

---

*Plan sponsors had enjoyed tax breaks since 1919, but until the Second World War they were not very significant because corporate tax rates were so low. In 1938, for example, Canadian corporations paid only $85 million in federal taxes. By 1943, however, income and excess profit taxes cost employers $740 million and, as Morton and McCallum point out, "even discounting full employment and soaring economic activity, taxes had become a burden worth shifting."

the lead of the Auto Workers, their members demanded the protection of a pension plan and the right to bargain for benefits. In 1946 about a quarter of Canadian industrial employees had some pension coverage; by 1951 that percentage had risen to forty-five percent. Even today, union members are about twice as likely to be covered by private pension plans as employees in non-unionized workplaces, and benefits levels under plans which are subject to collective bargaining are also significantly higher, on average, than benefits in plans which are not.

By the end of 1979, Statistics Canada figures showed that there were 14,586 employer-sponsored pension plans in Canada covering about 4.4 million employees, figures which sound very impressive. But there is a flip side of the coin. Since the great expansion of the private pension system after the Second World War, most Canadians have taken it for granted that employer-sponsored pension plans are an integral and necessary part of the pension system as a whole. This is an image which the private sector, and especially large employers, has been eager to foster and which it continues to guard jealously through well-financed lobbies and powerful professional organizations. The existence of such plans — and the private sector's assurances that coverage would continue to expand with time — has provided the business community with a potent argument against the expansion of the public pension system and the resulting shift of control over fund assets from the private sector to the federal government.

Yet the private sector's performance has been uneven at best and downright scandalous at worst. By the mid-1970s, despite all the promises, only forty percent of all working Canadians belonged to an employer-sponsored pension plan and fewer than one working woman in four had any private coverage at all, primarily because so many women, then as now, worked in retail and service sector jobs where private pensions were the exception rather than the norm. Statistics cited in the 1982 federal Green Paper on pensions indicated that in 1979 there was *no* coverage for 720,000 self-employed men and women, for 920,000 men and women earning between half and one and a half times the average wage, for 570,000 women in the private sector who earned less than $11,000, and for another 450,000 women earning between $11,000 and $22,000. Furthermore, only a fraction of those Canadians who had been enrolled in private plans ever collected anything like a full pension. They lost their pension entitlements because of vesting rules and lack of portability, and as a result retired on pensions which were totally inadequate to begin with.

Panic about the adequacy of the private pension system began to mount in the 1970s as it became increasingly apparent that most of the assumptions underlying its creaking framework had disintegrated over the years. For a decade thereafter, attempts to put things right turned into a major Canadian cottage industry. Yet, despite its manifest injustices and the many attempts to reform it, the system remained virtually untouched until the mid-1980s.

In the meantime, the expansion of the private system was long overdue. By 1986, the total membership of employer-sponsored plans stood at 4.6 million, with only about thirty-seven percent of the total labour force and forty-seven percent of all working Canadians covered by occupational pension plans. Of those who were covered, nearly half were members of public-, not private-sector plans. Instead of expanding to cover more Canadians, as the corporate lobby and the pension industry had promised it would, the private system was stalled at roughly the same levels it had been for two decades. Indeed, in some occupations and industries, predictably those which employ large numbers of women and low-income earners, there continued to be virtually no private pension coverage at all.*

Legislators defended their lack of resolve on the most critical problems of all — mandatory inflation protection and expanded coverage — as the private-sector pension lobby continued to guard its role in the pension system ferociously, mounting

---

*In addition to lack of coverage in entire industries such as farming and forestry, coverage varies widely from province to province, with employees in the poorer provinces being much less likely to have access to a pension plan. In 1984, for example, pension coverage extended to only 22.5 percent of the total labour force in Prince Edward Island and to only 31.7 percent in Newfoundland. By comparison, coverage in Ontario stood at 38.9 percent.

costly and elaborate campaigns to fend off its critics. Much of this energy was spent debunking anyone who had the audacity to suggest that most Canadians would be far better off in retirement with an expanded Canada Pension Plan. Even with all of the pitfalls of an unfunded plan, they argued, an expanded CPP would be better than the mishmash of employer-sponsored plans which left so many Canadians out in the cold and shortchanged so many others. At least it would compel *all* employers to contribute to their employees' retirement security.

That sort of loose talk was, of course, anathema to the corporate lobby, whose spokesmen continued to insist that, if given just a little more time, they would make good on their past promises. And when, in 1985, Ottawa and the provinces finally did reach an agreement in principle on the course that reform should follow, the business community asserted that genuine reform of the pension system was now complete. That assessment, though typical, was both premature and entirely self-serving. In fact, the battle over pension reform is far from over.

As a society, Canadians clearly believe that employers *should* bear some real responsibility for the well-being of their employees after retirement. As we saw in chapter two, the Canada Pension Plan is premised on the fundamental assumption that all employers must contribute to their employees' future security as part of the ordinary costs of doing business. And, until the high inflation rates of the 1970s plunged the pension system into disarray, most Canadians thought that their employers believed that too.

Take Mr. Manyshares, for example. In 1952 the president of Doodads Inc. decided that a pension plan was the very thing his firm needed to compete with all the other doodad manufacturers for the skilled staff it needed. With the economy booming, it was hard to find and keep good people and, with memories of growing up during the Depression still fresh, young employees were impressed by the security that a good pension plan could offer their families. So Mr. Manyshares hired a pensions and benefits expert who analyzed his company's needs. How much did the employees earn? How many were men, how many women? Were they young or old? What did they want from a pension plan? What was the turnover rate? What could the company afford? The expert, in turn, told Mr. Manyshares what kind of plan he should have: how much it would cost the company, what tax relief he could expect, how much the employees should contribute, how the plan would work. Mr. Manyshares made one or two modest suggestions — after all, it was *his* plan — paid the expert, registered the plan and that was that.

But Doodads Inc.'s plan was premised on one basic assumption: that inflation would stay within "manageable" bounds, increasing at a rate of no more than one or two percent per year. As a result, the plan, like most private plans then and now, made no provision at all for indexing pension benefits to the cost of living. When inflation rates started to edge up in the mid-1960s, Mr. Manyshares faced some major headaches. But his problems were nothing compared to the problems confronting the members of his pension plan who were approaching retirement. Most of them, like Fred, would have to make do on fixed-income pensions when they retired, and cross their fingers that Mr. Manyshares would take pity on them.

Many employers did take pity on their retirees, precisely because they *were* good and responsible corporate citizens who did care about their employees. Others made upwards adjustments to pension benefits because their retirees banded together and engaged in a mild sort of blackmail, lobbying their former employers publicly to cough up or to risk a smudge on their corporate images. Some unions, too, took their retired members' cases to the bargaining table, although many argued that they were not legally empowered to bargain on behalf of retirees. These tactics were sometimes successful in encouraging recalcitrant employers to make periodic ad hoc adjustments to benefits. Sometimes they weren't: as was their right under the terms of the pension plans, many employers simply ignored their retirees.

A 1987 survey of 284 Canadian companies by pension consultants Hewitt Associates submitted to the 1987 Ontario Task Force on Inflation Protection provides an overview of what happened. Fully a quarter of all employers who responded to the survey said that they had done nothing at all to improve benefits for retirees between 1976 and 1986. And among those who did, almost half made fewer than four ad hoc adjustments in the ten-year period. The Hewitt survey is revealing, but it may well have overestimated the extent to which employers rallied to restore the real value of pensions. We will never know. It is impossible to cite accurate and comprehensive figures for all private pension plans, because they don't exist.*

Moreover, even according to the pension industry's own figures, only a handful of employers made up anything like the full amount retirees were losing to inflation. The Hewitt survey showed that in the ten-year period from January 1, 1977 to January 1, 1987, when the cumulative rate of inflation was 110 percent, the cumulative average paid to retirees in the same period amounted to only 29 percent of the increase in the Consumer Price Index. That means that employers made up barely a quarter of what retirees had lost to inflation in those years. Translated into dollars, it means that a retiree with a monthly pension of $1,000 in 1976 needed about $2,100 in 1987 just to keep up with inflation, but in fact received only $1,290. And if an employer chose to do nothing at all, as did a quarter of all companies in the Hewitt survey, there was precious little retirees could do about it. They were, after all, now *former* employees, with little more than natural justice on their side.

While retirees helplessly watched their pensions vanish into thin air, pension-fund managers were enjoying a different kind of magic show. Beginning in about 1980, if they were any good — and indeed even if they weren't — the returns on their investments began to exceed their wildest dreams. Soon many pension funds boasted surpluses far, far greater than the plans required to meet their obligations, in part because the high

---

*The members of the task force admitted in their 1988 report that "ad hoc increases are commonly believed to have generally compensated for 40 percent of inflation. However, we have not been able to substantiate either this figure or the number of employers making them....Even with increases that have been reported to the Pension Commission of Ontario, government records do not clarify the details." Employers who dipped into corporate income to provide one-time-only payments to their retired employees displayed the ultimate hypocrisy: such payments do not increase the base of the pension benefit nor do they increase the liabilities of the plan.

inflation rates which were ravaging pension benefits also guaranteed good investment returns. The cause of these huge surpluses has been a bitter bone of contention between plan sponsors and their critics, as we shall see in chapter seven. The important point is, though, that wherever the surpluses came from, they did accumulate at a time when retirees had their backs against the wall. The market value of Canadian trusteed pension-fund assets grew from $59 billion in 1981 to $138 billion in 1986 — $40 billion more than plan sponsors had a right to expect based on the investment experience of the previous five years*. By insisting on bickering over the whys and the wherefores of the surpluses, the private sector effectively stonewalled the larger issue: the decline in value of their retirees' pensions.

As this manna from heaven — another act of God, no doubt — rained down upon them through the early 1980s, employers responded in very different ways. The good ones concluded that, indeed, there must be a connection between the erosion of the real value of retirement benefits and their own burgeoning pension funds. And they acted accordingly, using the surpluses to improve pension benefits for their retirees. But many employers, like Mr. Manyshares, didn't see it that way. They chose to view the huge surpluses as a golden opportunity to reduce their own contributions to the plans. As the surpluses grew, so did the numbers of "contribution holidays" and applications for surplus withdrawals.

At first, these withdrawals attracted little public attention and less controversy. But that was about to change. On June 26, 1985, when Ontario voters turned out the Tory government that had been entrenched in the province for forty-two years, the sluggish progress of pension reform took a dramatic and unexpected turn. Locked into an uneasy two-year accord with the New Democrats, Premier David Peterson and his neophyte ministers scrambled hard to claim exclusive credit for blowing the winds of change into the province. This was a happy

---

*According to Statistics Canada, the book value of assets in trusteed pension funds as of December 31, 1987 was $142.9 billion, up 12.3% from the previous year.

situation for pension reformers. Provincial NDP leader Bob Rae had campaigned on pension reform during the election campaign. Now the issue was one of the twenty-eight items mutually agreed to in the accord with the Liberals. And with the Liberals more responsive to pension reform than they might otherwise have been, the NDP applied the pressure and kept it on.

Ross McClellan, then NDP House leader and MPP for the Toronto riding of Bellwoods, recalls that his party had reached a measure of agreement with the Liberals on pension matters, including the urgent need for mandatory inflation protection, as early as 1981, when he and David Peterson, then finance critic, sat together on a legislative select committee for pension reform. The committee's recommendations had gathered dust on a shelf. So when NDP members finally found themselves in a position to force significant pension reform under the terms of the accord, it was a moment of great personal satisfaction for McClellan: "You never know when something is going to catch on with the public, and rarely are you able to make something a national issue," he recalls. And the discovery that Conrad Black was involved through the Dominion Stores surplus withdrawal made the issue even more savoury for the party, says McClellan. "Conrad Black put a face on capitalism and its most irresponsible aspects. That helped."

Years of NDP research into pension questions began to pay off. Months before the Dominion Stores case broke, McClellan and a dogged team of researchers had been digging into the use and abuse of pension funds across the province. But they were as surprised as everyone else by the recent spate of surplus withdrawals. In June 1985 — just after the election — McClellan had received a letter from Robert Baldwin, senior researcher with the Canadian Labour Congress, asking him to raise the question of surplus withdrawals with the Liberal Government by filing a written request on the daily order notices at Queen's Park. Baldwin had been looking into the subject at the federal level and he wanted to find out if employers were using similar tactics in Ontario.

"I didn't know what he was talking about: that's how much of a non-issue it was," McClellan remembers. Indeed, the party almost dismissed Baldwin's warning out-of-hand. McClellan even lost the letter. But Baldwin persisted. A couple of months later, he got in touch again; and this time McClellan paid attention.

Party researchers dug deeper into the surplus issue, and their findings staggered them. In the fiscal year 1984-85, they discovered, $248 million had been withdrawn from Ontario pension plans. Even today, McClellan is at a loss to explain the phenomenon, which seems to have been inspired by similar corporate tactics in the United States. "The Americans didn't discover they could steal this money until about 1983," McClellan says. "In 1981 nobody dreamed that this kind of corporate theft would even be considered."

Well-briefed by his researchers, Rae launched the NDP pension assault in the Ontario Legislature in January 1986 with his disclosure of the Dominion Stores withdrawal. Day after day, NDP members disclosed details of corporate manoeuvring, focusing on the sudden upsurge in surplus withdrawals from defined-benefit pension plans and exposing what he called the "haemorrhaging" of pension funds. In 1984, Rae pointed out, Inco Ltd. had been permitted to remove $105 million from its pension plan, despite the fact that an Inco miner retiring that year could look forward to a total pension package of only $1,000 a month after thirty years on the job.

Day after day, Rae demanded that the promised pension reforms include either an outright ban on contribution holidays and withdrawals from ongoing plans or tight new rules which would force employers to index pensions and devote at least a portion of any remaining surpluses in their plans to richer benefits for their retirees and current employees. Day after day he spoke of "legalized theft" from pension plan members, words which made the business community cringe.

The tactics were effective. When the details of the Dominion Stores withdrawal emerged, Canadians were finally ready to pay attention too. The revelations — with Conrad Black's name attached — sent reporters scrambling for more details about the withdrawal and for more information about the Pension Commission — certainly a low-profile body — which had approved it. How many other companies had applied to remove surplus funds from pension plans? How many had been successful? How much had they withdrawn? What was going on here, anyway?

The first thing reporters discovered was that nobody really knew the amount of surplus assets in private pension plans. Nor was there any way to get precise information. In Ontario alone, estimates of the surpluses in the plans ran as low as $4 billion and as high as $12 billion. Next they learned that right across the country, provincial legislation to protect plan members was weak and ineffectual, if it existed at all. Like most of the plans themselves, the rules governing them had been put in place long before the surplus "problem" developed. Ontario's Pension Benefits Act, which covers about sixty percent of all private pension plans in Canada, for example, made no mention of surplus assets at all.

The Ontario Regulations under the Act were no better. First, they ignored the question of the surplus in ongoing plans, stating in Section 21.(2) only that "no funds shall be paid out of a pension plan to an employer unless consent of the Commission is obtained." In the event that a plan was terminated, the regulations stated in Section 14.(6) only that "no part of the assets of the plan shall revert to the benefit of the employer" unless "provision has been made for payment of all pension benefits and other benefits under the terms of the plan to employees, former employees, pensioners, dependents and estates."

The Regulations, in other words, had left the question of the disposition of surplus funds in ongoing plans entirely to the discretion of the Pension Commission. Then, in 1982, another proviso had appeared in the Regulations: employers would not be allowed to use the surplus in terminated plans for their own purposes unless "the pension plan provides for such reversion." But that proviso did little to protect employees: a determined employer like Dominion Stores could simply persuade the Commission to amend the plan retroactively to comply with the new restriction.

In the last ten months of 1985, the Pension Commission had allowed 49 active companies to withdraw $187.2 million from surpluses in their plans, including a $75-million withdrawal by Noranda Mines Ltd. in September. Those Ontario figures were hard enough to pin down. It proved even more difficult, and in some cases impossible, to unearth information about surplus withdrawals in other jurisdictions. British Columbia and Prince Edward Island, for example, have no legislation to control or even monitor the use employers make of the surpluses in their plans and only Quebec forbids surplus refunds from ongoing plans. (An amendment to Bill 58 that would have permitted employers to use surplus assets to reduce their own contributions to private plans died on the order paper before the 1985 Quebec election.)

In June 1986, six months after the Dominion Stores withdrawal, Rae introduced a private member's resolution demanding legislation to forbid companies from withdrawing surplus funds and to mandate inflation protection for private pensions, a resolution that many Liberal and Tory members were now prepared to support. Their numbers increased as more bits and pieces of information began to emerge about the Pension Commission, most of it painting a most unflattering picture of a secretive, hypersensitive and biased agency.

The Commission, it seemed, had not approved a single withdrawal in the first three months of 1986, the period when the Liberal government was putting the final touches on its new pension policy. But as soon as Consumer Affairs Minister Monte Kwinter announced that policy in late March, the logjam broke: between April 1, 1986 and August 18, 1986, when the Dominion Stores decision was released, the commissioners had approved twenty-two corporate withdrawals — two more than had been allowed in the entire year of 1980.

Nor was the practice limited to Ontario, where most of the largest funds are registered. According to Statistics Canada, which is prevented by federal regulations from releasing details of the transactions (or even the names of the companies), firms across Canada withdrew at least $290 million from their pension plans in 1985.

The condemnation of the surplus withdrawals intensified throughout the autumn with Rae leading the attack. Companies were making billions of dollars "shuffling paper" at the expense of retirees, he charged, adding that Canadians were living in an economic system that had begun to eat its young — and its old. "Where does that money come from?" Rae demanded: "It comes from you."

With its Pension Commission under attack in the courts and in the Legislature, Ontario quickly became the main arena of the surplus debate that was heating up across the country. This was good news for committed pension reformers.* About forty percent, or 1.46 million, of all private-pension-plan members in Canada belong to one of the 8,752 plans registered in the province. A major victory in Ontario would have an enormous impact on the rest of the country as the provinces moved to bring a measure of conformity into their legislation.

Only two weeks after the Supreme Court judges rapped Domgroup and the Pension Commission over the knuckles — ordering the company to return $37.9 million plus interest to the fund — another surplus withdrawal case hit the headlines. This one involved Dominion Securities Pitfield Ltd., Canada's largest investment dealer, and its outcome was equally heartening for the angry employees who took that company to court. They were members of a pension plan set up in 1958 by A. E. Ames and Co. Ltd., an investment firm which merged with Dominion Securities Ltd. in 1981. And they had a grievance much like the one that prompted the Dominion Stores employees to take their employer to court.

The A. E. Ames plan, too, specified that it was designed for the exclusive benefit of members and that, in the event that it was terminated, the assets of the plan would be paid out to its beneficiaries. When the two investment companies merged in 1981, the A. E. Ames plan had a surplus of $3.5 million. In October of that year, the trustees of the fund approved the

---

*Pension plans are normally registered in the province in which the majority of their members are employed. Under a Memorandum of Reciprocal Agreement and a series of bilateral agreements between provincial governments and the federal Department of Insurance, plan members who work in a province other than the one in which their plan is registered fall under the jurisdiction of the province in which they are employed.

transfer of $1,732,000 to the merged company. A year later, the Pension Commission approved an amalgamation of the Dominion Securities and A. E. Ames pension plans retroactive to the day of the merger. Under the new plan, the surplus withdrawal was not prohibited. In a judgement released on August 29, 1986, Mr. Justice Eugene Ewaschuk of the Supreme Court of Ontario called the withdrawal "corporate piracy" and ordered Dominion Securities to return the $1.7 million plus interest to the employees. The trustees of the plan had acted "in flagrant breach of their trust," Ewaschuk ruled, and the withdrawal amounted to an appropriation of funds to which the company had "no right whatsoever." In approving the transaction, Ewaschuk added, the Pension Commission had acted in "blissful ignorance and undoubted negligence."

Coming so close together, the impact of the two court decisions was dramatic. First, Pension Commission spokespeople, under siege from the NDP and, by then, from the media too, admitted that perhaps there were a few, ah, problems which needed to be sorted out.

"Among the members, there is some difference in views as to how to interpret the political environment that we find ourselves in now," David Stouffer, a pension consultant for William M. Mercer Ltd. and a Tory appointee to the Commission, told *Toronto Star* reporter Sandro Contenta on September 2. That was something of an understatement. In fact, the Commission was in disarray. Tensions and disagreements between old-guard Tory appointees and three recent Liberal appointees, including consumer advocate Lynne Gordon and Monica Townson, a knowledgeable advocate for women's pension rights, had all but paralyzed its operations. As a result, the commissioners had decided to toss the ball squarely into the lap of the Liberal government. Kwinter had already been informed that all surplus withdrawal applications would be put on hold until the government instructed the Commission on how to proceed.

Kwinter, who had said earlier that he considered the Dominion Stores withdrawal both legal and ethical — even while the matter was then before the courts — began to backpedal from his earlier assurances to Bay Street that the Liberal pension reform package would not prohibit surplus withdrawals. At the same time he continued to assure the business community that he had no plans to amend party policy to include mandatory inflation protection. He told reporters, however, that the Cabinet might well want to review that position in light of the recent court decisions.

Three weeks later, Kwinter bowed to growing pressure to clean up the Commission by appointing John Kruger as its chairman. An elegant, Australian-born troubleshooter with a matched set of notches on his gun from years in the trenches of Toronto municipal politics, Kruger strode into his latest showdown with a firm mandate: to do whatever was necessary to put an end to the ineptitude, the secrecy and the bias — fast. But the possibility that such withdrawals might be more tightly regulated, or even prohibited, drove some employers into a frenzy of activity. By December, 152 employers had applied to the Pension Commission to withdraw $256 million from private plans. Of those applications, 74 were approved for a total of $70.5 million. Of that amount, $42 million was withdrawn from ongoing plans, the rest from plans which were wound up in whole or in part.*

Then, on December 9, the same day that the Liberal government introduced its long-awaited pension legislation, Bill 170, for its first reading in the Legislature, Kwinter anounced that there would be a moratorium on surplus withdrawals. Direct raids on pension surpluses were, for the time being, illegal and would remain so until a newly-created Task Force on Inflation Protection for Employment Pension Plans reported a year later on the questions of indexation and surplus assets in the plans. And notwithstanding Kwinter's earlier assurances to the corporate lobby, the legislation included a firm commitment to force employers to make inflation

---

*The largest refund, $10.7 million, went to AMCA International Ltd. of Toronto. Acres Consulting Services of Toronto, an engineering firm, withdrew $9.3 million; Brascan Ltd., $7.5 million; and Ford Glass Ltd., a division of Ford Motor Co. of Detroit, $5.3 million.

protection a feature of all private plans registered in the province.*

Thus it was that a fluke of politics, and a handful of employers who had stepped over the line of fairness in the eyes of the public, put the pension reform bandwagon on the road again. And thus it was that corporate Canada was obliged once again to dust off its briefs and position papers listing the 292 reasons why pensions should not be indexed to protect retirees against inflation, the 127 excuses for the failure of the private sector to live up to its promises to expand pension coverage and improve benefits for employees and the 223 reasons why the money in company pension plans belongs to them. This time round, though, there were a lot more Canadians saying, "Hey, that's not right, that's not fair." And this time round, somebody was listening.

Thank you, Conrad Black.

---

*Although the moratorium put a temporary stop to the withdrawals in Ontario, it had little influence on other jurisdictions. In January, 1987, for example, Mobil Oil Canada removed nearly $45 million from its pension fund with the approval of the Alberta superintendent of pensions. Unlike Dominion Stores, Mobil notified current employees and retirees of its application to withdraw the funds.

7

FALSE PROMISES
BIG BUSINESS
AND HIGH FINANCE

::

*"The action of the short-sighted amongst employers has brought
the entire structure of private pensions into disrepute."*

Ontario Federation of Labour,
Brief to the Friedland Task Force on Inflation Protection, June 1987

*"It cannot be assumed that the promise of pensions was either
made or understood in real terms."*

Towers, Perrin, Forster & Crosby, Actuaries and Consultants,
Brief to the Friedland Task Force on Inflation Protection, May 1987

..

Just as Ottawa and the pension industry were getting the
message out that the Great Canadian Pension Debate had
finally come to an end, public outrage over the surplus rip-offs
pumped new life into the reform effort. If the system had been
reformed, Canadians wanted to know, how was it possible for
employers like Dominion Stores to reap great gains at the direct
expense of plan members? Why were retirees who had worked
hard all their lives being forced onto the welfare rolls while their
corporate employers pocketed huge windfall profits? And what
lay in store for younger Canadians? If a decade of attempts to
reform a system which was clearly discriminatory had failed to
put a stop to the most glaring abuses of the rights and

expectations of older Canadians, were all members of private plans going to face similar risks in the future?

Against all expectations, the stage was set for still another round in the Great Debate. This time the battleground would be Ontario, the province where sixty percent of all private plans in the country are registered and the bellwether jurisdiction for further reforms across Canada. And this time the stakes would be immeasurably higher: not only would the Ontario initiative set the pattern for other jurisdictions, but its deliberations would raise fundamental questions about the fairness of Canada's pension system as a whole and the legitimacy of the private sector's claim to exclusive ownership and control of the billions and billions of dollars in private pension plans.

Ontario politicians had been chastened by the New Democrats' barrage of revelations of corporate greed and they had been shocked by the Ontario Pension Commission's failure to protect the savings of many members of private pension plans. They had learned that many retirees had lost more than half the purchasing power of their pensions over the last decade. Yet the provincial government had allowed their former employers to withdraw millions of dollars from company pension plans. They had heard how in 1985, the Ontario Pension Commission approved a request from Inco, the giant Ontario nickel producer, to withdraw $105 million from its plan even though long-time Inco employees had watched helplessly as their pension benefits lost more than half their value in fourteen years.*

The misfortunes of longtime employees of several companies in financial difficulty also provided another compelling reason to take a hard look at the legislation governing the plans and at the guarantees plan members could expect when they retired — or when their firms were sold or went bankrupt. CCM, a long-established Ontario sporting-equipment company, for

---

*The United Steelworkers obtained partial redress for longstanding pension grievances with Inco in May 1988, when the union won inflation protection for pensions up to an inflation rate of 7 percent. As well, all Inco retirees and all survivors of Inco workers will receive inflation protection.

example, had folded in October 1982. Nearly two years later, the firm's former employees discovered that for more than eighteen months before the bankruptcy the firm had made no payments into the pension fund. As a result, pensions for hundreds of longtime CCM employees would be reduced by as much as sixty percent. One former CCM employee who expected a deferred pension of about $1,100 from the company when he reached age sixty-five, for example, discovered that his benefits would be only $415.

Ontario politicians finally responded. In an unusual show of unanimity, all three provincial parties agreed in December 1986 that Ontario's new pension rules should address not only the question of plan members' rights, but the explosive problem of inflation protection as well. If employers insisted on dipping into the surplus assets in their pension plans without guaranteeing plan members a significant measure of protection from the ravages of inflation, they would have to be forced to mend their ways. Despite the overwhelming opposition of the private-sector pension lobby, the new legislation would have to make such protection mandatory.

Ontario's abrupt decision to push pension reform one stage further took the business community and the pension industry by surprise. This was, after all, a battle they thought they had already won. Despite incessant private-sector grumbling that the reforms would be too complicated and too costly for plan sponsors to bear, most employers had resigned themselves to the thrust of pension reform. By now their grousing was pure habit; in reality, employers had long since decided that they could learn to live with earlier vesting, coverage for some part-time employees, minimum interest rules, improvements in survivor benefits and a funding rule that required employers to provide at least fifty percent of pension benefits. In fact, corporate Canada had emerged bruised but hardly bloodied from the reform exercise, in large part because the reforms applied primarily to benefits earned in the future and did little to make up for past abuses.

When all was said and done, the consensus position did little more than set right the most flagrantly discriminatory aspects of the private pension system: its fundamental structural biases against part-time, low-income and mobile employees, its arbitrary calculations of interest rates and, in the fifty-percent funding provision, the most egregious form of corporate hypocrisy in which the employer contrives to contribute little or nothing at all to the pension plan over a period of years. Inadequate as they were, these reforms were genuine steps forward — or, to be more precise, they *would* have been genuine steps forward had they been adopted universally across the country. In fact, the delicate consensus began to unravel almost immediately as different provinces adopted different parts of the plan to suit themselves.

And there could be no question that the corporate lobby had won the big ones. Its spokesmen and political sympathizers had successfully held the line on the critical questions of mandatory coverage and mandatory inflation protection. On top of that, the question of who owned — or should own — the assets of private pension plans had never arisen in a serious and systematic way. Those matters would be left to the courts and to the consciences of individual employers, as they always had been, unless those consciences happened to be bound by the terms of a rock-solid collective agreement.

Historically, the employers who sponsored defined-benefit pension plans assumed that they also "owned" them. If a plan could meet all of its legal obligations, any extra assets belonged to the plan sponsor, who could deploy them as he saw fit, as long as the plan contained enough money to pay the benefits promised to members as well as a "cushion" to cover unexpected exigencies. As long as all the "defined" benefits were protected, it was no business of contributors what happened to the fund.

There is nothing particularly wrong with this assumption — if the benefits provided by the plan are adequate, if inflation is negligible and if the company stays afloat. Everything stays roughly in balance, employers run the plans on their employees' behalf, contributing whatever is necessary to meet the obligations of the plan. Plan members, for their part, get what they were promised on the day they retire.

But over the years, the problems with this arrangement have

become apparent, and they are big problems. In the first place, as soon as inflation rises above a percentage point or two each year, the plan design begins to discriminate against plan members, whose benefits are fixed, and to work in favour of the employer, who is under no legal obligation to share the excess earnings of the plan. In the second place, the traditional view of a pension as a gift of the employer doesn't correspond to most real life situations in Canada today.

In the real world, many pension plans are subject to contractual agreements and these agreements are based on a completely different assumption: that all contributions to the pension plan, employers' and employees' alike, are simply deferred wages to be negotiated at the bargaining table in precisely the same way as wage increases. If employees want a richer pension plan, they must sometimes be prepared to settle for lower increases in salaries. Employers, for their part, must be prepared to negotiate the entire package in the context of such variables as company profits, the amount of surplus in the pension plan and the relationship between the long-term goals of the corporation and the legitimate concerns of its employees.

In this scheme of things, contribution holidays and surplus withdrawals are possible, but only when economic conditions call for them and plan members agree to them. Employers cannot unilaterally decide to divert pension-fund assets to corporate uses. Indeed, in theory, if pensions are part of a negotiated wage package, then all of the assets of the plan *must* "belong" to the members of the plan because all of the money in the plan derives from their wages. As deferred wages they do not belong to the employer at all unless the employees agree that they should.

In practice, though, the equation of pensions with deferred wages is, to say the least, imperfect. Unless there is an explicit contractual understanding that the fund belongs to the employees, employers still insist that the fund belongs to them. And sometimes, as we have seen, employers have made that argument even when there *was* such an explicit understanding.

Indeed, the provision in the federal/provincial consensus most employers liked least was the fifty-percent-cost rule which made them nervous, precisely because it involves a calculation of employers' and employees' contributions to the plan and thus appears to accept the premise that a pension is simply a deferred wage. If that principle were to become entrenched, employees could argue that *any* surpluses generated by pension plan investments belonged to them exclusively. Moreover, while the fifty-percent rule would cost employers money, it could also embarrass many of them as well. After all, no employer wants to admit to younger employees that the company has made no contributions at all towards their pension benefits in the past few years.

These two notions — pensions as "gifts" from employers and pensions as deferred earnings — represent two completely different ways of looking at retirement benefits. The first is paternalistic, self-serving and arrogant. It takes for granted that plan sponsors and the pension industry know best, that they will always act in the best interests of employees and that they know and care what those interests are. It ignores the fact that plan sponsors are usually more preoccupied with the best interests of their shareholders and with their profit margins than they are with the best interests of their employees. It allows contributors no recourse if the plan is a poor one or if it is badly managed. And when plan membership is a condition of employment, as is usually the case, it forces employees to make an "investment" which may not be in their long-term best interests at all.

Yet, as employers and the pension industry never tire of pointing out, the notion of pensions as nothing more than deferred earnings ignores the fact that it is the sponsors of defined benefit plans who assume the risk if the plan cannot cover its obligations. As long as the company stays in business, employees will get what they were promised even if the pension plan runs into trouble. If the assets in the pension plan cannot keep pace with its obligations, it is the *employer* who will have to make up the difference in the event of a shortfall in the fund. And if the employer takes the risk, why should he not reap the benefits as well? Although the plan itself makes money in real dollars, plan members have no right to expect anything more than what they were originally "guaranteed" — in dollars which are constantly declining in value.

It is precisely this question of risk that has most bedevilled attempts to find a fair solution to the inequities which have resulted from private pension plans in the last decade or so. For to determine the level of risk, it is necessary to work out what the relationship is, if any, between inflation and the investment return on the money in the fund. And that may be the most difficult and complex question ever to arise in the entire history of the pension debate.

Or it may be one of the simplest. It all depends upon your point of view. For anyone who believes that pension plans owe their members nothing more than the promised benefit — no matter how much money the pension fund has earned by investing their money — benefits and surpluses are apples and oranges, two unrelated matters which ought not be discussed in the same breath. But for retired employees with fixed pensions, the situation looks rather different. What *they* see is that in the last decade billions of dollars in surplus assets have accumulated in defined-benefit pension plans at a time when the real value of their own pension investment was sinking like a stone in calm water. Worse, they see that these surpluses have accumulated at a time when more than half of all older Canadians were obliged to apply for welfare in the form of federal or provincial income supplements to survive.

These very different definitions of what a pension is have co-existed uneasily in Canada for decades. But until the surpluses in pension plans started to run into the billions, it didn't matter much that employers with defined-benefit plans were, in effect, operating two different systems: one for unionized employees, another for everyone else, based on contradictory and completely different assumptions. The end result was the same: the employers still claimed to "own" the plans and nobody bothered to challenge them. Indeed, even the unions who viewed the money in the plans as deferred wages and treated them as such at the bargaining table didn't go out of their way to force the issue. What was the point? Until the early 1980s, there was nothing to fight over. Indeed, although as a rule interest rates follow inflation up over time, there was a brief period in the 1970s when plan sponsors *were* out of pocket as investment returns stagnated and inflation rates soared.*

That situation changed dramatically in the last decade. Pension consultant D. Don Ezra estimated that, as of 1982, before the stock market boom increased them further, the surpluses in private pension plans had grown to at least $4 billion. Had different actuarial assumptions been applied, Ezra added, the figure might have been as high as $8 billion. Estimates of surplus assets in private plans in Canada today range as high as $40 billion or even more. In these changed circumstances, it was entirely reasonable for unions to argue that plan members and retirees should share in the profits earned on their own money. Yet, provincial pension standards laws across the country, if they existed at all, remained silent on the question of surplus ownership and generally supported the notion that plan assets belonged exclusively to employers.

Furthermore, union leaders tended to assume that their members either can't or won't focus on pension issues when to do so might mean a lower wage settlement. Young employees don't care about pensions, the argument ran. They would rather have the money in their pockets now and worry about the future later. Current employees, for their part, don't care about retired employees. They are not prepared to fight for better pensions for them because, in the end, it would take money out of their own pockets.

Such assumptions — which were not completely unjustified, especially in industries where wage levels were so low that employees simply could not *afford* to save anything for the future — caused both unions and employers to treat pensions as a take-it-or-leave-it proposition. They also worked against attempts to find fair and creative solutions to the blatant injustices in the system.

Many employees *have* been oblivious to pension issues. And in the case of younger employees, who would really expect or

---

*This situation was so unusual that a new word — "stagflation" — had to be coined to describe it.

want it to be otherwise? But the fact is that young employees were often obliged to contribute to pension plans whether they wanted to or not. Surely they had as much right to a sound investment as their older colleagues. Just because they were young and uninterested in pensions was no excuse for ripping them off through inequitable portability and vesting rules. Nor is it necessarily true that younger employees do not care about what happens to retirees, a proposition which employers and unions alike seem to have taken for granted. Most of them do care: too many young Canadians have witnessed firsthand the severe financial difficulties their parents and grandparents face when they retire. In any event — and this is the critical point — it wasn't current employees who were benefiting at the expense of retirees when unions eased off on demands for better pensions; it was their employers who reaped the gains.

Had unions been more aggressive about informing their members of the consequences of ignoring pension issues and of the enormous amounts of their own money accumulating in private plans, the pension debate of the last few years could not possibly have been as lopsided as it was. Had they understood what was going on, plan members would not have stood for it. By their indifference and, in some instances, their incompetence, union leaders came within a hair's breadth of allowing an issue of enormous social and political importance to slip from their grasp.

And they can't say they weren't warned. As long ago as 1976, U.S. economist Peter Drucker was writing about what he termed the "Unseen Revolution" in American society. Through their pension plans, he estimated, employees "owned" at least twenty-five percent of all businesses in the United States, a figure which he correctly predicted would rise to more than sixty percent by the mid-1980s. Indeed, Drucker pointed out, employees owned a greater share of the American economy than was "owned" by the workers in Castro's Cuba or than had been nationalized in East Bloc countries at the height of Stalinism. In the land of unbridled capitalism, pension funds had transformed workers into the owners of their own means of production. The plain fact was, though, that they didn't realize it and therefore had not exercised the enormous power in their hands.

These were heady ideas, and they should have given Canadian unions rich food for thought. After all, the same phenomenon was apparent in Canada. But, by and large, Canadian union leaders did not raise the question of pension-fund ownership at all. That would have required a massive educational effort of their union members in a hostile and uncomprehending environment. The private sector and the pension industry had long had a stranglehold on the debate, and regulatory bodies like the Ontario Pension Commission had failed to protect even the most basic rights of unions to know how the pension funds were being used. Still, even though the deck was stacked against them, unions and employee organizations could have put the pressure on much sooner.

There were exceptions to this widespread indifference and timidity, particularly in large public sector unions such as OPSEU, the Ontario Public Service Employees Union. A handful of private-sector unions were on top of the issue too. The Canadian Paperworkers Union, for example, announced at a 1977 policy conference that it would seek ways to gain control of industry pension plans, because the payouts in the plans were too low and members were tired of pleading fruitlessly for improvements. Failing that, CPU leaders said, they would explore ways to gain control of the windfall investment gains in the plans, to win equal representation on pension boards and to ensure full disclosure of plan assets and liabilities.

The Canadian Brotherhood of Railway, Transport and General Workers, too, spoke out strongly on the need for unions to pay more attention to pension issues. They advocated putting union plans to work to the advantage of their members by boycotting pension fund investments in non-unionized companies. But most unions in North America ignored the issue, despite the fact that employee participation in management decision-making about pension investment is the rule, and not the exception, in many European countries.

The unions' most critical omission, though, was in docilely allowing the private sector to dictate the terms of the debate. Throughout the reform process, it had been a fiercely-held tenet of the pension lobby that the only "experts" qualified to pass judgement on pension matters are plan sponsors and the actuaries who are in their pay.

That assumption should have been challenged seriously years ago by every union in the land. They might have begun by pointing out that virtually every actuary in Canada is in a potential conflict of interest. For so long as employers control the pension funds, they are also paying the actuaries. And actuaries, as anyone who has ever tried to pin one down in an effort to discover the "truth" about pensions swiftly discovers, can dodge every bullet, climb out of every hole, and squirm out of every tight corner with a flip of their computer programs and a fiddle of their assumptions.

Actuaries and the assumptions they make about pension plan funding are crucial to the controversy now raging over defined-benefit plans. Let's take a simple example of how an actuary — we'll call him Reg — goes about his business. In order to figure out how much money Doodads Inc.'s pension plan needed in 1970 to provide the benefits promised to an employee — let's call him Charlie — who would retire in 1982 at age sixty-five, Reg had to make several predictions. He had to estimate both what Charlie's pension benefit would be when he retired *and* how well the pension fund was likely to perform in the intervening years. Only then was he able to specify how much money needed to be in the fund to cover the plan's liability for Charlie.

But now let's see how Reg's assumptions can affect his calculations. When he estimated Charlie's cost to the plan in 1970, Reg assumed a six-percent return on the investment fund. And using that assumption, he told Mr. Manyshares that the plan would need about $13,000 to cover the probable cost of Charlie's pension when he retired in 1982. But what if Reg were a conservative chap, as actuaries are inclined to be? Then he might have decided that interest rates were unlikely to exceed four percent a year over the twelve-year period. In that case, he would have informed Mr. Manyshares that, in 1970, the plan needed $18,000 to cover Charlie's benefits.

Where does this leave the plan as a whole? Clearly, when every current employee's future claim on the fund was calculated, the range of possibilities open to Reg was very great and depended entirely upon the assumptions he made about the future. If his predictions about interest rates and investment returns were too low, the fund would accumulate a surplus. If, for example, instead of four or six percent, the money earmarked for Charlie's pension earned ten percent over the next fourteen years, there would have been more money in the fund than the company needed to pay his pension. If the fund earned sixteen or eighteen percent, there would have been *much* more money in the plan than the company needed to cover its future obligations. On the other hand, if Reg's predictions were too high, Doodads Inc., having promised Charlie a fixed benefit, would have had to make up the difference from corporate revenues.

This latter situation is at the heart of the argument the pension industry lobs at any critic who suggests that it should be possible to find a way to ensure that retirees get the pensions they were promised in currency which bears and will continue to bear some relationship to real dollars. If it is difficult to predict how much current employees will cost when they retire, industry spokesmen argue, think how much more difficult it would be to provide inflation protection for retirees. And since employers take all the risk, how can it be fair to force them into a position in which they might be required to pay out more than they have budgeted for?

But surely it is time to turn that question around. Since they have no recourse, how can it be fair to force retirees into a position in which their pensions lose a portion of their value each and every day? Just who, really, is at risk here?

That question is best answered by examining what happened to pension funds in Canada in the course of the last decade after interest rates began to rise in the early 1980s. First, and most dramatically, the earnings on the assets in the plans began to skyrocket. At the same time, the high interest rates pushed the cost of buying annuities for retirees down; with high interest rates, less money was required to provide the promised benefit.

Both of these factors, clearly, were good news for pension plans. How good was the news? Let's take as an example the third-quarter results for all Canadian trusteed pension plans in 1985 when, according to Statistics Canada figures, the income in these funds increased by 22.3 percent as profits on the sale of securities grew by a whopping 265 percent. A year later, the news was even better. The trusteed funds had total revenues of $4.9 billion and total expenditures of only $1.6 billion.

With this kind of money at stake, it is hardly surprising that employers and the pension industry have fought tooth-and-nail to maintain control over the assets of the plans. But what is surprising is that, in defending their position, they continue to deny categorically that there is a connection between the surpluses and the erosion of pension benefits and to resist all efforts to find a fair way to redress the imbalances.

In the paperstorm of surveys, charts, graphs and expert opinion flying around in the last decade, it seems not to have occurred to many employers to ponder the ethics of their good fortune — or even to ask the most obvious questions of all: what do employees want and how much risk are they prepared to take on themselves? Are they prepared, for example, to pay a few dollars extra each week into the pension plan in return for guaranteed inflation protection? Are they prepared to share the risk by investing a portion of their retirement savings in a money-purchase plan? After all, most retirees would be far better off today if they *had* shared some of the risk in the last decade. As it turned out, they ended up shouldering it all.

The second most difficult problem bedevilling attempts to find a fair way to treat private pension plans is the private sector's unshakeable conviction that shareholders' interests come before the interests of their employees and that therefore the only good reform is a reform which costs employers nothing. This argument arises solely because employers insist that they "own" the plans, yet it has circumscribed most attempts at reform up to now. And a disingenuous argument it is, too. Of course the improved coverage and improved benefits called for by pension reformers would cost employers more. That's the point. For years, pension plan sponsors benefited from out-of-date and inequitable pension rules. They had been relieved of their obligations every time an employee took a year or two off to raise her children or changed jobs or fell prey to lay-offs and closures. They had been allowed to credit departing employees with minimal rates of interest on their contributions to company pension plans. They had been permitted to use plan surpluses earned on employees' money to cover their own contributions to pension benefits. How could reform not cost them something? The reform measures were *meant* to compel employers to shoulder their fair share of the load.

Incredibly, it took nearly a decade for this proposition to be taken seriously enough to prompt Ontario politicians to act. It may be several decades more before many other provinces move to prevent similar abuses in the future. Indeed, unless voters demand protection, it may never happen at all.

Contribution holidays deserve special attention. Many Canadians were shocked and outraged by the handful of surplus raids that received widespread media attention when they were turned back by the courts. But in all the excitement over the surplus withdrawals, the most lucrative pension rip-offs of all — contribution holidays — have largely escaped the attention of most plan members. Few employees know, for example, that it is very likely that their own employers will not contribute a nickel to their pension plans this year and may well have contributed nothing last year or the year before or the year before that. Indeed, in most jurisdictions in Canada, employers are under no obligation to tell plan members that they intend to use the surpluses to reduce their own contributions to the plan. Yet these contribution holidays deplete the surpluses in the plans just as surely as do the seemingly more ethically suspect surplus withdrawals.

When a pension fund generates more earnings than expected, these "excess" or "surplus" earnings are reported in plan valuations as "experience gains." Employers who sponsor pension plans with large experience gain surpluses have several options. They can be allowed to accumulate in the pension fund, risking the wrath of Revenue Canada, which wants to collect tax on the money. They can be used to increase benefits for retired or current employees. With the permission of regulatory authorities, provincial pension boards or, in some cases, federal regulators; they can be withdrawn from the plan. Or, without permission from anyone, they can be used to reduce the employer's contribution to the fund.

As plan surpluses grew in the last decade, most employers, predictably, chose to interpret experience gains as a sign that they had paid too much into the plan, at which point they reduced or suspended altogether their own contributions to the plan. From one point of view, this practice seemed unobjectionable. As the sponsor of the plan, the company is legally obliged to ensure that its assets are sufficient to pay for the benefits employees have been promised. If the plan has an enormous surplus, employers argued, why should the company continue to contribute to it?

Just to complicate the issue, the federal Income Tax Act seemed to actually compel employers to take a contribution holiday when the surpluses in their plans grew too large on the grounds that no more money than is necessary to keep the plan afloat should be sheltered from taxes. For years, in fact, Revenue Canada refused to approve corporate tax deductions unless it was clear that the employer could not use the pension plan as a temporary tax shelter.

In the 1970s, Revenue Canada began to worry about pension plans as tax shelters for *employees* as well. An information circular issued in 1981 suggested an upper limit on the amount of tax relief a company could expect to claim for its contributions to a pension plan, and it also referred to an upper limit, for tax purposes, on the value of the benefits employees could receive from the employer's contributions. Not surprisingly, employers seized upon this suggestion and have used it ever since as a justification for cutting off their own contributions instead of improving benefits for plan members.

Furthermore, the tax regulations seemed to suggest that if a company terminated its pension plan, any surplus left in the plan "must" be refunded to the company. Yet, incredibly, for all those years, the legal status of the Revenue Canada directives was far from clear. A 1986 lawsuit, *Reevie v. Montreal Trust Co.*, for example, called the Revenue Canada guidelines into question. An employer, Canada Dry, had amended provisions in its pension plan which spelled out the disposition of the plan's surplus in the event that the plan was wound up. The amendment stated that the surplus would revert to the company, even though employees had been assured in the past that all contributions to the plan were "irrevocable" and to be used "exclusively for the benefit" of plan members. When employees complained, the company's lawyers argued that Canada Dry had amended the plan simply to bring it into conformity with the Revenue Canada rules. The court rejected that argument and refused to allow Canada Dry to recover the surplus. Why? Because the Revenue Canada rule in question was not in the Income Tax Act at all. It appeared only in the information circular and, in the court's eyes, it did not have the force of law.

And not only was the legal status of the Revenue Canada rule in question, but it also begged the question. There were, as we have seen, other, fairer alternatives open to employers. Pension plan sponsors, particularly sponsors of contributory plans, made an implicit or explicit promise to employees that they would continue to contribute to the plan. That promise was broken every time an employer unilaterally took a contribution holiday. If indeed the surpluses in their plans were too large to satisfy Revenue Canada or if benefit levels were truly too high, a simple solution was readily available: to provide adequate inflation protection for their retirees. And if there was still too much money in the plan to satisfy Revenue Canada, they might have offered their current employees a contribution holiday too.

Although most employers who sponsor defined-benefit plans have taken contribution holidays in recent years, employees, and especially non-unionized employees, rarely hear about them. There are, however, some dramatic exceptions to this deafening silence. In July 1986, for example, Ontario Hydro announced that it would make no contributions to its pension plan for 1986 and 1987, because the plan contained a substantial surplus. The corporation took the position that it was the sole owner of the $240-million surplus and its financial plan indicated that the money would be used to eliminate the employer contribution over a five-year period. (The plan contained assets of about $2.8 billion as of December 1985.)

Following that announcement, the Canadian Union of Public Employees (CUPE) Local 1000 commenced legal proceedings against the Crown corporation in the Supreme Court of Ontario on grounds of Hydro's non-compliance with the Power Corporation Act, which indicates that the employer contributions should be based on the current cost of the liabilities of the plan. The union's goal: to force Ontario Hydro to contribute the current service cost of $53 million for 1986 and to meet its legal obligations to the plan in future years. The Court decided in favour of Ontario Hydro by a two-to-one majority. But the dissenting opinion should give other unions with different language in their plans the courage to carry on.

"I can see no difference between Hydro giving itself an accounting credit in the fashion described and removing the equivalent amount from the surplus without the consent of the Pension Commission of Ontario," wrote Mr. Justice Robert Reid. The union appealed the decision and the case is still before the courts. The outcome will provide one side or the other with a major psychological victory in the battle over surplus ownership. Still, because the Ontario Hydro plan is not governed by the Pension Benefits Standards Act but by a separate provincial Act, it may be of little real help in future challenges to the legitimacy of unilateral contribution holidays.

In a case which could be even more significant, the unionized members of the Hospitals of Ontario Plan mounted a legal challenge to the disposition of surplus in their pension plan after the Ontario Hospital Association board, on the advice of its actuaries, announced that no employer contribution would be made to the plan in 1988. The three unions involved, the Ontario Division of the Canadian Union of Public Employees, the Service Employees International Union and the Ontario Public Service Employees Union, had long argued for substantial improvement in benefits, including full inflation protection for current retirees and deferred employees. Instead, the plan surplus has been used to provide occasional contribution holidays for plan members and to reduce employer contributions to the plan.

The outcome of the battle could have repercussions across the country. The Hospitals of Ontario Pension Plan is the fourth largest non-governmental pension plan in Canada with 70,500 active contributing members and 22,000 former employees now receiving pensions or qualified for deferred pensions. At the end of 1986, the assets of the plan stood at $3.6 billion with a surplus the unions estimated to be about $942 million. And, as is the case with many other large plans, the employers' contribution to the plan has steadily decreased in relation to plan members' contributions. Over a twenty-year period, OHA contributions to the plan have been reduced by almost sixty percent, with most of that reduction occurring in the last decade. Over the same ten-year period, ad hoc adjustments compensated retirees for barely half the rate of inflation.

The OHA characterized the contribution holiday as "an opportunity to meet many capital needs" and made an emotional public pitch that the money could be better spent to improve patient care in Ontario hospitals. The decision to suspend employer contributions, OHA spokesmen added, was "in line with acceptable business practices."

The three unions disagreed. They described the board's decision as a "cynical grab" for the money and accused the OHA of funding capital improvements to hospitals from the retirement savings of hospital employees. The money in the plan, union officials pointed out, was money they had negotiated in the form of pension benefits in place of dental plans, vacations or improved salaries. Now it was to be used for unspecified projects over which plan members had no control and no say.

The outcome of the legal action will be watched carefully by other employee groups who are alarmed and outraged by the rate at which many employers across the country are depleting plan surpluses. For at the moment there is no legal consensus on the question of surplus ownership. In *Little v. Kent-McClain of Canada Ltd.* (1972), employees successfully challenged an Ontario company's right to pass a resolution modifying its pension plan to give the surplus to the company, which was going out of business. That decision was upheld on appeal.

A ruling in a more recent case, *Campbell v. Ferrco Engineering Ltd.*, however, seemed to contradict that judgement. In 1984, the firm's employees went to court after the company amended the pension plan to allow surplus assets to revert to the employer when the plan was terminated. That plan, too, had provided that all assets were to be used "exclusively for the provision of benefits" to its members. This time, though, the employees lost, on the grounds that the company had amended the document a year before it folded the plan and that the plan had been amended primarily to bring it in line with Revenue Canada regulations. The employees appealed, but settled out of court before the appeal could be heard.

Far from solving the problem, legal precedent mirrors the conflicting "pension as gift" and "pension as deferred earnings" battle in contradictory case law. The courts have not established whether pension funds are contractual agreements whose only obligation is to ensure that employees receive the defined benefit promised to them, or whether they are trusts established solely for employees' benefit. And, because the language of every pension plan is different, it will take many more challenges in the courts before the ownership question is sorted out. If those challenges are not even initiated — and if employees and unions do not raise the ownership questions with their employers in the meantime — the situation will remain unresolved, with the advantage to the employers.

This is especially true in light of new federal rules which will explicitly prohibit employers from contributing to pension plans that have surpluses of more than two years of combined employer-employee contributions. The proposed changes require plan sponsors to submit an actuarial report every three years indicating the amount of surplus in the plan, finally giving the ambiguous Revenue Canada information circular the force of law. The new rules reflect the federal government's determination to put a stop to employers making "unnecessary" contributions to their plans in order to shelter corporate revenues from taxation. The consequences of the rules, though, will be that employers as well as provincial governments will now argue that they have no choice: Ottawa has ordered them to reduce the surplus in pension funds by means of substantial contribution holidays.

This will be a spurious argument. For were employers to provide automatic and retroactive inflation protection for retirees and former employees with deferred pensions, and to improve pension benefits for their current employees, the "surpluses" in the plans would swiftly be absorbed. In circumstances such as these, the battle over the ownership of the pension funds is becoming increasingly critical. Furthermore, it is equally clear that the weakness of the reforms that have been instituted in some jurisdictions in Canada is not that they oblige employers to spend more to run their pension plans fairly, but that they allow them to spend little or nothing at all to redress past wrongs.

Moreover, the greater inadequacies of the private pension system — its low coverage rates, its mishandling of contributors' money, its paternalistic attitudes and its inability to adjust quickly to economic and social change — have scarcely been addressed. For despite all the claims to the contrary, the system has never fulfilled its self-appointed role adequately. In fact, as we have seen, so great have been its shortcomings that many of its critics have argued persuasively over the last decade that the only genuine reform would either force all employers to provide inflation-adjusted pension coverage for all of their employees — or to shut the system down forthwith.

These solutions were not idle threats. Indeed, there were many moments on the long road to reform when it looked as though legislators might crank up their resolve and force the private pension industry to set its house in order. The Special Senate Committee chaired by David Croll recommended expansion of the CPP as the "only fruitful" way to protect retirees from inflation in its 1979 report, *Retirement Without Tears*. Ontario's 1980 Royal Commission on the Status of Pensions (the Haley report) concluded that the private pension system had fallen far short of delivering on its promises and stated that the chaotic system of employer-sponsored plans might have to be much more strictly regulated in the future and that expansion of the system might have to be made mandatory. And after the 1981 National Pension Conference, Liberal Health and Welfare Minister Monique Bégin put the private sector on notice: reform or face the consequences. The consequences, as she saw them, were mandated private pension coverage, or an expanded Canada Pension Plan which would pre-empt the private sector altogether.

Their arguments were hard to refute. The private system, with its apparent inability to provide portability, its blatant discrimination against retirees, employees whose pensions were deferred and women, its lack of universality and its hodgepodge of plans with widely varying benefit levels, was a dog's breakfast. Moreover, the administrative costs of the private plans were much, much higher than the costs of running a public plan. The private system demands an army of actuaries, regulatory officials and investment consultants, to say nothing of the enormous demands it places on many employers, especially those running small businesses, in terms of personnel and technology. And if the plans were badly managed, as many were, the implications for employees could be very serious indeed. After paying in a substantial percentage of their lifetime earnings to a company plan, they could wind up with little more than broken dreams.

Not surprisingly, both of these options, mandated private coverage and an expanded CPP, made corporate Canada tremble with fear and loathing. Permit government to force employers to provide coverage? Relinquish control of pension fund assets to the federal government? Not on your life. Even a reform measure as obvious as mandatory inflation protection was like a red rag to a bull. So strenuously did the employers object to the concept that the issue was pushed aside and ultimately abandoned on the grounds that no consensus was possible and that any attempt to force one could jeopardize the entire reform initiative. As a result, when Ottawa and the provinces steered a course through the Scylla of mandated private pensions and the Charybdis of an expanded CPP, Canadians were left roughly where they had been before: waiting patiently for the private sector to make good on its promises.

If not for a fluke of politics and the bad behaviour of a few greedy employers, they would be waiting still. But when the Ontario New Democrats, full of vim and vigour after more than four decades in the provincial political wilderness, decided to target pensions in their 1985 accord with the Liberals, they gambled that the outrageous behaviour of some employers and the failure of regulatory bodies to prevent such abuses as CCM's failure to maintain its pension fund would finally catch the attention of voters. They were right, even though the issue paid them no immediate political dividends and even though the Liberals contrived to claim much of the credit themselves for reopening the pension debate.

In fact, the surplus issue had caught the Liberals by surprise. David Peterson's strategists initially had no intention whatever of upsetting the consensus or of enraging their corporate backers by mandating inflation protection. But the NDP's litany of questionable surplus withdrawals and unsound funding practices had forced them into an uncomfortable position. The Liberals were bound by the terms of the accord with the New Democrats to move ahead swiftly on pension reform, and they also had public outrage over the Dominion Stores case to consider. As one senior Liberal official acknowledges privately, they believed that the greatest danger of all was that voters would identify the Liberals with questionable corporate practices. "No one," he says, "wanted to line up behind Conrad Black except Monte Kwinter."

NDP critics saw Kwinter as a stumbling block in the way of reform — and as an Achilles' heel for Peterson's Liberals. The minister for consumer and commercial relations was himself a businessman who had run the family business, J. Kwinter Gourmet Hot Dogs, and bought and sold real estate. And throughout the ruckus over the Dominion Stores withdrawal, he had made it clear that his sympathies lay with Conrad Black. In the eyes of the NDP, he was a very loose cannon indeed. "We targeted Kwinter as vulnerable and went after him," says Ross McClellan, then NDP House leader and the party's pension strategist.

And the NDP strategy had worked — for a while. With a commitment to inflation protection in hand, the New Democrats believed that they had won a major victory, and that they had identified and captured a potent campaign issue for themselves. The Liberals, for all their promises, they believed, would succumb to corporate pressure and denature their inflation protection promises with an indexation formula which was weak and ineffectual. But NDP spirits fell when the Liberals appointed a task force, chaired by University of Toronto law professor Martin Friedland, and instructed its members to come up with a formula and phase-in procedures for the inflation-protection measures. "We were thrilled that our daily firing in the legislature had forced the moratorium," McClellan says. But he admits that the NDP had been outfoxed. The task force would put indexation on hold for at least a year, effectively killing pensions as an election issue when the two-year accord expired in September 1987. Says McClellan ruefully: "We didn't dream that they would design legislation with a trip wire."

And indeed, this time around, it was the Liberal strategy that succeeded. The task force effectively buried the indexation issue, and as a result pensions did the NDP no good at all in the September election. In fact, no issue helped them. Peterson's Liberals, riding a wave of economic prosperity and personal popularity, had managed to convince Ontario voters that the reform initiatives of the previous two years had had little to do with the accord or with the relentless NDP pressure on them. The task force had served its purpose, clamping a heavy lid on what McClellan calls "the very best issue we had...an issue people saw as something that directly affected them."*

And there was another disappointment as well, one which is spoken of gingerly in NDP circles. Against Bob Rae's wishes, Clifford Pilkey, the former head of the Ontario Federation of Labour, had agreed to serve on the task force, giving the exercise

---

*Before they lost all political leverage, the NDP pushed through another little-noticed pension reform. McClellan shepherded through last-minute amendments to the new Pension Benefits Act just before it was passed by the Ontario Legislature on June 25, 1987, which provide guarantees that groups of workers who leave one union will not lose their pension entitlements in multi-employer plans when they join another. The changes make it possible for Canadian workers to break away from U.S. unions without loss of pension benefits.

a legitimacy which the NDP was convinced it did not deserve. It was not the first time that a government had attempted to co-opt prominent labour leaders in the reform process, sometimes successfully, but the NDP was determined that it would not happen this time. In separate meetings, Rae, McClellan and party strategist Robin Sears all begged Pilkey not to sit on the task force. With the support of the labour movement, Pilkey turned them down.

The Liberals breezed through the September landslide election, decimating the NDP opposition benches and costing McClellan his seat. Even so, Peterson remained wary of the pension issue. Recognizing that the issue was still a "political time bomb," as one party insider puts it, the premier handed the pension portfolio over to Treasurer Robert Nixon, one of his most trusted and powerful ministers, and awaited the task force report.

However disappointed the New Democrats may have been that the task force allowed the Liberals to shelve inflation protection until after the election, they could nonetheless claim a substantial moral victory. The Friedland deliberations confirmed that the NDP offensive had moved the debate over pensions into a critical new phase, one that might well have taken years to build again without their timely intervention. By providing yet another forum for the critics of private pensions to air their grievances, the task force reopened old issues and raised some new ones as well. And this time around, those critics were better organized and better prepared than they ever had been before.

They had more to complain about, too. The unusual economic climate of the last few years had thrown the deep-seated problems with private pensions into even higher relief. And whereas many of the previous pension inquiries had taken place at a time when pension-fund managers were struggling, not always successfully, to ensure that their investments would cover plan liabilities, the task force convened at a time when even the most poorly managed plans had accumulated large surpluses.

The danger was that the surplus scandals could themselves become yet another stumbling block in the way of genuine reform. The result of unusual economic conditions, they muddied the indexation waters by providing employers and their critics with one more red herring to squabble over. *Of course* something needed to be done about the surplus windfalls: it was simply not fair that retirees had no claim on them. But inflation protection was a legitimate goal whether or not the surpluses existed.

Still, because the surpluses had dangled irresistible temptation under the noses of many pension plan sponsors, they provided the most compelling argument of all for indexation: if employers refused to provide adequate inflation protection voluntarily — even when their coffers were bursting at the seams — how could they ever be trusted to be fair if left to their own devices?

As the task force got under way, it was clear that corporate Canada intended to fight the same old battles all over again, and to downplay the surpluses as a mere fluke. But the actions of those employers for whom the temptation had been too great were impossible to ignore. Indeed, the greediest among them had managed to shine a very bright light on the shortcomings of the entire private pension system one more time. And this time the debate would venture into what had been forbidden territory before. For the first time since the reform exercise began, a duly appointed body would examine closely the legitimacy of the most fundamental tenets of the private pension system: employers' claims to exclusive control and ownership of pension fund wealth and their adamant refusal to accept a legislated remedy to the problem of inflation.

By the time the Friedland Task Force got down to business, Canadians' faith in private pensions had been badly shaken. And as the corporate lobbyists prepared to launch yet another pious and predictable defence of the system, its critics were preparing to let them know that their avowals of good faith were no longer good enough. Nobody believed them any more.

· 8 ·

TO GROW OLD IS TO GROW POOR

THE PUSH FOR INDEXED PENSIONS

::

"The majority of people in this province are not prepared to accept that in Canada to grow old must inevitably mean to grow poor. It is now widely understood that the poverty of many older Canadians proceeds directly from inadequate pensions and particularly from the deficiencies of the private pension system on which so many are forced to rely."

Clifford Pilkey, Minority Report to the Ontario Task Force on
Inflation Protection for Employment Pension Plans, February 1988

· ·

The law professor, the union boss and the insurance executive were a study in contrasts: Martin Friedland, friendly, self-effacing, a good listener; Clifford Pilkey, stocky, florid of face, inclined to gruffness; Sydney Jackson, gaunt, grey, supremely confident — three movers and shakers from different worlds thrown together by a government determined to buy a little time.* Against all odds, The Great Canadian Pension Extravaganza was on the road again in the summer of 1987, two years after everyone had thought the show was over. For the men in the dark summer suits who paraded into the dreary government

·

*Friedland is professor of law at the University of Toronto. Sydney Jackson is chairman of the Manufacturers Life Insurance Company of Toronto. Clifford Pilkey is a past president of the Ontario Federation of Labour.

conference room in downtown Toronto, briefcases firmly in hand, there must have been a sense of déjà vu. After all, the corporate pension lobby is such a tight and self-enclosed community that most of them had been in rooms like this before, explaining patiently to the members of countless hearings, panels, commissions, task forces and subcommittees why Canada's private pension system was sacrosanct and why it should remain so.

Here they were again, fighting a battle against government interference and union meddling which they believed they had already won. And, indeed, the actuaries and the personnel managers, the consultants and the vice-presidents of finance who took their places in front of the task force didn't seem terribly pleased to be there. Ontario, they pointed out severely, had stepped badly out of line. Why should employers suffer the indignity of yet another inquiry into the workings of the private pension system? How could the Canadian business community conduct its business at all if politicians insisted on threatening them with constricting rules and regulations, especially at a time when they faced a rapidly changing and competitive world economy? How dare the Liberal government — at the urging of the NDP, for heaven's sake — violate the spirit of the federal/ provincial consensus, an agreement that had been ten years in the making and was properly silent on the question of mandated inflation protection? Why was government setting out to beggar corporate Canada?

The Investment Dealers of Canada, for example, complained that the Ontario action "destroys a hard-won consensus among federal and provincial governments on mandatory pension indexation." Falconbridge Ltd. charged that pension indexing "represents an uncontrollable and unpredictable BLANK CHEQUE from all sponsors of Defined Benefit Pension Plans in the Province of Ontario FOREVER." William M. Mercer Ltd. declared flatly that the company objected to legislation which "may not be in the best interests of plan sponsors and plan members." It would be "ideal" if every pension plan were fully indexed for inflation, the Mercer brief to the task force said, "but Utopia cannot be legislated."

Not only were these representatives of corporate Canada cranky, a few of them were pugnacious too as they delivered their message: that employers and the pension industry *still* did not like the idea of indexed pensions. And if the province wantonly carried out its naive and misguided threat to force them to provide automatic inflation protection, corporate Canada would make them sorry they had. If employers are obliged to index pensions, they chorused, we will wind up our plans, we will reduce benefits, we will make our employees wish they had never heard the word "indexation." Day after day, in June and July of 1987, the men in the dark summer suits, carefully-crafted presentations at the ready, greeted each other gravely and waited for their turns to explain to the law professor, the union boss and the insurance executive why nothing had changed and why the huge surpluses in private pension plans bore no relationship whatsoever — well, hardly any — to the precipitous decline in the value of pension benefits.

Despite the fact that Ontario's Liberal government had already made a firm commitment to introduce some form of mandatory inflation protection for pension benefits, the briefs to the committee from employers and the pension industry, virtually without exception, opposed even minimal standards for such protection. Even a modicum of government coercion, they pointed out sternly, would cause employers to punish plan members by converting their defined-benefit plans into money purchase schemes.*

"There is no requirement for an employer to have a pension plan. If mandatory inflation protection is legislated for defined-benefit plans, many employers have indicated that they will shift to money purchase plans or wind up their pension plans entirely," said the Wyatt Company, Actuaries and Consultants,

---

*In a defined-benefit plan, annual pension benefits are defined in dollar terms and are usually related to income levels. Money-purchase (defined-contribution) plans, by contrast, produce pension payments which vary depending upon the pre-retirement investment experience of the pension fund and the price of an annuity at the time of retirement. More than ninety percent of all Canadians covered by employer-sponsored pension plans belong to defined-benefit plans.

in its submission. "A significant number of Ontario Chamber employers have already indicated their intention to wind up their defined benefit pension plans if inflation indexation is mandated," said the Ontario Chamber of Commerce. The government should use a carrot, not a stick, suggested the Life Underwriters Association of Canada, who insisted that "instead of any proposal for mandatory inflation protection for employment pension plans, more attention [should] be given to encouraging employers to adopt voluntary periodic pension adjustments through contractual or ad hoc arrangements to relieve pensioners from undue hardship."

Now, this was a strange state of affairs. Ontario's commitment to inflation protection had already been made; that was not the issue. Employers and industry professionals had been invited to the hearings to present their ideas on how it could best be implemented. What, they were asked, would be the fairest way to insure that all employers would provide at least a minimum amount of inflation protection in their pension plans? But all they wanted to talk about was why pensions should *not* be protected from inflation by law, no way, never.

Yet, nobody had suggested that the province was committed to one hundred percent indexation, nobody had hinted that full retroactivity was in the cards, nobody had threatened to seize every last dollar of surplus money in the private plans and turn it over to oldsters with their eyes fixed firmly on luxury condos in Miami Beach. The point was to find a fair middle ground which would protect the rights — and the solvency — of *both* employers and employees. Indeed, the mandate of the task force was to seek fairness in the context of the existing pension system.

Perhaps it was the principle that bothered them. Whatever the problem was, the task at hand was to find a compromise position and this seemed to be a difficult concept for many of the corporate participants in the debate to grasp or, certainly, to acknowledge. General Motors' brief to the task force, for example, declared that the company recognized the need for reform of the legislation governing employer-sponsored pensions in Canada despite the fact that it would involve significant cost increases. Indeed, GM had supported the "thrust" of the federal/provincial reform package. But the company wanted no part of indexation, now or ever. "We believe," said General Motors, "that ad hoc improvements are the only acceptable form of indexation for Ontario."

Company spokesman Rick Wagoner, Vice-President, Finance, told task force members on July 10 that GM's actuaries estimated that full indexation would cost the company an additional $321 million in the first year, with similar cost increases each year for many years thereafter — an annual increase of 611 percent, or 19.5 percent of total payroll costs for the company's 46,000 employees. Full inflation indexation, Wagoner explained, would increase the compensation levels of employees by about $3.57 an hour. And that, he said, represented an additional cost of $550, including tax, on every GM car sold to Canadian consumers that year.

Wagoner's astronomical figures seemed to puzzle the panel. David Conklin, the executive director of the Friedland Task Force and a practised pension hand, suggested a meeting at a later date with the company's actuaries "to find out how you do your arithmetic." Even Sydney Jackson, the private sector's advocate in the deliberations, and often its conscience as well, commented dryly that either there was "not very good funding of the pension plan" or the company "had built into its estimates every cost disadvantage known to man."

The General Motors submission, complete with a slide show, was one of the more belligerent of the corporate presentations to the task force, and it was sadly typical in its determination to ignore the task at hand. It was also one of the more ironic, given the fact that only four months later the company, which had adamantly insisted that it would fight the good fight against inflation protection to the bitter end, docilely agreed to index company pensions in its contract settlement with Bob White's Canadian Auto Workers Union.

Wagoner and the GM team concluded their presentation at 11:30 on that fine Friday morning in July. Within minutes, another group took their place, with a markedly different message to the task force and a markedly different style as well. Bob White, Bob Nickerson and Sam Gindin did not wear dark summer suits — and they didn't think much of what General Motors had had to say. The CAW, White said, had never believed private sector assurances that retirees would be protected against inflation by voluntary ad hoc adjustments — and with good cause: despite all the talk of risk to plan sponsors, the logic of the corporate position was, in fact, that *retirees* should bear all of the cost and risks of the system.* And, far from persuading Canadians that the private pension system was doing a good job for them, the louder such companies as General Motors railed against inflation protection, the more convincing they made the case for the expansion of the public pension system.

The CAW agreed that full indexation imposes "risks and uncertainties" on employers, especially in the short term. But the union took issue with the pension lobby's contention that the funding costs of mandated inflation protection would erode corporate profits, destroy competitiveness and weaken the economy. On the contrary, White said, the union's experience was that pension costs — even with ad hoc negotiated increases in pensions of fifty to sixty percent of inflation — had actually *fallen* as a percentage of total labour costs in the previous decade. Even if the increases had matched inflation, costs to the automobile manufacturers would still have been a lower proportion of overall labour costs today than they were ten or fifteen years ago. The cost of most benefits — wages, health care, drugs, insurance — had increased by at least the rate of inflation, White pointed out, but pension costs had been greatly restrained by the highly successful returns of pension funds.

The heart of the CAW's argument was that it is not that indexation is too costly in real terms, but that employers, with the tacit approval of regulatory bodies, have contrived to make it *appear* so by arbitrarily adopting funding rules that guarantee that it *will* be too costly. Existing funding rules, for example,

---

*As a rule, defined-benefit plans which provide the least generous pensions on retirement are the plans which also generate the greatest surpluses. The larger the surplus in the plan, the more likely it is that an employer will take contribution holidays or apply to withdraw a part of the surplus from the plan.

require companies to put money aside for recently negotiated benefits. And because indexed pensions create obligations far into the future, if these obligations are funded according to the current rules, they require very substantial amounts of money to be set aside today. Thus employers are justified when they complain that the burden on them is too heavy.

But such funding rules, the CAW pointed out, are completely unnecessary. If inflation protection were to be based on a longer funding period than that for regular benefits, the cost of indexing would look completely different. For example: with full inflation indexing, the projected pension for a worker who is aged thirty today and who belongs to a defined-benefit plan that now provides a $1,000 monthly pension would be about $5,500 a month and growing when he turns sixty-five in the year 2023. Funding that amount immediately under current rules would be prohibitively expensive. Yet it is also unnecessary. Because indexed benefits stretch so far into the future, it makes more sense to fund them over a longer time period, thereby reducing the up-front funding costs dramatically.

Current Ontario regulations stipulate that unfunded liabilities should be amortized over a fifteen-year period. Yet if the regulations allowed for amortization as a constant percentage of payroll, there would be a marked decrease in costs to employers. If amortization of a $1 million unfunded liability, for example, requires fifteen years at a rate of 8.682 percent of payroll, amortization over twenty-five years would be at a rate of 6.194 percent of payroll.

These differences are significant. Yet most employers and the pension industry as a whole have flatly refused to cost pension benefits differently — even for the sake of discussion — or even to acknowledge that there might be a fairer way of doing business. And until employers and governments agree to look at alternative funding rules, the battle over inflation protection would continue to be fought on an actuarial technicality, CAW pointed out, and not on its merits as a political, social and ethical issue.

The details of pension-plan funding are technical and complex, but the basic assumptions underlying defined-benefit plans are straightforward. And it is these assumptions that are absolutely critical in making sense of the battle over inflation protection. In a non-inflationary environment such as existed when most pension plans were established, plan sponsors assume a "real" rate of return on investment of about three or four percent. This growth rate has nothing at all to do with inflation; it is simply what the investment is expected to "earn" in real dollars.

When inflation *is* a factor, there are two different rates of return on the money: the "real" rate of three or four percent — which the money would earn anyway — and the "actual," or "nominal," rate — which includes inflationary gains. And, whenever the actual rate of return exceeds the rate that plan actuaries have predicted (the "assumed" rate), a surplus will be created in the plan — *unless benefits keep pace with inflation.* To put it another way, a fully-funded pension plan which earns its forecast real rate of return can provide indexed benefits at no more cost to the plan sponsor than the cost of an unindexed plan when there is zero inflation.

That would appear to be a reasonable and fair argument for indexing retirees' pensions to cover the losses in purchasing power they suffer when inflation rises. But over the years, these two very different rates have been lumped together in most plans, because actuaries routinely adjust their estimates ("valuations") of interest rates upwards to reflect anticipated long-term inflation. In so doing, they have built inflation into the *funding* of benefits. But, unfortunately for plan members, they have not built similar assumptions into the benefits themselves. As a result, while the plans experience inflation-driven gains, plan members suffer inflation-driven losses. In these circumstances, employers are the big winners from inflation — they pay less into the plan because benefits are fixed — while retirees suffer significant losses: as inflation rises higher, so the real value of their pensions declines.

Indeed, defined-benefit plans are *designed* to generate surpluses over the long run. And if they do not, the actuarial assumptions underlying the plan can be adjusted to ensure that they do. If this sounds like a no-win situation for employees, that's because it is.

Take Louise, for example. If she retires at age sixty-five with a benefit of $500 a month, the cost to the pension plan in a non-inflationary economic environment at a real interest rate of 3.5 percent would be $73,641. With even modest inflation of 4.5 percent (a "nominal" interest rate of 8 percent), the cost of providing Louise's benefit drops to $54,419. The difference of $19,222 is the result of inflation. But Louise doesn't benefit from the interest earned on her money. That is a bonus for Doodads Inc., which will use the surplus money in the plan as an excuse to take a contribution holiday next year. Louise's "bonus" is rather different. Her pension will begin to lose its value as of the day she retires. Some bonus.

As we have seen, the pension industry is fond of pointing out that any legislation designed to put a stop to this injustice would have dire implications for employers — implications which they would immediately transform into dire consequences for defined-benefit plans. To underline the reality of this threat, several pension-consulting firms surveyed their corporate members and presented the task force with their likely responses to mandatory indexation. Some adopted a wait-and-see attitude, but many others took a much harder line.

The Association of Canadian Pension Management, which represents 500 corporations that sponsor non-negotiated pension plans, for example, polled its members on the issue and reported their comments to the task force. "We are already considering changing from a defined-benefit to a defined-contribution plan or terminating our plan as a result of legislation changes. Indexation could be the final straw," said one. "Eliminate future improvements to plans," said another. "In our opinion, the cost implication for private employers will result in severe negative results for pension reform (switching to defined contribution or RRSP, etc.)," said a third. In short, most of the plan sponsors said that the additional costs of inflation protection would either force them to convert their plans to money purchase or, at the very least, to reduce benefits and raise employee contribution levels.

Well, fair is fair. When *they* were promised personal anonymity, the money managers of some of the largest defined-benefit plans in Canada saw little reason to fear significant mandated inflation protection. "There is no reason at all to believe that employers cannot afford indexing," said one. "Over the last fifteen years, interest has been more than sufficient to make up 100-percent indexing." "A surplus only exists in terms of what the actuaries predict will happen in the long run. In the past, they have responded to very conservative guidelines laid down by provincial pension commissions," said another. "You could say that indexation of benefits wouldn't cost anything. If there is a proper management team, it should not. Often the mandate of such a team is just that: to outperform inflation. A well-managed fund should do that, and if it does indexation is no problem," said a third. But perhaps the most telling comment of all came from the manager of a billion-dollar fund. "If I couldn't keep up with inflation," he said, "I would lose my job."

So where does that leave us? Can defined-benefit plans provide their members with significant protection against the ravages of inflation without bankrupting the employer, or can they not? As always with pensions, the answer to that question depends in large part on your perspective. In the Great Canadian Pension Debate, truth is very much a matter of assumptions — and the assumptions of the two sides in this debate have very little in common. And, as the GM and the CAW positions illustrated, the difficulties confronting policy makers caught in the cross-fire between critics of the private pension system and the corporate lobby are almost insurmountable.

So who is right and who is wrong? Well, that depends. Were the two sides in the controversy even discussing the same issues? Well, yes they were, but from very different starting points. Were employers and the pension lobby who appeared before the task force even prepared to listen to a reasoned attack on their assumptions? Well, they surely didn't seem to be. Against powerful evidence that retirees had suffered greatly while their employers had laughed all the way to the bank, they continued to insist that, left to their own devices, plan sponsors will see to it that retirees are not bilked of their fair share of windfall profits earned on their own money. Indeed, so thick was the overlay of political ideology and obfuscating rhetoric that the whole enterprise seemed at times to be nothing more than an exercise in actuarial bafflegab.

Nowhere was this stonewalling approach clearer than on the critical question of retroactivity. For despite all their protests to the contrary, many Ontario employers had already resigned themselves to the fact that they were going to have to live with at least minimal inflation protection for their current employees' future service. So while they complained about indexation in general, they saved their biggest guns for an all-out attack on the concept of retroactivity. In its mildest form, retroactive inflation protection means that all former employees receiving pensions will have them indexed in the future. In its more extreme form, it can mean that all employees who retired ten or twenty years ago would automatically have their pension benefits increased to the level they would have been had inflation protection been in place throughout their retirement.

Without some form of retroactivity, of course, current retirees gain nothing whatsoever from inflation protection. Indeed, they might be even worse off than they were before, because employers forced to index future pensions might well be tempted to pay for the indexation by making no further ad hoc adjustments for retirees. And even more frightening for plan sponsors than providing pensioners with retroactive indexation is the prospect of being forced to provide retroactive indexation for the previous service of employees yet to retire. Yet without such retroactivity, employees due to retire in the next decade or so have very little to gain from indexation.

It is fair to say that employers and the pension lobby spoke with a single voice on the subject of retroactivity: virtually every one of their submissions to the Friedland Task Force pointed out that such a course would be expensive, difficult to implement in declining industries and unfair to every employer who had been conscientious about providing voluntary increases in the past. And, underlying their position was the familiar argument that there is no relationship whatsoever between the surpluses in the plans and the plight of retirees and older employees.

And instead of concentrating on the task at hand — how to spread the pension risk more evenly between employers, current employees and retirees in the future and make up for some of the injustices inflicted on current retirees — the pension industry spokesmen continued to insist that it is unreasonable to expect pension funds to earn a moderate "real" rate of return over the long run and to deny that the surpluses had anything whatever to do with inflation or with employees' money or employees' rights.

So where, in the view of the pension lobby, *did* the surpluses come from, if not from inflation-driven investment windfalls earned on employees' money? According to Hewitt Associates, they came mainly from four different sources: investment earnings in excess of conservative funding requirements; salary increases below what had been assumed in actuarial calculations; release of reserves caused by downsizing; and release of reserves caused by the adoption of less conservative and more realistic assumptions.

What did those words mean? Basically they meant that huge surpluses had accumulated in private pension plans because employers earned more money on employee contributions than they had expected to earn, because they had paid less for retirement benefits than they expected to pay, because they had given their employees lower salary increases than they expected to give them, because they had laid off a lot of people and pocketed their pension entitlements, and because they had managed their pension funds over-cautiously and badly.

An objective observer might be forgiven for thinking that this is more or less what their critics had accused them of doing, and that on the face of it there was not a lot to be proud of in that litany of excuses and explanations. But in the Alice-in-Wonderland world of pensions, these were the *best* arguments the pension lobby could muster for letting employers off the indexation hook. Clearly there was more at stake here than met the eye.

Indeed there was. The real battle raging before the Friedland

Task Force was buried under a mountain of actuarial projections, cost accountings, funding formulas — and nonsense. At issue was nothing less than the legitimacy of the entire private pension system and the nature of its "right" to exercise total control over the vast surplus assets in pension funds. Put simply, it was a battle over whether or not Canadians should continue to trust the private sector with their retirement savings in light of employers' actions in the highly charged investment climate of the 1980s.

After all, there are other alternatives to private-sector pension plans and they are alternatives which increasing numbers of Canadians either have endorsed or would endorse if they understood the magnitude of what is at stake. And *that* is a political threat which the pension industry and its corporate and political friends hope will remain deep-sixed for the foreseeable future. But, hard as they tried, it was an issue which refused to be buried, despite the limited mandate of the task force: to find a way to reform the private system, not a way to dismantle it.* For it is impossible to discuss indexation without touching on the three fundamental questions which will shape the Great Pension Debate in the years to come: Whose interests does the private pension system serve? What, if anything, should be done about the enormous amounts of pension-fund capital accumulating in private hands in this country? And whose money is it, anyway?

Since the end of the Second World War, enormous reservoirs of power and money have concentrated in the hands of four private financial industries — chartered banks, trust companies, trusteed pension funds and life-insurance companies. In the last decade, the rapid growth of these pools of capital has outstripped every prediction and every expectation. And it should surprise no one that the last thing corporate Canada wants is government

---

*The task force's terms of reference precluded an examination of the expansion of the Canada Pension Plan as an alternative to the private plans. Its report noted that although Pilkey "believes that plan, which is fully indexed and universal, would be the best solution" and Jackson "takes the opposite view," the members "collectively express no opinion" on the CPP.

intervention in this lucrative arrangement. But this concentration of power and wealth has not been a great boon to those Canadians who entrusted their money to private pension plans. They have watched their own pensions plummet in value as the financial institutions — and their own employers — reaped great gains. And that, in a nutshell, is what the escalating pension fight is all about.

A few years ago Keith Ambachtsheer's *Pensions and the Bottom Line* took employers to task in no uncertain terms for their ineptitude and, in some cases, for their sheer incompetence in managing their pension plans. Employers, Ambachtsheer suggested, were painfully slow to recognize the enormous profit-making potential of the pension plans they controlled. Instead they administered them as they always had in the past, with no particular sense of urgency, turning any real risks over to the insurance industry and operating the plans as nothing more than a service to their employees. What they *should* have been doing, Ambachtsheer says, was looking at the pension plan as a serious business and running it accordingly. Employers were most impressed with his arguments.

And Ambachtsheer was right. But as long as employees were the only beneficiaries of the plans, many employers simply didn't take them very seriously. It was only when a plan threatened to cost them money, as many plans did in the late 1970s, that they sharpened their investment strategies or fired their consultants or attempted to analyze the fund's performance in a serious and systematic way. Then, when investment returns began to surge upwards in the early 1980s, creating huge surpluses in the funds, formerly indifferent employers began to view the plans in a different light altogether.

And why not? The sheer size of many of the plans *demanded* new strategies and new management styles. Pensions had become very big business in Canada. Gone are the days when a poor investment return on the pension fund was a matter of no concern. Gone are the days when most funds were managed internally, almost as an afterthought, or by life insurance or

trust companies.* A new breed of money managers who take
the view that it is their job to maximize the performance of the
fund by treating it like any other corporate investment has
moved into the once-sluggish pension scene.

If all were right with the world, this development would be
very good news for all of us who have a sizeable chunk of our
retirement savings tied up in a private pension plan. But hold on
a minute; we've been here before. It's all very well to want our
pension funds to be well managed, but the question remains:
who ultimately benefits from the enhanced performance of a
well-managed fund? By now, the answer to that question should
be clear. Unless inflation withers away to nothing — or the benefits of our plans are indexed — it's not likely to be you or me.

The typical pension fund in Canada earned 14.1 percent a
year during the ten years ending in 1985. During this period, the
Consumer Price Index rose by 7.8 percent a year. This means that
the typical fund earned more than 6 percent a year in real terms.
There are more than 4,000 trusteed pension plans in Canada
today. According to Statistics Canada, the book value of their
assets on June 30, 1986 was about $118 billion — an increase of
371 percent in a single decade.† By the first quarter of 1987, the
assets of the plans had grown to about $130 billion and in that
quarter alone their total income topped $5 billion. At the same

---

*According to *benefits canada*, trust companies in 1981 managed nearly 39 percent of
pension-fund assets. By 1986 that share had dropped to 5.4 percent. Investment
counsellors who managed about 33 percent of assets in 1981 controlled 76.4 percent of
fund assets five years later. The intense competition for pension-fund business, and
the trend towards deregulation of financial institutions in Canada and the United
States, have forced the life insurance and trust companies to fight back. By 1987 the
large financial institutions owned one in three investment counsellors in Canada.

---

†During 1985 alone, the book value of assets held by trusteed funds increased by
$13.9 billion — a growth rate of 14.4 percent. Plan expenditures were $6 billion, up
from $5.2 billion in 1984. Statistics Canada reported that the largest increase was
observed in a category called "other expenditures," which grew from a previous high of
$58 million in 1984 to $328 million the following year. At least $290 million of this
amount, Statistics Canada estimated, was paid in the form of surplus refunds to
employers.

time, the plans reported total expenditures of only $1.6 billion. That left a net cash flow of $3.4 billion *in a single quarter* — hardly peanuts by anyone's standards.

Today trusteed pension funds are the largest institutional investors in Canada, surpassing the traditional leaders, insurance companies and chartered banks. Much of this wealth is concentrated in a few hands. In 1986, according to the industry publication *benefits canada*, the twenty largest plans in the country — among them several public employer plans — had total assets of $47 billion, with sixteen of the plans reporting assets of more than $1 billion each. The assets of the largest of them, the Ontario Municipal Employees Retirement System (OMERS), grew to $8.2 billion in 1986 from $7 billion a year earlier. Canadian National Railways (CN), with assets of $5.8 billion, and Bell Canada, with assets of $4.7 billion, ranked second and third. Also included on the list were the Hospitals of Ontario Pension Fund, Ontario Hydro, Canadian Pacific, Hydro-Québec, Air Canada, General Motors, the Aluminum Company of Canada, the Canadian Broadcasting Corporation, the Royal Bank of Canada, Imperial Oil, Stelco, Northern Telecom, the Ford Motor Company of Canada, the Canadian Imperial Bank of Commerce, Shell Canada, Inco and the Bank of Montreal.

And the plans would be even richer if they were not constrained by federal legislation. Since 1971, tax restrictions have discouraged pension funds from leaving Canada by penalizing plan sponsors who invest more than ten percent of the book value of plan assets outside Canada. Under the ten-percent foreign-property rule, pension plans which exceed that amount face a one-percent monthly penalty tax on the excess, a rule which also applies to RRSPs.*

Keith Ambachtsheer has noted that while the Toronto Exchange stock index produced average annual gains of about

---

* In 1985, Finance Minister Michael Wilson offered a three-for-one incentive, allowing funds to invest three dollars outside Canada for every dollar they invested in "venture-capital" enterprises at home. New federal legislation outlining other changes to the investment rules is in the offing, but had not appeared at the time of writing.

23 percent in the five year period up to 1987, comparable returns for the U.S. and combined European/Far East stock markets were much better — at 28 percent and 36 percent respectively. If Canadian pension funds had invested 20, not 10, percent of their assets in foreign markets in those years, he estimated, they would have earned at least $5 billion more than they did, increasing their 1986 assets from $150 billion to $155 billion.

Needless to say, the pension industry has supported the removal of the rule, ostensibly on the grounds that lifting the restriction would make pension plans more efficient and thus enable them to deliver better benefits to retired employees. There is every reason in the world to doubt their word on this. Given the industry's stance on retroactive inflation protection for retirees — that no matter how large plan surpluses grow, employers will never be able to *afford* to index their pensions — it is clear where the excess profits would wind up: in employers' — and not retirees' — pockets.

As a result of the ten-percent rule, vast amounts of pension money are channelled into Canadian stocks, often into inferior investments which do not perform as well as many foreign investments would. And because the number of market issues available in Canada is limited, the rapidly expanding funds have been forced to buy larger and larger chunks of individual companies.

Prior to the implementation of the Ontario Pension Benefits Act, 1987, for example, the choice of investments open to pension funds was limited to a "legal list" prescribed by the Canadian and British Insurance Companies Act. This restriction forced the funds into a tightly circumscribed market. It has not been unusual, for example, for forty percent or more of the outstanding common shares of an "approved" corporation to be owned by a handful of pension funds — a potentially dangerous situation in which the fund could encounter great difficulty in selling its shares without adversely affecting their price. Ontario's new pension legislation replaces the list with a "prudent person" approach. Under the Act, every pension plan administrator must "exercise the care, diligence and skill in the administration and investment of the pension fund that a person of ordinary prudence would exercise in dealing with the property of another person."

That change is an improvement, but it is no guarantee that employees' best interests will be better protected than in the past. As we have seen, weak regulatory bodies such as the Pension Commission of Ontario allowed companies to view their pension plans as profit centres, without making it clear that the plans' first obligation should be to the plan members whose wages provide the capital for the fund. That legacy has led to great mischief. By allowing inflation to be integrated into the financial structure of most pension plans, the regulators have made the immediate costs of inflation protection much higher than they needed to be. And, given their dereliction of duty, it cannot be surprising that employers have come to feel that the best pension plan is one which costs them as little as possible — even if that view ignores the implicit promises they have made to their employees in the past to provide them with a pension benefit *in real dollars*.*

While task force members mulled over the seemingly irreconcilable theoretical arguments swirling around them, a real-life scenario was about to be played out which would have a direct impact on their deliberations. Four days after General Motors and the auto workers made their positions clear to the committee, CAW president Bob White served notice to the automobile industry that his members wanted indexed pensions. General Motors' cost estimates, White charged, were nothing more than a "worst case scenario" designed to mislead and intimidate the task force. His members wanted a decent wage increase and they wanted indexed pensions — and they saw no reason whatsoever that they should not have them — regardless of the terms of the forthcoming provincial legislation.

The CAW chose Chrysler Canada as its first target, in part to

*In the last decade, the ratio of employer-to-employee contributions to trusteed plans has changed dramatically. In the first quarter of 1987, for example, employer contributions were 10 percent lower than in the same quarter of the previous year. Until 1979, employer contributions had increased each year since Statistics Canada began to track the statistic in 1970, and until 1981 they were the plans' major source of revenue, accounting for as much as 52.4 percent of total income. Since 1978, that proportion has gradually decreased to a low of only 17.6 percent in the first quarter of 1987.

avoid getting tangled up in U.S. negotiations between the United Auto Workers and Ford which were underway at the same time. "We knew that this was a hell of a hurdle," said Bob Nickerson, CAW's secretary-treasurer and a member of the union's high-powered negotiating team, "and we didn't need any interference from anybody."

Chrysler's profit picture made the company a logical choice too. Chrysler Canada earned $193 million in 1986 and its parent corporation reported world-wide profits of $1.2 billion. "There is no question of their ability to pay," said White at the time. He added that Lee Iacocca himself, chairman of Chrysler, would "have trouble resisting our argument after giving himself $20 million last year." Chrysler spokesmen, for their part, said simply that they were "opposed in principle" to inflation protection. The issue, company spokesmen said, had no place on the bargaining table at all in view of the forthcoming provincial legislation on indexation.

On September 14, White made good on his threat. About 10,000 Chrysler employees walked off the job, vowing to stay off until their demands for indexation were met. After three days of hard-nosed bargaining in the middle of the four-day strike, Chrysler and the CAW — negotiating its first major contract since the union had broken away from its U.S. parent in 1985 — reached agreement on September 17. The deal improved basic pension benefits. An employee who retired with at least thirty years' service would receive a monthly benefit of $1,505 (up from $1,205 a month) — but there was nothing revolutionary about that. Improvements in basic pension benefits had long been subject to the collective bargaining process in the automobile industry. What was new in the settlement was an automatic indexation formula for retirees' pension benefits.*

Under the terms of the agreement, retiring employees would receive annual increases equivalent to 90 percent of any rise in the Consumer Price Index. These increases, however, could not

---

*In June, the Canadian Paperworkers had also negotiated pension indexing with the Eastern Canada pulp and paper industry with much less fanfare.

exceed increases in the basic rate for current employees, to prevent retirees receiving greater inflation protection than current employees. The Chrysler settlement was not retroactive, although in a separate clause the company agreed to increase pension benefits for employees who had already retired. Nor did it apply to the deferred pensions of employees who had left the company. Moreover, it had a life of six years — a provision which the pension industry seized upon to downplay its significance. But in fact, the six-year limit allowed Chrysler to sidestep funding regulations. In effect, the company adopted funding procedures similar to those the CAW had called for in its brief to the task force.

White was jubilant, calling the settlement a "milestone for our union and a milestone for all workers in this country." The union, White claimed, had made the largest improvement ever in pensions, both for current and future retirees. Best of all, the settlement would serve as a model, not only for future CAW negotiations, but also for other industries as well.

Chrysler's chief negotiator William Fisher was philosophical. "Sometimes in collective bargaining you do change your position and we certainly did here, no question about that," he told reporters at a press conference after the deal was announced.

With the Chrysler settlement in hand, union negotiators took a deep breath and plunged into preparations for the next round. The union had given Ford a deadline of October 1 to endorse a similar contract or face a prolonged strike. Ford, in the meantime, had reached a settlement with the UAW in the United States which included improvements in profit sharing and job protection, but did not address the pension issue. It wasn't clear, Nickerson said, whether the company would accept the Chrysler settlement or try to force the U.S. settlement on the union. Five hours before the strike deadline announced by the union, that question was answered. Ford agreed to a settlement similar to the one Chrysler had already agreed to — and Bob White had another first in his pocket: the first agreement in Canada which differed fundamentally from its U.S. counterpart.

With two settlements in hand, the union moved on to

General Motors, which, Nickerson says, the CAW considered the most "reasonable" of the three auto makers. Even as GM was telling the Friedland Task Force that indexation was absolutely out of the question, Nickerson says, the union was getting indications from company officials that there was room to negotiate on the issue. "There were good vibes from GM," he recalls. The good signals rang true; the settlement with the company was marginally better than those at either Ford or Chrysler. Since then, the union has carried its "pattern" settlement into contract talks in the auto parts industry, providing a precedent for other industries which has proved impossible to ignore.*

The auto workers' successes contrasted sharply with the prevailing mood of caution and gloom that had dominated the Friedland hearings. But the second intrusion of reality seemed to confirm employers' fears. Predictably, Black Monday, the dramatic stock market crash on October 19, 1987, provided another weapon for the pension lobby, coming as it did just as the Friedland Task Force was completing its work. A wave of "We-told-you-so's" echoed through the financial community from employers who maintained that their cautions to the task force had been vindicated.

For his part, Ontario Treasurer Robert Nixon, the man who bore ultimate responsibility for the government's decision on inflation protection, indicated that the crash might bring the provincial reform exercise to an abrupt end. "It will certainly make it more difficult for [pension reform] to be applied, because many of the surpluses in the various pension plans have essentially changed if not disappeared," Nixon told reporters. The principle of indexing, he added, was "not at issue.... It is the position of the government to go forward with the indexation of pensions. But we certainly can't have a program

---

*In December 1987, after a series of rotating strikes and a company lock-out, the Machinists and Aerospace Workers won a much weaker indexation provision from Air Canada. In February 1988, brewery workers in Ontario secured dramatic improvements in pension benefits, although indexation remained capped at 2 percent, as it had been under earlier contracts. Since then, pension indexation has become a commonplace on union shopping lists at contract renewal time.

that can't be funded. So it will have to be reviewed when this thing straightens out."

Yet because the average pension plan invests less than half of its assets in common stocks — and fund managers never buy on margin — the immediate impact of Black Monday on pension funds was far less than the doomsayers suggested. Few money managers panicked — most had been expecting a market correction — and few sold off shares at the market's low point. Some even plunged into the market immediately in search of bargains. The market, after all, had lost only the profits it had gained in the previous year. Indeed, in February 1988, less than four months after the crash, *The Financial Post* reported that "corporate Canada" had shown "remarkable resilience" in the aftermath of Black Monday. The ninety-four companies surveyed by the paper had posted an average 48 percent jump in after-tax fourth-quarter earnings in 1987, compared with fourth-quarter earnings a year earlier. Black Monday had not been as devastating as Canadians had been led to believe.

The Friedland report, when it was finally released in February 1988, was hailed in some quarters as a major breakthrough in pension legislation, ensuring that Ontario would become the first jurisdiction on the continent to legislate indexed pensions.* Its key recommendations — that current and deferred pensions should be protected from inflation to a minimum level of 75 percent of the Consumer Price Index minus 1 percent [(75% of CPI)-1%] up to an effective maximum of 6.5 percent — accepted many of the arguments put forward by critics of the private pension system. For example, many employers have eyed Group RRSPs as an alternative to their defined-benefit plans; the report recommended that they too be subject to the same rules as other pension plans, that sponsors of money

---

*Nova Scotia's new pension legislation requires employers to index deferred pensions, but the province has not yet implemented the provision. See also Appendix A.

purchase plans be required to offer indexed annuities to retiring employees and that the Pension Commission help plan sponsors "and their actuaries" find ways to provide better inflation protection than the suggested formula.

But as welcome as the report's conclusions were, the task force did little to ensure that retirees and older employees would benefit from the new rules. The report's proposals would give employees who retire in the distant future some protection against the erosion of their pension benefits by inflation, but they required no inflation protection at all for current retirees, who have no redress for the losses of the past two decades, during which time there has been a clear transfer of wealth from pensioners to employers and shareholders. In fact, the report demanded no significant protection for anyone who will retire in the next decade or so.

On the contrary. Instead of directing employers to use their vast surpluses to make up for past injustices, the recommendations handed the surpluses in private pension plans over to employers, in effect forcing them to do little more than they had been doing anyway in periods of low inflation. Ironically, the report paid lip service to the need to protect retirees from "the arbitrary redistribution of income that accompanies inflation." But by "encouraging" employers to voluntarily make provisions for pensioners *over the next five years* at a rate of 75 percent of CPI minus 2.5, it ignored the significance and magnitude of plan assets being siphoned from private pension plans by means of contribution holidays.

By endorsing contribution holidays, the recommendations would permit plan managers to continue to deplete the surpluses for the foreseeable future. And by allowing employers to withdraw surplus funds if they provide "adequate" inflation protection, the report ignored the escalating dispute over plan ownership and the need to protect pension funds until the courts have dealt with the growing numbers of ownership challenges.

On February 8, 1988, Ontario treasurer Robert Nixon extended the ban on surplus withdrawals from plans still in operation and broadened the moratorium to include plans in the process of being wound up. He also apppointed David Slater, former chairman of the Economic Council of Canada, to conduct yet another round of consultations with labour groups and government policy-makers. But as the target date for the new legislation, January 1, 1989, approached, the Liberals dithered, unable or unwilling to muster the political will to move beyond the timid recommendations of the report — and the rhetoric and the constant threats of the corporate lobby — to tackle the real question: the legitimacy of the private pension system and its "pension deal."*

On March 2, 1989, two months after indexation was scheduled to take effect, the Ontario government finally announced its intentions. Murray Elston, Nixon's successor as minister of financial institutions, released a lengthy consultation paper detailing several revisions to the Friedland recommendations. The document made it clear that the Liberal government had caved in to pressure from the corporate community. Not only would there be no automatic retroactivity — and no restrictions on contribution holidays — but plan sponsors would once again be allowed to make withdrawals from ongoing plans, as long as they promised to make a matching contribution towards retroactive indexing, a compromise which, in effect, turned half of the surplus money in defined-benefit plans over to employers. On top of that, the proposals weakened the Friedland recommendations by calling for a lower cap (effectively 5 percent instead of 6.5) on indexation. Worse, the formula would apply only to 60 percent of the Year's Maximum Pensionable Earnings as defined by the Canada Pension Plan.

•

*The "pension deal," a phrase of which employers and actuaries have become very fond lately, takes into account an employer's willingness and ability to establish a pension plan, the marketplace in which the employer operates, the legal and regulatory situation and any bargaining that may have taken place between employer and employees in the past. It has become a buzzword for everyone who insists that employees in defined-benefit plans have "agreed" to accept a pension benefit defined without reference to "real" dollars — and that the only interest of members in the plan is that the employer's funding policy and the pension fund itself will be adequate to provide that benefit.

Not surprisingly, the new proposals were greeted warmly by large employers and the pension industry.

For the hundreds of thousands of Canadians who retired in the last two decades counting on their private pension plans to deliver what they believed they had been promised, the pension "deal" — a deal they had little choice but to make — has been a very raw deal indeed. The New Deal spelled out in the Friedland report and substantially weakened by the proposals in the consultation paper is not much better: in return for the surpluses in their plans, employers must build in a modest level of inflation protection for current employees in the future. Under these terms, the plight of today's retirees would still be a matter to be negotiated between plan sponsors and their consciences.

In the course of the last decade, the notion that pension plans exist primarily for the benefit of employers has become recognized as both socially disruptive and morally suspect. It is not a notion which the majority of Canadians today supports. An Ontario Federation of Labour public opinion survey in 1986, for example, indicated that 67 percent of those polled said that they believed employers should not be allowed to remove funds from employee pension plans no matter who "owns" the funds. And after years of watching the real value of pensions plummet, it should also be clear by now that there is no defensible argument for allowing retirees to subsidize their former employers and their shareholders with money that is rightfully theirs.

Until now older Canadians have lacked the political muscle — and the numbers — to protect their rights and their futures from governments and employers who, for narrow and self-serving reasons, have had no compunction about ignoring and exploiting them. That is about to change.

..

PART THREE

THE POLITICS OF PENSIONS

::

THE SEARCH FOR A
BETTER TOMORROW

::

"If working people are going to make their money work for them instead of the insurance companies and investment firms, they are going to need more than representation. They need joint control over investment policies."

John Fryer, President of the National Union
of Provincial Government Employees, 1981

"If shareholders do not receive the lion's share of rewards accruing from placing the pension fund at risk...there is no corporate rationale for doing so."

Keith Ambachtsheer, pension consultant,
Pensions and the Bottom Line, 1986

::

The incensed grandmothers who shook their fists and shouted insults at the politicians who were threatening to tear yet another strip off their dignity and their pride on that fine June day in 1985 forged an unforgettable image in the minds of many Canadians. Their anger at the Tory government's decision to partially de-index Old Age Security benefits captured the frustration thousands of older Canadians living on fixed incomes have felt in the last decade. It is an image for the future, too, because age will become an increasingly potent force as a greying Canada mobilizes its energies and flexes its political muscle. In the coming years, today's false and demeaning stereotypes of impotent, witless senior citizens whiling away their sunset years in bingo halls and shopping plazas will give way to new perceptions of what it means to grow old. And as the vast baby boom generation approaches retirement, the Grandmothers' Uprising of '85 will be remembered for exactly what it was: an early warning of the potency of the politics of age.

Yet it is a misleading image, too. For, despite what many harbingers of doom and gloom for the pension system would have us believe, Canada's population is aging in demographic terms, but it is not yet old. And although the implications for Canadian society of plummeting birth rates and increasing life expectancies are enormous, they should not be permitted to obscure the fact that *today* Canada enjoys a young and vigorous population, a rapidly expanding labour force and a golden opportunity to correct many of the flaws in the retirement security system *before* the demographic shifts of the coming decades reach unmanageable proportions.

It has been an article of faith among conservative politicians and policy makers in recent years that the only way to prepare the country for the coming changes is to slash social spending, including expenditures for old age security, *now*. Indeed, the Mulroney government, like conservative governments in Great Britain and the United States, has devoted much of its energy to finding ways to cut back on funding for everything from education to job-creation programs, invoking the dark spectres of overwhelming deficit, national bankruptcy and economic ruin to justify their actions.

Especially the deficit. Like Margaret Thatcher and Ronald Reagan, conservative politicians have fashioned a rhetorical straw-man out of the government deficits to justify their unrelenting attacks on the "welfare state," a term which in today's conservative lexicon is synonymous with waste, greed, sloth and fiscal irresponsibility. And, like market-obsessed governments everywhere in the industrialized world, they have then attempted to knock the straw-man down at the expense of those who are least able to defend themselves: the poor, the disadvantaged, the politically impotent and, above all, the elderly, who make up a large proportion of all of those categories.

But in targeting OAS pensions, the Tories made a serious miscalculation. Deficit or no deficit, most Canadians were not prepared to stand idly by as the elderly took it on the chin from the politicians, as they had taken it for more than a decade from the private pension system. They agreed with the angry grandmothers on Parliament Hill that older people had subsidized the country's economy for too long as it was.

In the end, the Tories were forced to back down and paid a high price in humiliation for insulting the intelligence of older Canadians and for underestimating their latent political clout. But it was certainly no higher a price than many retirees had paid in the last decade as they struggled to make ends meet in an affluent society whose political and corporate leaders seemed determined to ignore them. By introducing a measure that was utterly insensitive to their real needs, Brian Mulroney and Michael Wilson had demonstrated that the government neither fully understood nor had much sympathy for the thousands of older people who live below the poverty line across this country. While there is a legitimate argument to be made that not every Canadian needs or should receive Old Age Security, the Tories had chosen not to make it. Instead, they opted to take money from the poor as well as from the well-to-do, on the grounds that the country could no longer afford to guarantee even a minimal monthly income, in real dollars, to those who needed it most.

That was a mistake. In reality, the country can no longer afford *not* to take the concerns of older Canadians seriously, notwithstanding the shortsighted arguments of the corporate lobby and its friends in high places who have so effectively dominated the debate over old age security for so long. Their message — that Canada is headed for fiscal catastrophe because of wasteful and ineffective spending on social programs — has come to be seen as a truism by many Canadians, even by those who believe that the network of social services established in this country since the Second World War is in large part responsible for the enviable quality of life most Canadians enjoy today.

The proposition that the federal deficit will destroy that quality of life — and that the only way to reduce the deficit is to reduce the incomes and expectations of the elderly and slash social programs in general — should not go unchallenged. For the argument that social spending must be reduced today to avoid fiscal disaster in the future is in many ways misleading. Canada *has* made progress in reducing poverty levels among the elderly. Statistics compiled by the National Council of Welfare indicate that many older Canadians are significantly better off than they were in the 1960s.

This improvement, however, is almost entirely due to increases in welfare payments by federal and provincial governments, especially to women, and to the fact that the Canada and Quebec Pension Plans subsidized those — mostly men — who retired without having been in the plans long enough to earn a full pension.* Yet even with such supports in place, the National Council of Welfare reported in April 1988 that 46.1 percent of all unattached Canadian women over age sixty-five and 31.9 percent of unattached men still live below the poverty line. The body found that one Canadian in five over age sixty-five lived below the poverty line in 1986 and that the threat of poverty was still significantly greater for women than for men. Women, the Council reported, make up 71.7 percent of the elderly poor.

Worse, the statistics show that six out of ten children being raised by single mothers in Canada are poor. Their deprivation will ensure that they will become the victims of the pension system in the future, as lack of educational and cultural opportunities force them into low-paying jobs in sectors of the economy which provide little opportunity to build retirement savings. Statistics Canada figures released in early 1988, for example,

---

*The Guaranteed Income Supplement was increased by $25 a month in July 1984 and by an additional $25 a month in December for those receiving the GIS benefit at the single rate.

showed that by 1986, 56 percent of all Canadian women were in the work force, including 62 percent of women with children under the age of six. Between 1981 and 1986, women accounted for 94 percent of all employment growth in Canada. Most of the 500,000 new jobs they filled, however, were in the service sector and little progress had been made in closing the gap between men's and women's earnings.

Yet, with unemployment rates declining and labour force participation growing in Canada, especially among women, government expenditures on social programs as a proportion of Gross Domestic Product will, in fact, decline substantially over the next two decades — reaching current levels again only when the first of the baby-boomers reach retirement age in the second decade of the next century. Instead of cutting back on services and income support for lower-income earners, policy makers should be looking at ways to ensure that the next generation will start saving for retirement on a sounder footing.

And there are, after all, other ways to reduce a deficit. Canadians would be far better served now and in the future if, instead of targeting basic social programs, their governments sought fairer ways, such as more rigorous corporate taxes, to keep the deficit under control. Indeed, as Canada enters the 1990s, it is arguable that governments should be spending a great deal *more*, not less, to provide a broader range of social services and to raise the income levels of poorer Canadians while there is still time to do so.

At the same time they were attacking the incomes of the elderly poor, the Tory government was also increasing the taxes of all working Canadians through higher contribution rates to the Quebec and Canada Pension Plans, justifying the rate increases with two arguments: first, that Canadians needed the improved benefits the plans would be able to offer as a result of the higher contribution rates and, second, that the country would soon be unable to pay for the benefits guaranteed by the plans because of the demands placed on federal coffers by an aging population.

The first argument, as we have seen, was largely bunk. Although some Canadians will enjoy improved benefits for their extra contributions, most will not. The changes to the CPP increased disability benefits to the same level the Quebec plan already provided, ensured that survivor benefits would no longer cease on remarriage and that pension credits could be split on divorce or separation. They also improved orphan's benefits. They did not, however, change the basic formula governing benefit levels.

The second argument was partly bunk. As the population ages and the plan matures, Michael Wilson correctly pointed out, CPP expenditures will increase, as will other social expenditures — health care, community services and housing among others — associated with an aging society. That is true. But Wilson might also have mentioned that the CPP is running out of money many years before it needed to, because governments have frittered the money away — and that there are many compelling arguments for significantly expanding benefits under the plans as well as for raising contribution rates.

Today, significantly improved benefits under the public plans may well be the single most effective way for any government to prevent other expenditures from overwhelming public tax revenues in the future. Virtually without exception, every study that has been conducted into the economics of aging has shown that people who have enough money to live on comfortably are emotionally and physically healthier, more productive and more independent than people who do not. They are also much less likely to require the massive government expenditures for health care, drugs and housing which politicians so fear. Older people who are financially secure remain in their homes longer, are able to care for themselves longer and do not succumb as readily to the debilitating malaises which accompany financial deprivation and loss of independence.

Aging populations *do* demand more public spending on social support services. At the same time their growing numbers at the ballot box make it more difficult for governments to raise extra money by taxing capital income to pay for these services. As many European countries have discovered in recent years, older voters are perfectly capable of exercising their political power to ensure that capital taxes are minimized. This in turn has forced governments to introduce consumption taxes, in the form of retail sales taxes, value added taxes or expenditure taxes, to raise the extra money they need. The sad fact is, though, that while consumption taxes provide a stable revenue source with minimal economic and political costs, they also erode the progressiveness of the tax system, placing an unfair burden on those who can least afford to pay.

Consumption taxes hit rich and poor equally hard, whereas a tax on income enables governments to oblige the rich to pay progressively more as their income rises. This is a fundamental concept which most Canadians fully support. Yet under the Mulroney government's tax reforms, which call for an all-inclusive national sales tax, Canada is moving inexorably in the direction of consumption taxes. And unless retirees — and all other low-income earners — are given significant protection in the new tax system in the form of tax credits, they will find that a large chunk of their already inadequate incomes is taxed away.*

Today, despite its reputation as an example to the world in its health-care and social-support systems, Canada spends very little to maintain retirement income levels and on social welfare in general. Most European countries will soon be spending as much as one-third of their Gross Domestic Product on social programs. By comparison, a 1986 International Monetary Fund study, which took into account changes in birth and aging rates as well as social and economic trends, such as increased participation of women in the work force, estimates that Canada's social expenditures will actually *decline* dramatically in the next two decades — to about seventeen percent of the GDP from the current rate of about twenty percent.

Far from leading the list of big spenders, as many Canadians seem to believe, Canada today spends less on social benefits and

---

*The Mulroney government has already introduced another tax "reform" which eats into the income of the elderly. As a part of changes brought in four years ago, the government eliminated full indexing of most personal deductions as well as full indexing of tax brackets in order to oblige all taxpayers to pick up the first 3 percent of inflation themselves. For older Canadians living on fixed incomes, this change was a genuine blow: a 6-percent increase in their income could translate into as much as a 50-percent increase in their income taxes.

social programs than almost any other industrialized society in the world. The most recent figures available, for example, show that Canada spends just 5 percent of its Gross Domestic Product on the poorest 20 percent of its citizens. Of that amount, only 1.5 percent goes to the poorest 10 percent. Japan, by comparison, spends 7.9 percent of GDP on the poorest 20 percent and 3.2 percent on the poorest 10 percent; Sweden, Australia, the Netherlands and West Germany all spend significantly more on social programs for the poorer members of society than does Canada, as does Great Britain, at 6.3 and 2.4 percent. Even the United States, that bastion of laissez-faire free enterprise, will soon overtake Canada in spending on the poor if it has not already done so.

Canadian expenditures for public pensions are also much lower than in most other industrialized countries. In 1983, for example, costs for public pensions in both West Germany and France amounted to more than 12 percent of GDP. Canada, by comparison, spent only 5 percent on public pensions. Yet the monetarist policies favoured by conservative politicians and social policy makers in recent years demand major cutbacks in social spending and the privatization of social programs. The benefits of privatization, the theory goes, will magically "trickle down" to the disadvantaged in the form of more jobs, higher salaries and general economic prosperity.

In Canada, we have seen these policies, which are today largely discredited, at work at both the federal and provincial levels. They are usually embedded in passionate appeals for deficit reduction and fiscal responsibility and their primary victims are invariably the poorest members of society: those dependent upon welfare — including half of all retirees — the working poor and the unemployed, because any trend towards privatization is necessarily a trend towards a system in which basic social services are available to people solely on the basis of their ability to pay.

Canadians need look no further than to the deepening crises in health care and education and at the appalling racial and class tensions and urban decay in Margaret Thatcher's England or at the horrendous insurance and health-care costs in the United

States to see where such short-sighted policies can lead — and to see how quickly they can lead there. Yet Canada, with its still-inadequate OAS and its low ceiling on CPP benefits, is well on the way to privatizing the retirement security system. When average OAS and CPP benefits together do not provide anything resembling an adequate minimum income, Canadians have had little choice but to entrust the largely unregulated private sector with their retirement security.

Indeed, the greatest irony of Canada's old-age-income system as a whole is that many retirees who today must depend on welfare in order to survive believed that they *had* guaranteed their retirement needs through their contributions to the Canada and Quebec Pension Plans. So they were told and so it was meant to be: the Guaranteed Income Supplement, after all, was originally intended as a temporary welfare measure to be quickly supplanted by an earned pension. Yet even though the Quebec and Canada Pension Plans are maturing, welfare supplements in the form of GIS or provincial programs are more important to retirees today than ever before. As a result, in the eyes of many politicians at least, older Canadians have come to constitute a new breed of welfare bums — yet another drain on the economy and yet another contributing factor to the almighty deficit.

For years, the private sector has insisted that older people don't really need as much money to live on as they would have us think they do. The financial needs of a retired person, Geoffrey Calvert ventured in the 1970s, probably decrease at a rate of around 2 percent a year. Others have pointed out that most Canadians owned their houses and that, because houses were a perfectly sound investment, most Canadians didn't need and shouldn't expect much in the way of pensions. Others said that old people don't eat very much and have simple pleasures. Still others, like William Mercer, said bluntly that Canadians as a people had become lazy, soft and greedy.

Over the years this debate has raged on in all its paternalistic glory. It would be a harmless debate except for one thing: such sentiments make the elderly an obvious target when governments set about reducing their deficits. Yet the "problem" of the deficit is as much a matter of political ideology as of economic necessity. Canada's deficit, after all, is mainly money Canadians have borrowed from themselves. Governments can ignore deficits or they can turn them into things that go bump in the night, depending upon their philosophies and their goals.

Conservative policy makers would have us all believe that the only hope for the future lies in an unrestricted marketplace with government in full retreat from the interventionist policies of the past. But that proposition is, at the very least, questionable. The very best guarantee against crippling deficits in the future may well be a concerted effort now — through further legislative reforms which include expansion of the Canada and Quebec Pension Plans and mandatory indexation of *all* employment pensions — to ensure that all working Canadians have income levels when they retire which will enable them to live with dignity — without having to rely on welfare to survive.

Unless benefit levels under the public-pension system expand, the majority of Canadians will continue to be at the mercy of the private sector when it comes to saving for retirement. A privatized pension system is not necessarily a bad thing, provided that it is fair and provided that it delivers on its implicit promise to guarantee that its beneficiaries will, in fact, get what they have paid for. In the last decade in Canada, that promise has not been kept.

And while the "problem" of the private-pension system is less obviously subject to political forces than the government programs, a political problem it is nonetheless. For decades, corporate Canada trumpeted its commitment to social welfare — and its willingness to assume responsibility for a fair share of Canadians' retirement security. Yet, when the chips were down, the rhetoric took on a decidedly hollow ring. And a familiar ring too, as the business lobby retreated to its traditional argument that older people don't really require much money to keep body and soul together and therefore shouldn't complain when their pensions lose their value because of inflation.

That argument surfaced again, as we have seen, in assertions by employers to the Friedland Task Force that ad hoc adjustments to benefits in the range of 30-to-40 percent of inflation constitute exemplary generosity on the part of plan sponsors. Such glib and insensitive arguments are not helpful. Instead, they would seem to be the best argument for a simple proposition: that, short of turning all employment pensions over to the CPP, the best thing Canadians can do today to protect their retirement savings is to elect politicians who are committed to insuring *through legislation* that Canadians who work diligently throughout their lives will never again have their retirement savings dissipated by inflation, government irresponsibility and corporate greed.

In the last decade inflation has forced retirees on fixed incomes to transfer a very substantial percentage of their retirement savings to corporate employers and their shareholders.* In its adamant refusal to provide indexed pensions, it is clear that corporate Canada still considers the continuation of that transfer of wealth to be a fair and sensible way to go about the business of private pensions. Indeed, when the surpluses in private plans began to accumulate early in the 1980s, the business community made it perfectly clear that social responsibility had slipped a few notches in their collective consciousness.

The problem with Canadian business in the past, we were told, was that it was too insular, too soft, too uncompetitive, too set in its unprofitable ways. Perhaps so. Yet if the solution to these perceived shortcomings is for employers to get leaner, meaner and more competitive at the direct expense of their employees and their retirees, are we really going to be much further ahead in the years to come?

Nowhere has corporate Canada's new tough-guy image been more visible than in the on-going battles over inflation protection

---

*If the Gross Domestic Product is stable or rising in real terms, *any* reduction in the value of income paid to individual retirees constitutes a continuous transfer of wealth from those individuals to the government. Similarly, if corporate profits are rising, any reduction in the real value of pension benefits means a continuous transfer of wealth from retirees to the corporation and its shareholders unless inflation is zero or pensions are fully indexed.

for current employees and over retroactive compensation for the retirees whose incomes have been so badly battered by inflation in the last decade. That battle, as we have seen, is now being waged primarily in Ontario. Its outcome will have a major impact on the future of private pension plans right across the country.

The battle lines are clearly drawn: corporate Canada wants no part of retroactivity and is not pleased with the prospect of having to protect future pension benefits from inflation.* Lined up against them are all those who believe that significant inflation protection is affordable and should be mandatory in defined-benefit plans in the future — and that it is self-evident that any significant surplus in private pension plans should be used, first, to adjust pension benefits for retirees and, second, to improve benefits for current employees.

The Friedland report accepted the corporate proposition that all decisions involving retroactivity must be left in the hands of individual employers on the grounds that it is "uncommon" for legislation to be retroactive and that retroactivity is "tantamount to changing the rules of the game in mid-stream." Employers, the report agreed, should not be forced to do something they have never done before, especially when they didn't expect to have to do it. "Individuals bargain and enter into contracts in light of the existing legislative framework," the report said, adding that "if the government retroactively alters this framework, individuals may become reluctant to rely on prevailing rules."

These words echoed the sentiments of the pension industry. The brief to the Task Force from the large actuarial and consulting firm of Towers, Perrin, Forster & Crosby, for example, pointed out that sponsors of defined-benefit plans established those plans "based on both their economic circumstances and the

---

*The private sector's favourite argument against any formula involving retroactivity is that it would penalize employers who have voluntarily upgraded benefits by providing early retirement options or improving benefit formulas — and that bad employers or firms without employment pension plans would suffer no losses. In fact, under the voluntary retroactivity guidelines suggested in the Friedland report, good employers would pay very little, bad employers would pay a lot more. That is as it should be.

legislative environment at the time. To make a mid-stream change in the rules would leave the sponsor bereft of any remedy."

But wait a minute. The rules of the game *have* changed in the last fifteen years. Just ask the thousands of retirees who have watched helplessly as the value of their pension benefits plummeted in real terms while pension funds and corporate profits grew by leaps and bounds. When most of the pension plans were developed, inflation was running at 1 or 2 percent and it was assumed that pensions would decline in value at that rate. When inflation rose to 4-to-12 percent, the rules of the game changed substantially — in favour of plan sponsors.

Until private employers and the pension industry are prepared to acknowledge the fact that their employees have not received full value for their money, to agree that redress is possible — instead of pretending that there is no relationship whatsoever between surpluses and the declining value of pensions — and to accept that there must be guarantees in place that the same thing cannot happen again in the future, why should anyone, governments included, trust them with anybody's money or expect them to behave any differently in the future?

The Friedland report, in its concern for the rights of employers and shareholders, downplayed the inequities of the last decade and the immensity of the consequences of allowing a similar situation to arise again in the future. Yet if Canadians cannot count on the pensions they have earned to maintain their value, we could all be in very big trouble in the years to come. Canada cannot afford a generation of retirees who must depend upon diminishing numbers of taxpayers to support them, simply because their employers refuse to acknowledge that a pension should be paid in a currency which bears some relationship to real dollars.

It is not employers who are in need of a remedy, for heaven's sake. Retirees are the ones in need of a remedy: for fifteen years their money has disappeared into the gaping maw of a private pension system which would prefer to pretend that they don't exist.

The surpluses that exist in most private pension plans today are central to the question of what can be done to redress the wrongs inflicted on current retirees. But it would be foolhardy for employers *or* employees to count on the surpluses in the future. As we have seen, they arose suddenly and as the result of economic forces which may or may not recur in the future. The widespread layoffs of the early 1980s, the trend toward job creation in non-unionized, low-paying industries and the longstanding discrimination against women, part-time employees and low-income earners all played a part in creating them. There is no reason to believe that all of these factors will coincide with an over-heated investment climate in quite the same way ever again.

But there is every reason to believe that current surpluses should be used to retroactively improve the pensions of those already retired. If we start with the proposition that significant inflation protection for current employees in the future *is* affordable in well-managed defined-benefit plans *without recourse* to current surpluses — a proposition which even many corporate spokesmen reluctantly admit is entirely defensible — the surplus issue becomes much clearer. It remains to be seen how clear it has become to the legislators who have it in their power to redress the wrongs of the last decade.

If politicians in Ontario — and, following their example, politicians across Canada — do muster the political will to legislate retroactivity, they will do so over the dead bodies of the pension industry — and of many employers as well. For in their threats and their posturing, many of them seem to have completely forgotten the promises they have made to their employees, and to all Canadians, in the past. Worse, they seem to have forgotten that their overwhelming interest in pension-plan surpluses as sources of corporate revenue is of very recent origin. Most employers, after all, set up their defined-benefit plans to attract and keep employees, to build a good corporate image and to be socially responsible members of society — not to create a profit centre for the corporation. Those goals, presumably, are as compelling as they ever were, although in the current frenzy over pension plans as money cows, matters of corporate responsibility and social justice rarely arise.

The Ontario initiative on inflation protection, from corporate Canada's perspective, was an unwarranted intrusion by a troublesome provincial government into the debate over the country's pension system. However, there is another way to look at it. Far from being a disruptive force, the province has moved the reform process along another step and, in so doing, has raised the critical question which the provinces and the federal government, under pressure from the pension lobby, swept under the table in its rough-hewn consensus position. For that, Canadians can thank the twist of political fate which briefly made the Ontario NDP the surprised and delighted bedmates of the equally surprised and not-so-delighted Ontario Liberals. Without that intervention, it could well have been many years more before the next stage of the reform process got under way.

But whatever the outcome of the latest round in the Great Pension Debate, it will by no means resolve all of the questions swirling around pensions today. These questions will be on the public agenda for many years to come and their resolution could well spell the difference between financial security and financial desperation for many Canadians in the future. They could also have an enormous impact on the quality of life this society as a whole can expect in the years to come.

The most important of these questions for the future of Canada's pension system revolve around Free Trade and the business community's growing pressure on Ottawa to significantly relax the rule that imposes penalties on pension funds that invest more than ten percent of their assets outside Canada. The danger to Canadians in any comprehensive free-trade deal with the United States is twofold as far as pensions are concerned. In the first place, Canadian corporations will find themselves under great pressure from their U.S. counterparts to bring pension practices into line with their own. By and large, those practices are even less generous and fair to employees than existing Canadian schemes and would constitute a giant step backwards in the effort to reform the system further.

In the second place, insofar as Free Trade opens the door to foreign ownership, Canadian employees are likely to suffer from the pension policies of new corporate owners unless inflation protection is mandated. Indeed, the Hewitt survey presented to the Friedland Task Force shows clearly that not only are U.S. pension practices generally inferior, but that their failings are readily apparent in the subsidiaries of U.S. firms operating in Canada today. "While Canadian employers appear to be granting more [ad hoc] increases over time," the survey found, "the trend among U.S. employers is definitely a downward one." The Hewitt report noted that while 70 percent of Canadian employers surveyed granted a retirement increase during 1980-84, only 48 percent of the 577 U.S. employers surveyed had done so in the same time period. Moreover, far fewer Canadian subsidiaries of U.S.-based companies provided pension increases for retirees in the years 1977 to 1986. In 1981, for example, 61 percent of Canadian companies provided some increase. By comparison, only 38 percent of the U.S. subsidiaries did. These comparisons suggest that concerns about Free Trade and the pension system — and about Free Trade and Canadian social programs in general — are entirely justified.

The ten-percent rule, which was already relaxed somewhat when Finance Minister Michael Wilson introduced changes in 1985 which allow pension funds to invest $3 outside Canada for every $1 they invest in "venture capital" enterprises in Canada, poses a different kind of dilemma for the future. As a direct result of the ten-percent restriction, many large pension funds have become significant shareholders in Canadian companies almost by accident. Having bought pretty well everything worth buying in Canada, the funds have now been forced into investments they would prefer not to make. Pension-related savings today finance between one-third and one-half of *all* of Canada's investment needs — and they will play an even greater role in the country's capital markets in the future as the funds continue to grow.

The Friedland Task Force, to its credit, did not buy the corporate lobby's very favourite contention: that mandatory inflation protection would have an adverse effect on the economy, because it would reduce the amount that Canadians save and thereby reduce the amount of capital available for business investment. According to the report, "some factors suggest that mandatory inflation protection might increase aggregate savings, while other factors point to a decrease." Empirical studies using Canadian data, the report added, suggest that aggregate saving is "insensitive" to whether or not pension payments are indexed.

But the report did take another favourite corporate threat very seriously indeed. As we have seen, employers and pension-industry spokesmen never weary of bullying their critics with the threat that, if they are pushed too far, the defined-benefit plan will become a thing of the past. And this, they insist, could have drastic implications, not only for plan members, but for the Canadian economy. If employers rush to convert their defined-benefit plans to money-purchase plans in order to avoid compulsory indexation and the high costs of implementing the recent reforms, they say, billions and billions of dollars could shift from stocks and corporate bonds to more secure short-term bonds and guaranteed-interest certificates. Why? Because, left to their own devices, individual Canadians tend to direct their retirement savings into "safe" short-term, interest-bearing investments.

Whereas about half of the assets in employer-sponsored defined-benefit plans are invested in corporate stocks and bonds, real estate and venture capital, less than a quarter of the money in individual RRSPs finds its way into the higher-risk investments. Under a money-purchase plan — which is similar to an RRSP — the investment risk is shifted to plan members, who, the pension industry notes, will value safety over high returns, thereby diverting billions of dollars away from corporate investments and into the "safer" accounts of insurance companies, banks and trust companies. And even if employers continue to offer defined-benefit plans, they say, new portability rules, which allow an employee who leaves a company before retirement to transfer accumulated contributions into a locked-in RRSP, will have a significant effect on the availability of risk capital in Canada, because the RRSPs themselves will be directed into safer investments.

These threats and this obsession with capital-market considerations to the exclusion of broader social goals should be taken for what they are: a large measure of political blackmail overlaid with a heavy veneer of paternalism and arrogance. At the very least, those who make them would have us believe that the private sector has done a good job in providing pension coverage for Canadians. In fact, as we have seen, fewer than forty percent of Canadians have access to a private pension plan — after more than a decade of efforts to reform the system. Moreover, many retirees would be better off today if their retirement savings *had* been in a money-purchase plan or an RRSP all along.

Given the reluctance of many employers to improve benefits under their plans, even though those plans contain huge surpluses, it is difficult to avoid the conclusion that large corporate employers are much more interested in preserving the private-pension money-machine than in protecting the best interests of Canadians. And so long as no employer is *required* to sponsor a pension plan with prescribed benefit levels, a principle the business community has defended tooth-and-nail for years, there is little that can be done to ensure that private coverage will expand or that benefit levels will rise where coverage exists.

The notion that corporate Canada's only responsibility is to serve its shareholders, and that employers are justified in claiming all profits earned on pension contributions simply by fulfilling a promise to pay a pension benefit defined without regard to inflation and real dollars, should also be taken for what it is: a political statement that most Canadians would find repugnant if they fully understood its implications. To accept that proposition is to accept the old cliché, slightly altered to fit the circumstances, that what is good for General Motors is good for Canada. Despite the rhetoric of a market-oriented government and the dire economic predictions of the business community, many Canadians still believe that people are the country's greatest economic asset and that the economy should serve their needs first.

In the years of optimism and economic prosperity after the Second World War, Canadians decided that they did not want a society in which the rich get richer and the poor paid the price. Yet in agreeing to take corporate Canada at its word when its spokesmen promised that they, too, were committed to reforms that would put an end to the appalling poverty levels among the elderly, many Canadians have paid a very high price indeed. Today, the question is: how high a price are Canadians prepared to pay in the future for greater corporate profits and satisfied shareholders? With the examples of Margaret Thatcher's Britain and Ronald Reagan's America before us, do we really want a privatized pension system with no legal guarantees that pension benefits will retain their real value in the future?

There are other dangers in allowing the private sector to exercise exclusive control over the billions of dollars in pension funds. In the last few years, many pension-fund managers have begun to act like the powerful shareholders they are, insisting on their right to become actively involved in management decisions. And, understandably, when pension funds become significant or even principal legal owners of the companies in which they invest, their interest and involvement in management questions will escalate. As a result, increasing numbers of corporations are coming under attack from institutional investors whose proxies constitute a powerful weapon in boardroom skirmishes.

Nor is it surprising that fund managers may consider it their duty to complain when the goals of the corporation are at odds with the long-term goals of the fund. A company that is more interested in quick profits than in long-term performance, for example, will likely not provide maximum returns to its pension-fund investors. Similarly, a company determined to protect itself from hostile takeover bids may deliberately dilute the value of its holdings to the detriment of its pension-fund shareholders. In response, some funds have gone so far as to put forward their own candidates for directorships in an effort to ensure that corporate policy works for, not against, the interests of the fund.

Because most money managers take the view that their primary obligation is to improve the performance of the fund without reference to broad social and ethical criteria, it is understandable that they would want to get involved. Yet it is also entirely reasonable to ask whether this is a happy state of affairs, and whose interests it serves. For as long as the excess earnings of the funds benefit only the employers who control the plans, Canadians are perfectly justified in wondering whether or not important investment decisions are taken in their own long-term best interests.

More than a decade ago, Robert Perry raised these questions in a provocative article in *The Financial Post Magazine.* In the years between 1973 and 1976, Perry pointed out, trusteed pension funds had taken unto themselves more than $1 billion in employees' money. Yet with the exception of Manitoba which in 1976 introduced a law requiring plan sponsors to produce full financial reports for members, the vast majority of plan sponsors operated "like KGB spooks," telling members nothing about "what they do and how they do it."

The stakes are much, much higher today. Just as Peter Drucker predicted they would more than a decade ago, pension funds have become the most powerful investors in the country, making all of us major shareholders in the Canadian economy. The great institutional investors — the insurance companies, banks, pension funds and mutual funds — move in and out of the market with but one aim in mind: to maximize their profits. They are very good at that and they are getting better at it all the time — within the narrow range of "acceptable" investments under federal tax laws. Yet many provinces still have weak and ineffective disclosure rules, if they have such rules at all (see Appendix A). And many employers still operate like KGB spooks.

Most plan members still have had no input into their pension plan's investment policies and little information, if any, about their own rights. Indeed, most members of private pension plans have had no way of finding out how their money is being invested. With new disclosure rules in effect in some jurisdictions, that may change — if plan members exercise their right to know where their money is being channelled. But for now, the political debate which should accompany the broad questions of pension fund investment and whether or not pension money should leave Canada has not even been initiated at the grassroots level.

In the years to come, private savings for old age will come to dominate the world's capital markets, as they have already come to dominate capital markets in this country. And as Canada's aging population looks for safe havens and long-term prospects for its savings through its institutional investors, the growing economies of Third World countries will provide fund managers with tempting alternatives to investing in Canada itself. Given the huge amounts of money in pension funds today, the removal or relaxation of the ten-percent rule has very great political and social implications for all Canadians and for the members of the private pension plans who are forced to "contribute" a significant percentage of their earnings to them.

At the same time there are many kinds of investments money managers are unwilling to make in Canada — even if the rates of return on these investments would be as good or better than the traditional investments made by pension funds in bonds and the stocks of mainline corporations or as good or better than they might be in offshore investments. Provincial regulations, Revenue Canada rules and the bottom line mentality of fund managers have actually prevented pension funds from investing in ways that might directly assist plan members.

As a result, pension money rarely finds its way into such socially "useful" areas as low-income housing, education or health-care. Ontario, in its new Pension Benefits Act, has attempted to loosen the stranglehold of outmoded investment rules by replacing its prescribed list of allowable pension-fund investments with a "prudent person" approach which frees plan administrators to make a broader range of investments. Ontario's sweeping new disclosure rules also guarantee the right of plan members to know how their money is being invested and to claim representation on the boards which control the investments of the fund. Most jurisdictions, however, are still in the Dark Ages when it comes to such fundamental questions as these.

At the same time, it is routine for pension funds to make investments which most plan members, if they knew what those investments were, might well prefer to avoid. Unions have long grappled with such questions as whether the pension funds they control should be invested only with an eye to maximizing returns — or invested with reference to such criteria as the labour practices and product of the companies in which they invest. The Canadian Labour Congress pension committee, for example, frowns on investment in the shares of anti-union companies — even if such investments would yield higher returns for their members.

More than a decade ago in the United States, some unions did begin to focus clearly on the potential power of their funds. In 1978 the union movement's umbrella organization, the AFL-CIO (American Federation of Labor-Congress of Industrial Organizations), recommended that unions channel their pension investments into mortgages and construction as a means of creating jobs for their members and urged that the substantial financial power of negotiated pension plans be entrusted to financial institutions whose investment policies are not "inimical to the welfare of working people."

The organization had discovered that much of the movement of industries and jobs to non-union Southern states and foreign countries was being financed by workers in Northern U.S. states through their pension funds. One way to stop the economic haemorrhage, the organization said, was for union pension funds to withdraw from non-union companies altogether and to invest only in companies with unions or with sympathetic labour practices. Indeed, the promise of pension investment, the organization pointed out, could be a powerful tool to force unionization on recalcitrant employers.

At about the same time, many church leaders realized that their own portfolios, including pension funds, were managed with no regard whatsoever for the social implications of the investments and some of them decided to do something about it. More than a decade ago, for example, Quakers in the United States set a precedent by directing that no church monies should be invested in any company involved in the production of war materials. Since then, many more churches and other institutions have taken stands on the ethics of investing in the economies of countries which violate human rights or in companies whose products destroy lives or the environment in which we all must live.

Recently, a coalition of labour groups, community organizations and churches concerned about the social implications of pension-fund investment has emerged in both the United States and Canada. In 1986, for example, the Canadian Council of Bishops set up a committee with representatives from churches, labour groups and community organizations with the primary goal of protesting the market-oriented policies of the Tory government. In 1987 its Working Committee for Social Solidarity released a document which challenged the government's responses on social policy, Free Trade, deficit reduction and privatization. Canada, the report said, is becoming a divided society of "winners and losers" because of the government's shortsighted reliance on the private sector and its priorities.

Nowhere have the consequences of this shortsightedness been plainer than in the private pension system in the course of the last decade. These consequences have been largely obscured by corporate stonewalling, actuarial mumbo jumbo and self-interested rhetoric on the part of the pension industry. Yet, at the very least, the vast sums of money accumulating in private pension plans today is worth a much broader political debate in this country than has yet taken place. There is little reason to think that corporate Canada will change its ways unless it is compelled to do so.

That debate could take many years more. But there are two fundamental pension issues which need to be addressed and addressed quickly before it is too late. First, retirees on fixed pensions, particularly those who have been retired for five years or more, are still paying an enormous price to inflation while many of their employers are enjoying the benefits of overflowing pension plans. At the same time, many current employees who have a legitimate claim to surplus assets in these plans will soon have nothing to lay claim to if employers are allowed to take contribution holidays at will before those claims have been heard. The longer their employers are permitted to deplete their pension funds through surplus withdrawals and contribution holidays, the more impossible it becomes to set such injustices right. Once the money leaves the plan, it is gone forever.

Secondly, reforms which do nothing to ensure that the abuses of the past cannot happen again in the future are just not good enough. Without significant guarantees that plan members will be protected against inflation, most of the reform measures of the last decade are meaningless. What good are improvements in the pension system if they are not accompanied by guarantees that benefits will maintain their real value after retirement? That should be self-evident to everyone who takes the time to think about the purpose of a pension plan. Yet the most striking feature of the offensive mounted by the corporate lobby in the last ten years has been its adamant opposition to rational dialogue on that critical point and its refusal to admit that there are fairer ways to go about the business of providing retirement security.

There is no reason at all, for example, that private pension plans cannot co-exist with an expanded Canada Pension Plan, providing whatever additional coverage they see fit to meet their own corporate goals. There is no reason the private plans cannot have two tiers: an indexed defined-benefit component invested in "safe" but relatively low-yield investments and a money-purchase component which could be invested more adventurously, at some risk to the plan member. There is no reason that governments cannot create new investment vehicles for pension funds which take inflation into account. There is no reason that pension funds cannot be managed jointly by plan members and their employers, a routine practice in many European countries.* And there is no reason at all for Canadians

---

*Ontario's new pension legislation, for example, gives plan members the right to establish an advisory committee in cases where there is not already a pension committee with at least one employee representative, and to appoint one representative to the committee from each class of employee covered by the plan. Every plan member across Canada should fight for that right too.

to put up with the paternalistic corporate argument that employees don't, can't or won't know what's good for them.

The battle shaping up over the billions of dollars in private pension plans will be a prolonged and bloody one. Yet its outcome will affect the retirement security of every Canadian in the future. Those who argue for increased governmental control over private pensions, whatever form it takes, must make it clear that their remedy will give governments the power to transfer wealth arbitrarily, just as an expanded QPP/CPP would inevitably make losers of the industry built around the private retirement system. The botched efforts to achieve uniformity in private pension legislation across the country have created a boom for the firms on which employers rely to sort out the complexities of a system which has become even more complicated as a result of the failed reform process. The number of pension-management firms has grown by leaps and bounds in recent years and the revenues of the ten largest actuarial firms in the country grew from $131 million at the end of 1984 to $218 million at the end of 1987. These statistics alone are among the most compelling reasons for shutting down the private pension system if the provinces cannot bring themselves to legislate uniformity in the rules governing private pension plans.

Those who would see hell freeze over before they would agree to turn over significant control of the billions of dollars in retirement savings currently in private hands to the federal government to distribute as it sees fit should remember that the private sector has been arbitrarily transferring wealth from retirees to shareholders at the direct expense of plan members for more than a decade. Perhaps it is now time to redress that imbalance — either through tough legislated controls on both the private plans and RRSPs or through a swift expansion of benefits under the Quebec and Canada Pension Plans.

As the next stage of the Great Pension Debate heats up in the coming months, Canadians will once again be bombarded with the all-purpose corporate cop-out: that it would be nice to improve the system, but employers really can't afford it. It is time that all of us took that excuse with several large grains of salt. If you find this book disturbing, try asking your own employer about your pension plan — if you have one. What has the company done for its retirees in the way of ad hoc adjustments in the last decade? How much has it contributed to the plan in the last five years and how have benefits been improved in that time? How large is the plan surplus? What interest has been paid on contributions to employees leaving the plan before their pensions were vested?

Demand employee representation on pension boards, if the law in your province gives you that right. If it does not, raise the question of pension standards and employee representation at election time in the jurisdiction in which you live. Find out just what your rights are by phoning the Pension Board or Commission in your province. Ask to see the plan. If you don't have a plan, ask why not. Give some thought to the simple fact that women will always have inferior pensions unless governments force employers to revise their salary policies and pay women the same salaries as men for doing work of equal value. Stop and think before you joke about "pay police" and "radical feminists." Ask your employer what the company is doing to ensure that salaries are fair and equal. Ask your political representatives what *they* are doing to ensure that salaries are fair and equal.

Then listen carefully. And if the answers to the questions you ask are unsatisfactory — or not forthcoming at all — make a fuss. For when all is said and done, if you don't, there are few guarantees that anyone else will do it for you. After all, we're all in this together, and whose money is it, anyway?

··

APPENDIX A

Pension Legislation Across Canada

::

Ottawa and the provinces reached an unofficial consensus on pension reform in the winter of 1984-85. Since then the federal government, Alberta, Ontario and Nova Scotia have all adopted new rules for the occupational pension plans under their jurisdiction. Manitoba and Saskatchewan introduced reform legislation prior to 1985. A 1985 Quebec White Paper detailed proposed changes to that province's twenty-two-year-old legislation, but the Quebec reforms died on the order paper when the Parti Québécois government was voted out of office later that year. New legislation is expected soon. New Brunswick's Pension Benefits Act, assented to in June 1987, has not yet been proclaimed and its fate is uncertain after a change of government in that province. British Columbia and Prince Edward Island have no pension standards legislation at all.

This appendix pays special and detailed attention to the Ontario legislation, because it covers more pension plans and more employees than any other and because the Ontario reforms are likely to influence further change in other jurisdictions. In 1984, the last year for which comprehensive statistics were available on occupational pension plans at the time of writing, about 4.6 million Canadians — 37 percent of the total labour force and 47 percent of all employed paid workers — were enrolled in employer-sponsored pension plans, with about 45 percent enrolled in public sector plans. Of the total 4.6 million, 1.8 million (44 percent of all private-sector plan members and 33 percent of all public-sector plan members) were in Ontario.

These summaries briefly describe some of the rules — and in many cases the absence of rules — in federal and provincial legislation which directly affect plan members. They are not a comprehensive description of the provisions of the legislation or of the regulations in force under the legislation, but are intended to give an overview of the situation across Canada. Sadly, they also serve as an illustration of how far short the reform process has fallen of its goal of securing uniformity in provincial legislation across the country. The summaries are based on legislation in effect on January 1, 1988, except for New Brunswick, where the legislation described was intended to take effect on January 1, 1989, but is now in limbo.

FEDERAL
(including Yukon and Northwest Territories)

Pension Benefits Standards Act, 1985 (effective January 1, 1987)

Coverage and Eligibility:

- Full-time employees are eligible to join a company pension plan, if there is one, after two years of continuous employment. Membership is voluntary, but may be made compulsory by the employer, who may also denote different classes of employees for pension purposes.

- Part-time employees who have earned at least 35 percent of the Year's Maximum Pensionable Earnings in two consecutive years after December 31, 1984 are eligible to join the plan available to full-time employees in the same class, although employers may provide a separate plan for part-time employees if it is "reasonably comparable" to the plan covering full-time employees. Membership is voluntary, but may be made compulsory by the employer. Employees who are plan members and are employed continuously may remain in the plan even if their income subsequently falls below 35 percent of YMPE.

Vesting and Locking-In: Benefits earned *after* December 31, 1986 are vested after two years of plan membership. Benefits earned *before* January 1, 1987 are governed by the old requirement that an employee must be age forty-five and have ten years of continuous service before the pension is vested. Everything that is vested is locked in, although that rule may be waived if the deferred pension is less than 2 percent of the current Year's Maximum Pensionable Earnings at the date of termination.

Portability: The entire vested benefit, or any unvested employee contributions plus interest, may be transferred to the new employer's pension plan (if there is one and if the employer will accept the transfer), to a locked-in RRSP or to a deferred life annuity. Employee contributions plus interest may also be taken in cash.

Minimum Cost to Employer: Employer contributions must provide at least 50 percent of the cost of a vested pension earned after December 31, 1986. However, pension plans that provide inflation protection equal to 75 percent of the rate of inflation minus one percent (or any other formula that would provide comparable protection and which is approved by the Superintendent of Financial Institutions) are exempted from this provision. Excess employee contributions plus interest may be taken in cash, transferred to a locked-in RRSP or used to provide additional benefits.

Survivor Benefits:

- Before Retirement: After December 31, 1986, if a member of a defined benefit plan dies *before* becoming eligible for early retirement and has a spouse, the full commuted value of the deferred pension plus any excess contributions may go to the spouse as a deferred annuity *or* may be transferred to the spouse's locked-in RRSP or pension. A member of a defined-benefit plan who dies *after* becoming eligible for early retirement and has a spouse is deemed to have retired on date of death and to have elected a joint and 60-percent survivor pension and the surviving spouse will receive the post-retirement benefits described below. The surviving spouse of a member of a defined-contribution (money-purchase) plan will receive the full value of the account.

· After Retirement: After December 31, 1986, the surviving spouse must receive at least 60 percent of the full pension benefit payable when both spouses were alive. Actuarial adjustments and spousal waivers are allowed.

· Upon Remarriage: A surviving spouse who remarries must continue to receive survivor benefits.

Marriage Breakdown: Pension benefits are subject to provincial property laws and will vary from province to province.

Retirement Age: Pensionable age is defined as the earliest age at which a member may retire on an unreduced pension without the consent of the plan sponsor. Normal retirement date must be defined in the plan. Early retirement is allowed any time within ten years of normal retirement date, but the pension benefits may be actuarially reduced.

Discrimination by Sex: Differentiation by sex in employees' contributions and benefits in a defined-benefit plan is not permitted.

Interest on Employee Contributions: Interest must equal at least the net rate earned by the fund, *or* in the case of a defined-benefit plan a rate fixed by the Superintendent of Financial Institutions which reflects "reasonably current" interest rates.

Disclosure: Each member of a pension plan (and each employee who is eligible to join the plan) and the member's spouse must be given a written explanation of the provisions of the plan and of all amendments. Plan members — and their spouses — must be given a written statement specifying the benefits to which the member is entitled at the end of each year, the value of accumulated contributions and the funded ratio of the plan. Each member and the member's spouse is entitled to examine documents relating to the plan and to order a photocopy of them. The employer may demand a written request for such information.

Surplus Withdrawals: Allowed, but must conform to current regulations and be approved by the Superintendent of Financial Institutions. The regulations state that surplus may be refunded if the employer establishes his entitlement to a refund and the surplus exceeds the greater of two times the contribution of the employer to the normal cost of the plan *or* 25 percent of the liabilities of the plan, and the employer has given notice in writing to plan members, retired members and any other person who is entitled to a pension benefit under the terms of the plan.

Inflation Protection: No rule.

ONTARIO

Pension Benefits Act, 1987 (effective January 1, 1988)

Coverage and Eligibility:

- Full-time employees are eligible to join a company pension plan after two years, although nothing in the legislation prevents an employer from allowing employees to join the plan within the first two years. The employer may make membership in the plan mandatory for all employees.

- Part-time employees who earned at least 35 percent of the Year's Maximum Pensionable Earnings or worked at least 700 hours for two consecutive years may join the company plan. Plan sponsors may also set up separate plans for part-time employees as long as the plan benefits are "reasonably equivalent" to those provided for full-time employees.

Vesting and Locking-In: Vesting and locking-in occurs after two years for benefits earned after December 31, 1986. The old rule of forty-five years of age and ten years of continuous employment applies to benefits earned before January 1, 1987 unless plan sponsors choose to make the new rules retroactive. Under the old rules, an employee could choose to take up to a quarter of the value of a vested pension in cash. That option now applies only to that part of the pension earned before January 1, 1987. Deferred pensions worth less than two percent of the Year's Maximum Pensionable Earnings may also be taken in cash.

Portability: The lump sum value of the entire vested benefit or the employee's own accumulated contribution plus interest may be transferred to the new employer's plan (if there is one and the employer will accept the transfer), into a locked-in RRSP or into a deferred life-annuity.

Minimum Cost to Employer: After December 31, 1986 the employer's contributions must provide at least 50 percent of the commuted value of the pension or deferred pension earned after that date. If the employee's contribution plus interest exceeds 50 percent of the commuted value of the benefit, the plan member is entitled to a refund from the pension fund.

Survivor Benefits:

- Before Retirement: The full lump sum value of the pension earned after December 31, 1986 goes to the surviving spouse as an immediate or deferred annuity *or* as a lump sum in cash *or* it may be transferred to the spouse's RRSP or pension plan. If there is no spouse, the beneficiary will receive the commuted value of the deferred pension. If there is no beneficiary, the estate will receive the commuted value of the pension. The act defines a spouse as "a man and woman who, (A) are married to each other, or (B) are not married to each other and are living together in a conjugal relationship, continuously for a period of not less than three years or, in a relationship of some permanence if they are the natural or adoptive parents of a child." It excludes the claim of any "spouse" who was living "separate and apart" from the employee on the date of death.

- After Retirement: For pensions commencing after 1987, the surviving spouse will receive at least 60 percent of the pension payable when both spouses were alive. Actuarial adjustments and spousal waivers are allowed and the pension may be reduced on the death of either spouse.

- Upon Remarriage: A surviving spouse who remarries must continue to receive survivor benefits.

Marriage Breakdown: Depends upon provincial law, and does not require compulsory splitting of benefits.

Retirement Age: Normal retirement date must be defined, and may not be later than age sixty-six. Early retirement is allowed within ten years of normal retirement date. Actuarial reductions are allowed.

Discrimination by Sex: Not permitted for contributions, benefits or eligibility.

Interest on Employee Contributions: Prescribed rates will be published in the Regulations each year.

Disclosure: The employer must provide to all plan members and to any employee eligible to become a member an annual statement detailing, among other things, the earliest date the member will be eligible to receive an unreduced pension, the amount of required contributions made to the pension fund and the accumulated amount of required contributions. The employer must also explain any special payments from the fund, the treatment of any surplus in a continuing plan on wind-up, and any amendments affecting the member. In addition, employees are entitled to see — on written request — the provisions of the current pension plan, including any amendment, any documents relating to the pension plan that are filed with the commission, the provisions of any previous pension plan, the provisions of any document that sets out the employer's responsibilities, copies of information returns, financial statements, correspondence with the Pension Commission, statements of investment policies and copies of any financial statement on file with the Pension Commission.

Surplus Withdrawal: An employer who wishes to remove surplus must obtain the prior consent of the Pension Commission of Ontario. On application for withdrawal, the employer must notify all beneficiaries of the plan and other interested parties, such as unions and pension advisory committees of the application. In December 1986, all surplus withdrawals were frozen until the Friedland Task Force submitted its report. In January 1988, that moratorium was extended until a formula for inflation protection is in place.

Inflation Protection: Mandatory indexation of deferred pensions; formula to be determined.

BRITISH COLUMBIA

British Columbia has no pension standards legislation.

ALBERTA

Employment Pension Plans Act (effective January 1, 1987)

Coverage and Eligibility:

- Full-time employees are eligible to join a company pension plan, if there is one, after two years of continuous employment. Membership is voluntary, but may be made compulsory by the employer, who must specify the class or classes of employees to be covered.

- Part-time employees who have earned at least 35 percent of the Year's Maximum Pensionable Earnings for two calendar years of continuous service after January 1, 1985 are eligible to join the same plan provided for full-time employees in the

same class or a separate plan providing benefits of comparable value. Membership is voluntary, but may be made
compulsory by employers.

Vesting and Locking-In: Benefits earned between January 1,
1967 and December 31, 1986 are governed by the old rule of
forty-five years of age and ten years of continuous employment.
Benefits earned on or after January 1, 1987 are vested after five
years of continuous service. The value of the vested deferred-
pension is locked in, unless it is less than two percent of the
Year's Maximum Pensionable Earnings or its commuted value
is less than four percent of YMPE. Excess employee contributions are not locked in.

Portability: The vested benefit may be transferred to the new
employer's pension plan (if there is one and the employer will
accept the transfer), to a government-approved locked-in RRSP
or to a deferred life annuity.

Minimum Cost to Employer: Employer contributions must
provide at least 50 percent of the cost of a vested pension earned
after December 31, 1986. Excess employee contributions plus
interest are refundable.

Survivor Benefits:

· Before Retirement: After December 31, 1986, if a plan
  member dies before retirement, the spouse receives whichever
  is greater: 60 percent of the commuted value of the deferred
  pension earned after January 1, 1987 plus the excess
  employee contributions *or* the employee's contributions
  with interest. If the employee has no spouse, the beneficiary
  is entitled to a refund of employee contributions with
  interest. If there is no beneficiary, the estate receives the
  refund.

· After Retirement: For pensions beginning after December
  31, 1986 each spouse must receive 60 percent of the pension

payable to the other, unless the non-member spouse waives that right. If one spouse dies, the pension may be actuarially reduced.

· **Upon Remarriage:** A surviving spouse who remarries must continue to receive the survivor benefit.

Marriage Breakdown: Rules are determined by the Alberta Provincial Matrimonial Property Act. There is no mandatory splitting of benefits.

Retirement Age: Pensionable age must be specified in the plan. Early retirement is allowed any time within ten years of pensionable age. Pension benefits may be actuarially reduced and the pension must commence before age seventy-one.

Discrimination by Sex: No rule.

Interest on Employee Contributions: In a defined-benefit plan, the interest rate must equal the annual average yields on five-year personal fixed-term charter bank deposits (CANSIM Series B14045) or a rate equal to the earnings of the fund.

Disclosure: The employer must provide plan members or former members with an employee booklet outlining plan provisions and the employee's entitlements and duties under the plan as well as an account of how the assets are invested and the method of calculating interest, an annual statement of the employee's contributions and benefits, and statements at termination, retirement or death outlining accrued benefits and available options. On request, the employer must provide access to the plan document and other related documents, data relating to calculation of benefits and prior notice of the employer's intention to withdraw excess monies in the plan or wind up the plan.

Surplus Withdrawals: Surplus on wind-up may revert to the plan sponsor subject to withholding amounts and any contractual restrictions. Withdrawals from ongoing plans are permitted, subject to similar withholding amounts and contractual restrictions, if the plan provides for such withdrawals and the withdrawal is approved by the Superintendent of Pensions.

Inflation Protection: No rule.

SASKATCHEWAN

Pension Benefits Act (January 1, 1969, amended July 1, 1981)

Coverage and Eligibility: No rule.

Vesting and Locking-In: The pension is vested after one year of continuous employment if the employee's age plus years of continuous service add up to forty-five or more. A deferred pension worth less than $25 per month is not locked in.

Portability: No rule

Minimum Cost to Employer: Employer contributions must pay at least 50 percent of the cost of the vested pension. Excess employee contributions plus interest are transferable or may be used to provide additional benefits.

Survivor Benefits:

- Before Retirement: No rule.

- After Retirement: At least 50 percent of the pension is payable to spouse on member's death, although actuarial adjustment and spousal waivers are allowed.

- Upon Remarriage: No rule.

Marriage Breakdown: No rule.

Retirement Age: No rule.

Discrimination by Sex: No rule.

Interest on Employee Contributions: Prescribed rates are published each year and can vary depending on the year in which the plan was created.

Disclosure: An employer must provide each plan member with a written explanation of the pension plan, the member's rights and duties and any other information that may be considered necessary for the purposes of clarification, as well as a written explanation of any amendments to the plan. Plan members must be provided with an annual statement of their contributions and benefits, the rate and amount of interest and total accumulated pensionable service. Employers must also make available for inspection a text of the plan, the trust agreement, a statement of revenues and expenditures and a summary of the most recent actuarial valuation. Among other things, the plan administrator must make available an itemized statement of all expenditures paid from the fund that year, including the amount paid to each person who rendered services to the plan, had transactions with the plan or attended seminars, meetings or conferences paid for by the fund.

Surplus Withdrawals: Allowed, but must conform to current regulations and be approved by the Superintendent of Financial Institutions. The Regulations to the Pension Benefits Act require the consent of the Superintendent of Pensions prior to any withdrawal.

Mandatory Inflation Protection: No rule.

MANITOBA

Pension Benefits Act (January 1, 1984, amended January 1, 1985)

Coverage and Eligibility:

- Full-time Employees: Membership in the company pension plan (if there is one) is compulsory for full-time employees after two years of continuous employment.

- Part-time Employees: Membership in the company pension plan is compulsory for part-time employees who have earned at least 25 percent of the Year's Maximum Pensionable Earnings for two consecutive years.

Vesting and Locking-In: Benefits earned before January 1, 1985 are governed by the old requirement that an employee must be aged forty-five and have ten years of continuous service before the pension is vested. Benefits earned after December 31, 1984 are vested and locked in after five years' employment. A two-year vesting and locking-in period is expected no later than 1990. Excess employee contributions are not locked in, nor is a deferred pension worth less than $25 a month.

Portability: Not mandatory, but allowed for employees who change jobs, if the new employer has a plan and is willing to accept the pension, and for spouses eligible for pre-retirement spousal benefits.

Minimum Cost to Employer: Employer must provide at least 50 percent of the commuted value of the pension earned after January 1, 1985. Excess employee contributions plus interest are refundable.

Survivor Benefits:

- Before Retirement: After 1984, the full commuted value of the pension earned goes to the surviving spouse or common-law spouse as an immediate or deferred annuity. If the employee has no spouse, the beneficiary or estate receives the commuted value of the deferred pension.

- After Retirement: At least 66⅔ percent of the pension payable during the spouses' lifetimes must continue to the survivor. Actuarial adjustments and spousal waivers are allowed.

- Upon Remarriage: Survivor benefits must continue.

Marriage Breakdown: A 50/50 split based on the length of the marriage or relationship is compulsory and takes precedence over court orders or separation agreements.

Retirement Age: Normal retirement age must be specified and early retirement is allowed after "reasonable" age and service requirements are met. Actuarial reductions are allowed for early retirement.

Discrimination by Sex: Not permitted for contributions, benefits, commuted values or eligibility criteria.

Interest on Employee Contributions: Must equal either the rate of return on the fund minus one percent or a rate paid by a financial institution on deposits or investments such as a non-chequing savings account.

Disclosure: Employers must provide a written explanation of the plan to all employees. Each active plan member must receive an annual statement indicating, among other things, normal retirement date, the first date on which an early retirement pension is available and information concerning the reduction of pension benefits on early retirement. Employers must make available the text of the pension plan within thirty days of a member's written request, including all amendments, all documents and the most recent annual information return and cost certificate filed with the Commission, as well as a written explanation of any amendment to the plan which may affect the member's benefits or rights.

Surplus Withdrawals: An August, 1986 amendment to the *Pension Benefits Act* retroactive to January 1, 1986 provides that no funds may be paid out of a pension plan to an employer unless the provincial Pension Commission believes that it is "equitable" and consents to the withdrawal in writing. Because there are no regulations which determine what is "equitable," this rule amounts to a moratorium on surplus withdrawals.

Mandatory Inflation Protection: No rule, but proposed surplus withdrawal guidelines state that "a surplus withdrawal will not be considered equitable unless the accrued benefits of plan members have been increased to offset the effect of past inflation. Other benefit improvements, of equal cost, would also be accepted." If the proposal is accepted, pension surpluses would have to be used to provide inflation adjustments or benefit improvements before they are available for withdrawal.

QUEBEC

Supplemental Pension Plan Act (January 1, 1966)

Eligibility: No rule.

Vesting and Locking-In: Pensions are vested after age forty-five and ten years' employment.

Portability: No rule.

Minimum Cost to Employer: No rule.

Survivor Benefits: No rule.

Marriage Breakdown: No rule.

Retirement Age: No rule.

Discrimination by Sex: No rule.

Interest on Employee Contributions: No rule.

Disclosure: No rule.

Surplus Withdrawals: No surplus withdrawals may be made from any pension plan unless the plan has been terminated and all benefits have been paid out.

Inflation Protection: No rule.

NOVA SCOTIA

Pension Benefits Act (effective January 1, 1988)

Coverage and Eligibility:

- Full-time employees are eligible to join a company pension plan, if there is one, after two years of continuous employment. Membership is voluntary, but may be made compulsory by employers.

- Part-time employees who have earned at least 35 percent of the Year's Maximum Pensionable Earnings for two consecutive calendar years are eligible for coverage. Membership is voluntary.

Vesting and Locking-In: Benefits earned after January 1, 1988 are vested and locked in after two years of plan membership.

Portability: Vested benefit may be transferred to the new employer's pension plan (if there is one and the employer will accept it), to a locked-in RRSP or to a deferred life annuity.

Minimum Cost to Employer: After January 1, 1988 the employer must cover 50 percent of the vested pension. Excess contributions plus interest are refundable.

Survivor Benefits:

- Before Retirement: The spouse will receive a payment equal in value to 60 percent of the commuted value of the vested pension earned after January 1, 1988. If there is no spouse, the member's estate receives a refund of employee contributions plus interest.

- After Retirement: Spouse must receive at least 60 percent of the pension payable when both spouses were alive for pensions commencing after January 1, 1988. Actuarial adjustments and spousal waivers are allowed.

- Upon Remarriage: After January 1, 1988, a surviving spouse who remarries must continue to receive the survivor benefit.

Marriage Breakdown: Determined by court order.

Retirement Age: Normal retirement age must be defined and be no later than sixty-six. Early retirement may be taken within 10 years of normal retirement date. Actuarial reductions are allowed.

Discrimination by Sex: Not permitted for contributions, benefits, eligibility or commutation of benefits.

Interest on Employee Contributions: Interest on contributions to be calculated and credited in accordance with prescribed rates.

Disclosure: The administrator of the plan must provide a written explanation of the provisions of the plan and of members' rights and duties to each person who will be eligible or is required to become a member. Under the regulations, the administrator must provide an explanation of any amendment to the plan within sixty days, unless the amendment does not affect members' benefits.

Surplus Withdrawals: Surplus on wind-up may revert to plan sponsor. In ongoing plans, withdrawals by sponsors are permitted, subject to withholding amounts and any contractual restrictions and to the approval of the Superintendent of Pensions.

Inflation Protection: Annual indexation of deferred pensions is mandatory, although implementation of this rule has been postponed.

NEW BRUNSWICK

Pension Benefits Act
Because the Act has not been proclaimed, New Brunswick currently has no pension standards legislation.

Coverage and Eligibility:

- Full-time employees are eligible to join a company pension plan, if there is one, after two years of continuous employment. Membership is voluntary, but may be made compulsory by employers.

- Part-time employees who have earned at least 35 percent of the Year's Maximum Pensionable Earnings in the previous two years are also eligible to join their employer's pension plan.

Vesting and Locking-In: Benefits earned after the effective date of the legislation will be vested and locked in after five years of employment.

Portability: Vested benefits may be transferred to the new employer's pension plan (if there is one and the employer will accept them), to a locked-in RRSP or to a deferred life-annuity.

Minimum Cost to Employer: The employer must provide at least 50 percent of the accrued value of vested pensions earned after the effective date of the legislation. Excess contributions plus interest are refundable.

Survivor Benefits:

- Before Retirement: The surviving spouse will receive 60 percent of the commuted value of the vested pension earned after the effective date of the legislation. If there is no spouse, the beneficiary is entitled to the commuted value of the deferred pension. If there is no beneficiary, the member's estate receives the commuted value of the pension.

  After Retirement: For pensions commencing after the effective date of the legislation, the surviving spouse will receive at least 60 percent of the pension payable when both spouses were alive. Actuarial adjustments may be made and spousal waivers are allowed. The pension may be reduced on the death of either spouse.

- **Upon Remarriage:** A surviving spouse who remarries must continue to receive the survivor benefit.

Marriage Breakdown: Will be determined by a separation agreement recognized by the courts or by court order.

Retirement Age: Normal retirement date must be defined and may not be later than age sixty-six. Early retirement is allowed within ten years of normal retirement date and actuarial reductions of pensions are allowed.

Discrimination by Sex: Not permitted for contributions, benefits, eligibility or commutation of benefits.

Interest on Employee Contributions: Will be specified in the regulations.

Disclosure: Will be specified in the regulations.

Surplus Withdrawals: Plan surplus on wind-up may revert to the plan sponsor. In ongoing plans, withdrawal by the sponsor is permitted, subject to withholding amounts and any contractual restrictions.

Inflation Protection: No rule.

PRINCE EDWARD ISLAND

Prince Edward Island has no pension standards legislation.

NEWFOUNDLAND

Pension Benefits Act (effective January 1, 1985)

Coverage and Eligibility: No rule.

Vesting and Locking-In: Pensions earned after December 31, 1984 are vested and locked in after age forty-five and ten years' employment.

Portability: No rule.

Minimum Cost to Employer: No rule.

Survivor Benefits: No rule.

Marriage Breakdown: No rule.

Retirement Age: No rule.

Discrimination by Sex: No rule.

Disclosure: The employer must provide an explanation of the plan in writing. The explanation may be a booklet highlighting certain provisions of the plan or a copy of the plan itself.

Surplus Withdrawals: Any surplus may be used to reduce the employer's future current service payments or to reduce the balance of any initial unfunded liabilities or deficiencies without government approval. Surplus withdrawals must be approved.

Inflation Protection: No rule.

..

APPENDIX B

Sources of Retirement Income

::

OLD AGE SECURITY

If you have lived in Canada for a total of forty years between the ages of eighteen and sixty-five, you will receive a full Old Age Security pension from the federal government as soon as you turn sixty-five. This pension will be paid to you whether or not you are still working, whether or not you are a Canadian citizen and whether or not you intend to live in Canada in the future. If you do not meet the forty-year residency requirement, you will be eligible for a partial pension if you live in Canada now and have lived in the country for at least ten years after your eighteenth birthday. There is also one circumstance in which the OAS benefit begins at age sixty. If you are receiving OAS, if your spouse meets the residence requirement and if your combined incomes are very low, your spouse may be entitled to a Spouses Allowance at age sixty which will continue until he or she begins to receive the OAS benefit at age sixty-five.

Old Age Security pensions are non-contributory; at no time have you made direct contributions to an OAS fund. The cheque you will receive in the mail each month from the federal government is drawn on general revenues, which all Canadians provide through their taxes. You must apply for the OAS pension, and once you start to receive it at age sixty-five it is considered taxable income.

The OAS benefit is fully indexed to the Consumer Price Index and, since 1973, it has been adjusted every three months. It is not enough to live on. For example, on January 1, 1985, the full monthly OAS pension was $273.80; a year later it had risen to

$285.20; two years later to $297.37. In January 1989 the standard rate of the full monthly benefit was $323.28.

If your income from all sources is very low, you may also qualify for the federal Guaranteed Income Supplement (GIS), which provides additional support as of January 1, 1989, to a maximum of $384.19 a month for a single person or $250.23 a month each for a couple with no other income — for a combined monthly OAS/GIS benefit of $707.47 for a single person or $573.51 each for a couple. Like the OAS benefit, the GIS is indexed and adjusted every three months.

The amount of the GIS supplement is determined by the amount of income applicants received the year before (excluding OAS and some other sources of income such as war pensions, workers' compensation, provincial supplements, CPP death benefits, family allowances). It is reduced by $1 for every $2 of outside income beginning at $2 per month. As of January 1, 1989 the maximum income for GIS eligibility was $9,240.00 for a single person and $12,048.00 for a couple over age sixty-five. The *maximum* benefit is payable only when other income is less than $24 per year. It is not taxed and recipients must reapply for it each year.

The OAS program is not writ in stone. The federal government determines how it will work and whether the rules which spell out how much the pension is worth will change. It is a universal program today. It may not be a universal program tomorrow.

CANADA AND QUEBEC PENSION PLANS

Secondly, if you or your spouse have contributed to the Canada or Quebec Pension Plans, as virtually all working Canadians are required to do, you will receive monthly income from either the Canada or Quebec Pension Plans (CPP/QPP). The amount of your pension will depend on how much you and your employer have contributed to the plan over your working life, up to a limit determined by yet another formula, based on the rate of increase in the Industrial Aggregate Wage Index, an indicator of the average annual wage in Canada. Both you and your employer have contributed equally to the plan unless you are self-employed, in which case you have paid both shares yourself. In addition to providing retirement benefits, the Canada and Quebec Pension Plans also provide death and disability benefits.

The Quebec and Canada Pension Plans provide similar benefits, but they are not identical. Both employ a formula which sets annual maximum and minimum limits on the amount of your earnings eligible for pension purposes. In 1989, for example, the Year's Maximum Pensionable Earnings — or CPP Max, as it is called by people who are accustomed to talking about pensions — was $27,700. If you earned more than that, the amount above the CPP Max was of no interest to the CPP/QPP. If you earned less than that, you paid less into the plan. If you earned less than $2,700, the Year's Basic Exemption or minimum, you didn't pay into the plan at all. The difference between the CPP Max and the Year's Basic Exemption is called your "pensionable earnings." In 1989, employers and employees will each have contributed up to $525.00 (2.1 percent of $25,000) to the plan.

When you retire, your monthly pension will be calculated as 25 percent of your average monthly pensionable earnings over your working life. Up to 15 percent of your pensionable career may be ignored if there were times when you were not working at all or if your contributions to the plan were negligible. In addition to this 15-percent drop-out rule, since 1978 any person whose earnings decreased because he or she was caring for a child under the age of seven may drop that period of time from the calculation. The maximum CPP/QPP pension in 1988 was $543.06 a month. Because it is indexed to the Consumer Price Index annually, it rose to $556.25 a month on January 1, 1989. It is fully taxable.

For more than two decades contribution rates to the Canada/Quebec Pension Plans remained fixed at 3.6 percent of pensionable earnings. You paid 1.8 percent; your employer paid 1.8 percent on your behalf. In 1987, after the federal government had obtained the necessary consent of the provinces to alter the formula, the contribution rate began to rise. The 1988 rate of 4.0 percent will rise by 0.2 percent each year for the next three years and then by 0.15 percent for each of the next twenty years. Thus, by the year 2011, the rate will reach 7.6 percent of pensionable earnings — unless the government increases it further in the meantime.

Some of the rules governing benefits changed in 1987 too. It is now possible to claim your CPP pension as early as age sixty or to postpone claiming it until you reach age seventy, a change which was introduced into the Quebec Plan in 1984. If you decide to take advantage of the flexible retirement provision, your pension will be adjusted downwards if you retire before age sixty-five. If you choose to continue working after age sixty-five, you have a choice. You can still claim your pension at sixty-five. Or you can continue to contribute to the Plan. If you choose the latter option, your pension will continue to grow.

In addition to the flexible retirement provisions, changes were also made to improve CPP/QPP pensions for spouses. Since 1978 spouses have been entitled to share all CPP credits earned during the years of their marriage. Under the new provisions, spouses or common-law partners — whether they were employed or not — may apply to split CPP credits upon separation or divorce. As well, CPP pensions to widows and widowers no longer cease when they remarry.

OCCUPATIONAL PENSION PLANS

Employer-sponsored pension plans are often referred to as "private" or "company" plans. These terms are somewhat misleading because occupational plans also include pension plans for government employees and plans sponsored, in whole or in part, by unions for their members (multi-employer plans). If you are employed by any level of government, you are likely to have access to an occupational pension plan. If you work for a private sector employer, particularly an employer with a small business or in the service sector, you are fortunate if you have an occupational pension plan at all. Current legislation governing private sector occupational pension plans varies from province to province. The most important of these rules, and recent changes in provincial legislation, are described briefly in Appendix A.

There are two basic kinds of occupational pension plans: defined-benefit plans and defined-contribution (or money-purchase) plans. The two plans sound as though they might be similar, but they are not.

Defined-benefit plans promise to pay you a fixed amount — usually calculated as a percentage of your salary — as a pension when you retire. The amount you will receive each month depends on a formula which can vary from plan to plan. In general, a formula which ties your pension to your earnings at the end of your career is more advantageous to you than a formula which averages your salary over your entire career. If your plan is based on "final earnings" or "final average earnings" or "average best earnings" it will have a measure of inflation protection built in and if your salary keeps up with inflation, your pension entitlement will too — until you retire, unless your benefit is indexed. Similarly, a plan which promises to replace 70 percent of your earnings when you retire is better than one which promises a replacement rate of 60 percent.

On the other hand, you may belong to a flat-benefit plan, which ties your pension to your length of service, not to a formula based on your salary. The great disadvantage of flat-benefit plans is that unless all benefits improvements over the years are made retroactive, they are very vulnerable to inflation.

The money for your pension comes from a fund to which you may or may not have contributed. If it is a contributory plan, a fixed percentage of your salary has been deducted from your paycheque during some or all of the time you have worked for the same employer. Some plans ("integrated plans") include your contribution to the QPP/CPP in the plan design, others do not.

In the past, eligibility rules often differed from plan to plan, but once you have joined a defined-benefit plan, your employer assumed the responsibility of ensuring that the plan's legal obligations to you would be met when you retire. This obligation does *not* require your employer to match your contributions to the plan each year. It means simply that the fund must be maintained in such a way that you will receive the pension you have been promised. It also does *not* mean that your employer must guarantee that your pension will keep up with inflation after you retire. Most public sector plans provide automatic protection against inflation; most private sector plans do not.

A defined-contribution, or money-purchase, plan is a different matter altogether. If you are a member of such a plan, you pay into a registered fund, usually through a payroll deduction calculated as a fixed percentage of your salary. Usually, although not invariably, your employer will match your contribution, dollar for dollar. If it is a non-contributory plan, your employer will pay the entire amount. The money, plus any interest it earns, is credited to an account in your name. You may, or may not, have some control over how your money is invested and you may, or may not, get advice from your employer about how best to move your money around as you get older in order to protect your investment.

The amount of your pension will depend on two things: how well your investments — or the investments made on your behalf — have performed and the prevailing interest rates when you retire. At that time, you will withdraw your accumulated capital from the fund and purchase the best annuity available. The higher interest rates are on that day, the higher your monthly pension cheque will be. If the day happens to be another Black Monday and your money was invested in the stock market, your retirement prospects will have taken a sudden and most unfortunate turn for the worse.

Thus, the pension you receive from a defined-contribution plan may be very different from the pension you expected to receive. The risk is entirely yours. Your employer must manage your investment prudently, but has no responsibility for ensuring that your pension is protected against market fluctuations — or for seeing to it that your benefit is as good as your co-workers' benefits when you retire. You and your friend may both have worked at the same job for the same employer for the same number of years. Your contributions to the pension plan may be virtually identical. But, if your friend retired two weeks before Black Monday and you retired three weeks later, the value of your pensions could be very different indeed.

REGISTERED RETIREMENT SAVINGS PLANS (RRSPs)

The federal government created RRSPs in 1957 to make it possible for — and to encourage — employees who have no access to employer-sponsored private plans to save for their retirement individually and to share some of the same tax advantages. The principle underlying RRSPs is straightforward: if you defer the receipt of part of your income until after you retire, you will pay less tax on the money because you will be in a lower tax bracket then. RRSPs offer an immediate tax advantage too. When you contribute to an RRSP, the government allows you to deduct your contributions from earned income when you calculate your income tax for the year, a tax break which, of course, members of occupational pension plans also receive.

RRSPs come in bewildering variety. Eligible investments range from the very safe — savings deposits, government bonds, guaranteed investment certificates — to the more adventurous — mortgages, common shares and mutual funds. It is possible to buy an RRSP which combines several different types of investment, just as it is possible to buy an RRSP which you administer yourself. You may hold as many different RRSPs as you like, but there are limits on the amount of your yearly contribution eligible for tax deferral. The rules governing how much you may contribute to RRSPs are complex. And they, too, are not writ in stone.

As of January 1, 1990, complicated but important changes are planned for the income tax treatment of contributions to pension plans and RRSPs.* Under the old rules, if you were not a member

*These changes were scheduled to take effect on January 1, 1989, but the federal government has delayed their implementation, adding to public confusion and depriving contributors of a promised tax break.

of an occupational pension plan, you were entitled to contribute a maximum of 20 percent of your earnings or $7,500 — whichever was less — to an RRSP. If you were a member of an occupational plan, you were allowed to contribute $3,500 minus any contributions you had made to the occupational plan.

The new system takes a different tack. It assumes that a contribution of 18 percent of earnings over a working lifetime would provide Canadians with a pension of 2 percent of final average earnings for each year of employment when they retire. Using that formula as a guideline, it then sets out to ensure that the tax laws treat everyone equally. To take full advantage of the tax break, however, you would need an annual income in excess of $83,000.

If you are a member of a defined-contribution plan, or if you are not in a pension plan at all, the new rules are fairly straightforward: employer and employee contributions to the plan or to RRSPs and employer contributions to a deferred-profit-sharing plan, taken together, must not exceed 18 percent of earnings up to a dollar maximum ($10,500 in 1990 rising to $15,500 in 1995 when it levels off) if they are to be tax deductible. If you are a member of a defined-benefit plan, the rules are much more complex. The overall limit on what you may contribute to an RRSP is 18 percent of your previous year's earnings, up to the same dollar maximum. But the maximum is reduced by a "pension adjustment," or PA, which is designed to ensure that access to RRSP tax deductions is roughly equal for everyone.

These new rules make it utterly impossible for most of us to calculate how much we are entitled to place in RRSPs each year. Recognizing that, the government has decided to do the work for us. In October of every year, you will receive a notice from Revenue Canada spelling out your individual contribution limit, based on information reported by your employer and on your tax returns for previous years.

As of 1991, it will be possible to accumulate RRSP "contribution room." In other words, if you don't have the money to contribute the maximum amount to an RRSP this year, you can make a larger contribution next year without losing the tax advantage.

This "carry forward" provision is good for seven years. If, in the past, you did not use up your contribution room, you will you will no longer be given another chance to do so. All past-service voluntary contributions have been eliminated.

There is nothing to prevent you from cashing in your RRSPs at any time. If you do, however, the money will immediately be taxed as income. You *must* dispose of your RRSPs in the year in which you turn seventy-one. You may cash them in then too, but if you do, the entire amount will be taxed in that one year. The alternative is to place your RRSP money in an investment which will spread the tax burden over several years.

There are several ways of doing this. First, you may buy a life annuity from an insurance company. Such an annuity provides regular monthly payments to you for life. Secondly, you may buy a fixed-term annuity from a life insurance company or a trust company. Such an annuity provides regular monthly payments for a specified number of years, usually until age ninety. Annuity payments are a mix of your own capital plus the interest you have been promised and they, too, are fully taxable. These annuities may be purchased any time after you reach age sixty.

Thirdly, you may transfer your money into a government-sponsored Registered Retirement Income Fund (RRIF). RRIFs were introduced in 1978 to provide an alternative to life annuities, which have no earning power. Unlike annuities, they are a form of investment. The money in them continues to be invested on your behalf, or you may invest it yourself under a self-directed plan. Every year, however, you must withdraw a fraction of the market value of the fund until you reach age ninety and the fund is exhausted. New rules allow you to have as many RRIFs as you want and to withdraw any amount over the minimum at any time.

Taken together, these plans will provide you with a comfortable life after you retire — assuming, of course, that you have been a full participant in the pension system for most of your life.

APPENDIX C

GLOSSARY

::

Accrued Liability: The value of benefits earned to date under a pension plan, actuarially discounted for future interest.

Accrued Pension: The amount of pension credited to a plan member up to a given time according to a formula which takes into account such factors as earnings and length of service.

Active Plan Member: A member of a pension plan who is currently working.

Actuarial Assumptions: Estimates of future experience, such as return on investment, inflation rates, employee turnover, mortality, salary increases, and retirement ages which actuaries must make to predict the cost of benefits provided under a pension plan.

Actuarial Valuation: An assessment of a pension plan by an actuary to determine the present value of the benefits the plan must pay out in the future.

Actuarially-Reduced Pension: A pension benefit which has been adjusted downwards from the benefit promised to a plan member at retirement under the terms of a defined-benefit plan. An employee who takes early retirement will usually receive an actuarially-reduced pension.

Actuary: A pension or insurance specialist and, in Canada, a member of the Canadian Institute of Actuaries.

Additional Voluntary Contribution: An optional payment made voluntarily by an employee to a registered pension plan. The payment is used to purchase additional benefits with no additional cost to the employer.

Ad Hoc Adjustment: An amount added to a pension by a pension plan sponsor after a plan member has retired. The adjustment is not the result of a prior commitment and is usually made on an irregular basis.

Annuity: A benefit which is paid out periodically (usually monthly) over a specified number of years or for the lifetime of the *annuitant.* A pension annuity may cease at death or it may continue, usually at a lower rate, to the beneficiary's spouse or for a specified period after the annuitant's death.

Annuity Rate: The price a seller of annuities charges to provide a dollar of annuity per month.

Asset Mix: The proportion of various kinds of investments — equities, bonds, mortgages, for example — held by a pension fund, usually expressed as a percentage of total investments.

Assets: All investments or cash held by a pension fund. These may include equities, bonds traded on capital markets, mortgages, real estate, venture capital and non-market government debt, among other investments.

Average Industrial Wage: Average earnings for the Industrial Composite of Wages and Salaries as measured by Statistics Canada. This statistic is usually expressed as an annual average wage for all Canadians although it does not, in fact, take into account the earnings of all members of the work force. This hypothetical average salary in turn determines the Year's Maximum Pensionable Earnings under the Quebec and Canada Pension Plans.

Beneficiary: A person who is entitled to a benefit under a pension plan upon the death of a current or former plan member or any person in whose interest a trust fund is established.

Benefit: Any form of payment owing to an employee under the terms of a pension plan, usually the normal pension provided by the plan formula.

Benefit Formula: A specified formula in a pension plan used to calculate a plan member's defined benefit.

Benefit Rate: The annual rate at which benefits accrue in a defined-benefit pension plan.

Best Earnings Formula: A defined-benefit formula which applies the unit of credit for each year of service to the plan member's best average earnings for a specified period.

Birth Rate: The number of live births per 1,000 population.

Bond: A certificate to show evidence of debt, usually indicating that specific assets have been pledged as security.

Book Value: The amount shown in the accounts as the cost of an asset.

Canada Pension Plan (CPP): A mandatory earnings-related pension plan for all working Canadians between the ages of eighteen and seventy who work outside Quebec. The CPP, which was introduced in 1965 along with the Quebec Pension Plan (QPP), is financed on a partial pay-as-you-go formula. The two plans are similar but not identical and are sometimes referred to jointly as the QPP/CPP. Both plans provide survivor and disability benefits as well as a pension.

Career Average Formula: A formula which relates the pension payable on retirement to average earnings over the entire period in which the employee belonged to the pension plan.

Cash Withdrawal: A return of personal contributions to a pension plan member whose employment has ended.

Commuted Value: The value of a pension, a deferred pension or a pension benefit as of a fixed date.

Compound Interest: Interest credited to an investor at a specified rate and on specified dates and added to the principal.

Compulsory Plan: A pension plan which eligible employees must join as a condition of employment.

Consolidated Revenue Plan: A pension plan in which contributions are paid into government revenues in the same way as taxes and are used for general government purposes.

Consumer Price Index: An index compiled by the federal government reflecting cost-of-living changes during a specified period of time.

Continuous Service: Period during which an employee is continuously employed by the same employer. Continuous service may be defined so as to include certain periods of absence and service with another employer.

Contribution Holiday: The use of surplus in a pension plan to reduce or eliminate employer and/or employee contributions to the plan for a specified period of time.

Contributory Plan: A plan which requires employee contributions by payroll deduction.

Cost Certificate: An actuary's certificate setting out the costs and contributions required under an employment pension plan.

Credited Service: Periods of employment counted in calculating the amount of a pension.

Credit Splitting: A provision in a pension plan whereby one spouse may obtain an equal division of the pension credits earned by one or both partners.

Current Service Cost: The cost of benefits earned during a year by members of a pension plan.

Deferred Compensation: Income paid at some future time, usually upon retirement or termination of employment.

Deferred Pension (Annuity): A specified pension determined at the time an employee terminates employment, or a pension plan itself is terminated, but not payable until some time after the date it is purchased, usually at normal retirement age.

Deferred-Profit-Sharing Plan (DPSP): A money-purchase plan, as defined in the *Income Tax Act*, to which an employer makes contributions out of annual profits for the benefit of employees.

Deficit: The amount by which the present value of estimated future liabilities exceeds current assets.

Defined-Benefit Plan: A pension plan in which the plan sponsor specifies the pension to be provided — usually related by a formula to previous earnings and years of service or defined by a fixed dollar amount for each month or year of service.

Defined-Contribution (or Money-Purchase) Plan: A pension plan in which employer and employee contributions are fixed — usually as a percentage of salary. The fund is invested (by hired pension-fund managers from outside the company, by internal fund managers or by a pension committee which may or may not include employees) and accumulates interest.

Demographic Projection: An estimate of the future size and composition of the population, based on past data and assumptions about future birth and death rates and estimates of levels of immigration.

Disability Pension: Any pension payable to an employee permanently incapacitated by physical or mental disability.

Drop-Out Provision: A rule which allows members of the Quebec or Canada Pension Plan to leave the work force temporarily for specified periods of time without penalty. Allowable drop-out time is not counted when QPP/CPP benefits are calculated.

Early Retirement: A provision in a pension plan for retirement earlier than normal. Early retirement usually reduces the amount of the pension benefit which would be payable at normal retirement age.

Earnings: Money acquired from employment or self-employment.

Eligibility Requirement: Any condition such as age or length of service that must be met before an employee is permitted or required to join a pension plan.

Employer-Sponsored Pension Plan: Any pension plan offered by an employer or a group of employers for the benefit of employees.

Employment Pension Plan: Any occupational pension plan.

Equity: Right of ownership.

Excess Earnings: Any earnings from the investments of a pension fund which exceed the rate of return assumed by the actuary.

Experience Deficiency: An unfunded liability, as defined by actuarial assumptions, resulting from a difference between the actual experience of a pension plan and predictions of that experience.

Fertility Rate: The number of live births per woman.

Final Average Earnings Benefit: A defined benefit formula based on average earnings over a short period just before retirement used to determine the amount of a pension.

Fixed-Return Investment: Investment offering constant returns over a period of time.

Flat-Benefit Formula: A defined-benefit formula which multiplies each year of service by a specified dollar amount of pension.

Flat-Rate Pension Plan: A plan which provides a fixed-dollar benefit for employees after they have fulfilled certain age and service requirements and which usually pays a specified amount of benefit for each year of service. Many flat-rate plans are the result of collective bargaining.

Fully Funded Plan: A pension plan which, at any given time, has sufficient assets to provide for all pensions and benefits earned by plan members as of that time.

Funding: All employer and employee contributions to a pension plan which, combined with the fund investment returns, are intended to cover plan liabilities.

Going-Concern Basis: The assumption that a pension plan will continue in operation indefinitely.

Group Annuity: A contract under which an insurance company agrees to provide retirement pensions to members of a group.

Guaranteed Annuity: An annuity which will be paid for the lifetime of the annuitant and will also be paid for a specified period even if the annuitant dies.

Hybrid Plan: A type of pension plan which promises members a pension benefit equal to whichever is greater: a minimum guaranteed benefit *or* employee and employer contributions plus investment earnings.

Income Test: Any method of determining the income of a person or family for the purpose of determining eligibility for payment under a government program.

Indexation: A formula which provides for regular adjustment to a benefit after retirement linked to a recognized indicator of price or wage levels such as the Consumer Price Index.

Inflation: Any increase in the general level of prices.

Insured Pension Plan: A plan in which all benefits are purchased from and guaranteed by an insurance company.

Integrated Plan: A common type of employment pension plan which relates plan contributions and/or benefits to those of the Quebec or Canada Pension Plans. Integrated plans may provide a lower level of contributions and/or benefits on all or part of a member's earnings up to the Year's Maximum Pensionable Earnings or they may provide for pensions to be reduced by all or part of the CPP benefits. When a plan provides for benefits to be added to QPP/CPP benefits, not reduced by them, it is called a *Stacked Plan.*

Interest Assumption: The actuarial prediction of the return to be earned on pension fund investment. The estimate is used to discount future liabilities to calculate their present value.

Investment Policy: The level of risk pension-fund managers and governors are prepared to assume, in terms of asset mix and financial rate of return.

Investment Return: Actual earnings of a pension fund including interest, dividends and capital gains usually expressed as a percentage of assets.

Joint Administration: Provision for a union-management committee or board to supervise a pension plan.

Joint and Survivor Annuity: An annuity payable until the death of the retired employee and continuing thereafter to the surviving spouse until that person's death.

Life Expectancy: Number of years a person of a given sex and age is expected to live.

Locking-In: A provision which prevents employees from withdrawing either their own or their employer's contributions to a pension plan in cash. A locked-in pension is payable only at the normal age of retirement.

Mandatory Retirement: A provision in pension plans, collective agreements or employment terms which requires an employee to retire at a certain age.

Market Investments: Assets which are bought and sold in a secondary market and may include stocks and bonds, real estate, mortgages, venture capital and private placements.

Means Test: Any method used to determine a person's assets as well as income.

Money-Purchase Plan: A plan in which contributions are specified but the pension which those contributions will earn is unknown. The pension is determined by the total amount of contributions accumulated, plus interest, at the time of retirement.

Mortality Table: A table showing expected rates of death at various ages for people born in different years and used by actuaries to make assumptions when they calculate the cost of pensions for a group.

Multi-Employer Pension Plan: An employment pension plan which covers employees of more than one employer. Usually such plans are set up by agreement with a union or a group of unions.

Mutual Fund: A portfolio of investment securities owned by those who have bought shares in a fund which is managed by investment specialists.

Needs Test: Any method of assessing an individual's or a family's income in relation to necessary expenditures used to determine eligibility for income support provided by government programs.

Net Replacement Ratio: A measure of the adequacy of retirement income in relation to pre-retirement income which takes into account such factors as income taxes and tax credits.

Non-Contributory Plan: A pension plan in which all contributions are made by the employer.

Normal Retirement Age: The age at which members of a pension plan are assumed to retire and on which actuarial calculations are based. Normal retirement age will not always be identical to actual retirement age. Where actual retirement age is greater than or less than normal retirement age, the retiree's pension will be actuarially increased or reduced.

Old Age Security: The federal program which provides a universal pension to all residents aged sixty-five and over and income-tested supplements to those with low incomes.

Pay-As-You-Go Plan: A pension plan which is not funded and in which benefits are paid out of current revenue or other sources outside the plan. A modified pay-as-you-go plan may have a small fund which is not sufficient to cover the plan's liabilities.

Pension Adjustment: An amount, calculated annually, used in determining the maximum annual RRSP contribution. The adjustment takes into account contributions made for pension benefits earned during the year under a registered pension plan or a deferred-profit-sharing plan.

Pension Benefits Standards Act: An Act of Parliament which establishes the minimum standards for federally-regulated pension plans.

Pension Fund: Assets which are accumulated and held separately to pay for members' pension benefits in the future.

Pension Plan: Any plan set up to provide a regular income for the lifetime of retired members and which may also provide payments in the event of disability or death.

Portability: The extent to which pension income recognizes all periods of employment with various employers.

Portable Pension: A pension which may be carried from job to job without loss of benefits.

Private Sector Plan: Any employment-related plan sponsored by a private employer. The plan may be a *trusteed* plan overseen by a trust company or a group of individuals or an *insured* plan overseen by an insurance company.

Public Pension Plans: Plans administered by governments for citizens at large, such as Old Age Security (OAS), the Guaranteed Income Supplement (GIS), the Canada and Quebec Pension Plans (QPP/CPP) and various provincial supplement programs.

Public-Sector Pension Plan: A pension plan established by an employer who may be classified as being in the public sector under the *Public Sector Prices and Compensation Review Act, 1983*, including government agencies, legislatures, municipalities, school boards, universities and colleges, hospitals, Crown-owned corporations or boards of health. Such plans may be trusteed or insured or they may be consolidated-revenue plans.

Quebec Pension Plan (QPP): A parallel, though not identical, version of the Canada Pension Plan offered in Quebec.

Real Dollar: A fictional unit of currency with a constant purchasing power.

Registered Pension Fund: A government-approved pension plan.

Registered Retirement Income Fund (RRIF): An investment vehicle permitted under the *Income Tax Act* for funds an individual has accumulated in an RRSP.

Registered Retirement Savings Plan (RSP or RRSP): A government-approved tax-sheltered plan which allows an individual to save for retirement with pre-tax dollars.

Seven-Year Carry-Forward: A rule which allows contributors to an RRSP who do not make the maximum contribution in any one year to retain the right to use that "contribution room" any time in the next seven years.

Severance Payment (Retiring Allowance): An amount received on or after retirement from an employer by an employee who leaves a job before retirement age.

Spousal RRSP: An RRSP arrangement in which one spouse makes the contributions to the plan and claims the tax deduction, but the title to the plan is held by the other spouse whose rate of taxation will prevail when income is taken from the plan.

Surplus: The excess of the actuarial value of the assets of a pension plan over the plan's accrued liability.

Survivor Benefits: Pension benefits which are transferred to the spouse of a pension plan member who dies.

Tax-Deferred Income or Benefits: Any income or benefits on which payment of taxes may be put off until some future date.

Tax-Sheltered Income: Income that is not currently subject to tax, but may be taxed in the future.

Trusteed-Pension Fund: The fund generated by an employer-sponsored pension plan, in either the public or the private sector.

Unfunded Liability: Any amount by which the value of benefits earned under a pension plan exceeds the value of the plan's assets.

Unisex Mortality Tables: Statistical projections, combining estimates for males and females in a single table, used by actuaries to calculate the expected rates of death at various ages for people born in various years. Unisex tables have replaced gender-specific mortality tables that gave higher retirement income to men than to women because of women's longer life expectancy.

Variable Annuity: A pension which depends on the market value of the pension fund. Such a pension varies in amount according to the performance of the fund.

Vesting: An employee's right to benefits accrued under a pension plan or a deferred-profit-sharing plan. Vesting provisions remove the obligation of a plan member to remain in a pension plan until retirement in order to qualify for pension credits. If their pensions are not vested, plan members are entitled only to their own contributions to the plan plus accumulated interest when they change jobs.

Wage Indexing: Automatic increases in benefits based on movements in average wages and salaries.

Waiting period: The time period before an employee fulfils eligibility requirements for membership in an employment pension plan.

Wind-Up: The discontinuance of an employment pension plan. Plans may be wound up by their sponsors voluntarily or involuntarily in the event of bankruptcy. The procedures covering terminated plans are regulated by pension benefits legislation.

Year's Maximum Pensionable Earnings (YMPE): The maximum amount of annual employment earnings, calculated annually using a formula based on the Average Industrial Wage. The YMPE — $27,700 in 1989 — is the earnings ceiling for contributions to the Canada and Quebec Pension Plans.

SELECT BIBLIOGRAPHY

::

Adell, Bernard, "Pension Plan Surpluses and the Law: Finding a Path for Reform." In *Task Force on Inflation Protection for Employment Pension Plans: Research Studies*, vol. 2. Toronto: Queen's Printer for Ontario, 1988.

Alexander Consulting Group, Submission to the Ontario Task Force on Inflation Protection for Employment Pension Plans, 1988.

Ambachtsheer, Keith P., "An Assessment of the Potential Impact of Mandated Inflation Protection in Employment Pension Plans on Canada's Capital Markets." In *Task Force on Inflation Protection for Employment Pension Plans: Research Studies*, vol. 2. Toronto: Queen's Printer for Ontario, 1988.

Ambachtsheer, Keith P., *Pension Funds and the Bottom Line: Managing the Corporate Pension Fund as a Financial Business*. Homewood, Ill.: Dow Jones-Irwin, 1986.

Ambachtsheer, Keith P., A. Asimakopulos and J.C. Weldon, "On the theory of government pension plans," *Canadian Journal of Economics*, vol. 1, 699-717 HBIC3.

Ambachtsheer, Keith P., *The Ambachtsheer Letter*, no. 38, Toronto: Keith P. Ambachtsheer and Associates Inc., July 16, 1987.

Anderson, Ronald, "Pension reforms have eased major stresses," *Globe and Mail*, September 4, 1987.

Ascah, Louis, "Evolution and Assessment of Reform Proposals for Pension Plans," Conference of the Canadian Association on Gerontology, 1986.

Ascah, Louis, "Recent Pension Reports in Canada: A Survey," *Canadian Public Policy — Analyse de Politiques* 10:4 (1984): 415-28.

Association of Canadian Pension Management, Submission to the Task Force on Inflation Protection for Employment Pension Plans, May 26, 1987.

Association of Canadian Pension Management and the Investment Counsel Association of Ontario, A Submission to the Pension Commission of Ontario, July 1986.

Barnes, Leslie W. C. S., "Pension Indexing — a new perspective," *The Labour Gazette*, July 1977.

Beattie, Earle, *Canada's Billion Dollar Pension Scandal: How Secure Is Your Future?* Toronto: Methuen, 1985.

benefits canada, Canada's Top 40 Pension Funds, April 1988.

Black, Conrad, "Of Pensions, Politicians and Pressure Groups," *Report on Business*. May 1986.

Bliss, Michael, *Northern Enterprise: Five Centuries of Canadian Business.* Toronto: McClelland and Stewart, 1987.

Bryden, Kenneth, *Old Age Pensions and Policy-Making in Canada.* Montreal: The Institute of Public Administration of Canada, McGill-Queen's University Press, 1974.

Business Council on National Issues, "Adequate Retirement Income: A Challenge Canadians Must Face," Submission to the Parliamentary Task Force on Pension Reform. October 1983.

Calvert, Geoffrey, *Pensions and Survival: The Coming Crisis of Money and Retirement.* Toronto: Maclean-Hunter Limited, 1977.

Canada. 1961 Census of Canada, vol. II, "Households and Families." Ottawa: Dominion Bureau of Statistics, 1961.

Canada. 1981 Census of Canada, vol. I, "Labour Force — Occupation by demographic and educational characteristics." Ottawa: Statistics Canada, 1981.

Canada. House of Commons, *Report of the Parliamentary Task Force on Pension Reform.* Ottawa: Queen's Printer for Canada, 1983.

Canada. Department of Finance press release, "Draft Legislation Issued on Retirement Compensation Arrangements," March 27, 1987.

Canada. Department of Finance, *Saving for Retirement: A Better Pension System.* Ottawa: October 1986.

Canada. Department of Finance, *Saving for Retirement: Improved Tax Treatment: Detailed Rules and Procedures.* Ottawa: October 9, 1986.

Canada. Departments of Finance and National Health and Welfare, *Better Pensions for Canadians.* Ottawa: 1982.

Canada. Dominion Bureau of Statistics, *Survey of Pension and Welfare Plans in Industry.* Ottawa: King's Printer, 1947.

Canada. Dominion Bureau of Statistics, *Trusteed Pension Plans: Financial Statistics: 1957-1972.* Ottawa: Queen's Printer, 1974.

Canada. National Council of Welfare, *1988 Poverty Lines.* Ottawa: Minister of Supply and Services, April 1988.

Canada. National Council of Welfare, *Poverty Profile 1988*. Ottawa: Minister of Supply and Services, April 1988.

Canada. National Council of Welfare, *Welfare in Canada: The Tangled Safety Net*. Ottawa: Minister of Supply and Services, November 1987, 1988.

Canada. National Council of Welfare, *Women and Poverty*. Ottawa: 1979.

Canada. The Senate, *Retirement Without Tears: Report of the Special Senate Committee on Retirement Age Policies*. Ottawa: Department of Supply and Services, 1979.

Canada. Statistics Canada, *Earnings of Men and Women*. Ottawa: Minister of Supply and Services, 1985.

Canada. Statistics Canada, *Pension Plans in Canada, 1984*. Ottawa: Minister of Supply and Services, August 1986.

Canada. Statistics Canada, *Quarterly Estimates of Trusteed Pension Funds*. Ottawa: Minister of Supply and Services, 1976-1987.

Canada. Statistics Canada, *Trusteed Pension Funds: Financial Statistics*. Ottawa: Minister of Supply and Services, 1976-1987.

Canada. Statistics Canada, *Women in the Work World*. Ottawa: Minister of Supply and Services, September 1984.

Canada. Statistics Canada, *Women in Canada: A Statistical Report*. Ottawa: Minister of Supply and Services, March 1985.

Canada. Task Force on Retirement Income Policy, 1979, *The Retirement Income System in Canada: Problems and Alternative Policies for Reform*. Ottawa: Supply and Services, 1980.

Canadian Advisory Council on the Status of Women, *Women and Pensions*. Ottawa: 1983.

Canadian Association of Pension Supervisory Authorities (CAPSA), *A Consensus for Pension Reform*, 1982.

C[anadian] A[utomobile] W[orkers]-Canada, Statement to the Task Force on Inflation Protection for Employment Pension Plans, July 10, 1987.

Canadian Chamber of Commerce, Submission to the Parliamentary Committee on Pension Reform, May 1983.

Canadian Conference of Catholic Bishops Episcopal Commission for Social Affairs, *Ethical Reflections on the Economic Crisis*. Ottawa: Concacan Inc., 1983.

Canadian Conference of Catholic Bishops Commission for Social Affairs, *Ethical Choices & Political Challenges: Ethical Reflections on the Future of Canada's Socio-Economic Order*. Ottawa: Concacan Inc., 1983.

Canadian Coordinating Committee for Jointly Trusteed Multi-Employer Pension and Benefit Plans, Submission to the Ontario Task Force on Inflation Protection for Employment Pension Plans, June 1987.

Canadian Institute of Actuaries, Brief to the Ontario Task Force on Inflation Protection for Employment Pension Plans, June 4, 1987.

Cassidy, Harry, *Social Security and Reconstruction in Canada*. Toronto: Ryerson Press, 1943.

Clark, Hart D., "Development of the Retirement Income System in Canada." In *Canada: Task Force on Retirement Income Policy, 1979. The Retirement Income System*, vol. II. Ottawa: Supply and Services, 1979.

Conklin, David W., Jalynn H. Bennett and Thomas J. Courchene, eds. *Pensions Today and Tomorrow: Background Studies*. Toronto: Ontario Economic Council, 1984.

Council of Ontario Construction Associations, Submission to the Ontario Task Force on Inflation Protection for Employment Pension Plans, July 6, 1987.

Coward, Laurence E., ed., *Pensions in Canada*. Don Mills, Ont.: CCH Canada Ltd., 1964.

Coward, Laurence E., *Report to the Treasurer of Ontario on Financing of Benefits Under the Superannuation Adjustment Benefits Act and Associated Superannuation Plans*, August 1987.

Delaney, Tom, *Delaney Report on RRSPs: A Buyer's Guide to Registered Retirement Savings Plans*. Toronto: McGraw-Hill Ryerson, 1988.

DeMont, John, "Post survey shows big profit jump," *The Financial Post*, Feb. 6-8, 1988.

Dingman, Harold, "Pension Poverty," *Maclean's*, March 1, 1949.

Drucker, Peter, *The Unseen Revolution: How Pension Fund Socialism Came to America*. New York: Harper and Row, 1976.

Dulude, Louise, *Pension Reform with Women in Mind*. Ottawa: Canadian Advisory Council on the Status of Women, March 1981.

Economic Council of Canada, *One in Three: Pensions for Canadians to 2030*. Ottawa: Minister of Supply and Services, 1979.

Ellmen, Eugene, *How to Invest Your Money with a Clear Conscience: The Canadian Guide to Profitable Ethical Investing*. Toronto: James Lorimer & Co., 1987.

Ezra, D. Don, *Understanding Pension Fund Finance and Investment*. Toronto: Pagurian Press, 1979.

Falconbridge Limited, Submission to the Task Force on Inflation Protection for Employment Pension Plans, 1987.

Fleming, James, *Merchants of Fear: An Investigation of Canada's Insurance Industry*. Markham, Ont.: Penguin Books, 1986.

Francis, Diane, *Controlling Interest: Who Owns Canada?* Toronto: Macmillan of Canada, 1986.

Friedan, Betty, *The Feminine Mystique*. New York: Dell Publishing, 1963.

Guest, Dennis, *The Emergence of Social Security in Canada*. Vancouver: University of British Columbia Press, 1985.

Hamilton, Colleen and John Whalley, "Reforming Public Pensions in Canada: Issues and Options." In *Pensions Today and Tomorrow: Background Studies*. Edited by David W. Conklin, Jalynn H. Bennett and Thomas J. Courchene. Toronto: Ontario Economic Council, 1984.

Hawkins, Freda, *Canada and Immigration: Public Policy and Public Concern*. Toronto: The Institute of Public Administration, 1972.

Heilig v. Dominion Securities Pitfield Ltd., 1986.

Hewitt Associates, Submission to the Task Force on Inflation Protection for Employment Pension Plans, June 1987.

International Monetary Fund, *Aging and Social Expenditure in the Major Industrial Countries, 1980-2025*. Washington D.C.: 1986.

Jacobs, Jane, *Cities and the Wealth of Nations: Principles of Economic Life*. Markham, Ont.: Viking, 1984.

Johnson, Arthur, "White Knights, Black Dreams," *Report on Business*. April 1985.

Kalbach, Warren E. and Wayne W. McVey, *The Demographic Bases of Canadian Society*. Toronto: McGraw-Hill, 1971.

Kennedy, Bruce, "Refinancing the CPP: The Cost of Acquiescence," working paper of the Institute for Research on Public Policy, 1988.

Kent, Tom, *A Public Purpose: An Experience of Liberal Opposition and Canadian Government*. Kingston and Montreal: McGill-Queen's University Press, 1988.

Kettle, John, *The Big Generation*. Toronto: McClelland and Stewart, 1980.

LaMarsh, Judy, *Memoirs of a Bird in a Gilded Cage*. Toronto: McClelland and Stewart, 1968.

Lametti, David, "Inflation Protection and Interprovincial Plans." In *Task Force on Inflation Protection for Employment Pension Plans: Research Studies*, vol. 1. Toronto: Queen's Printer for Ontario, 1988.

Leacy, F.H., ed., *Historical Statistics of Canada*, 2nd ed. Ottawa: Statistics Canada, 1983.

Lee, Don, "Pensions in Other Nations: The Implications for Reform in Canada." In *Pensions Today and Tomorrow: Background Studies*. Edited by David W. Conklin, Jalynn H. Bennett and Thomas J. Courchene. Toronto: Ontario Economic Council, 1984.

Life Underwriters Association of Canada, Memorandum Re Inflation Protection for Employment Pension Plans (Ontario), May 1987.

Longhurst, Patrick and Rose Marie Earle, *Looking After the Future: An Up-to-Date Guide to Pension Planning in Canada*. Toronto: Doubleday Canada, 1987.

Macintosh, R. M., "The Great Pension Fund Robbery Revisited." In *The Pension Fund Debate*. Toronto: Ontario Economic Council, 1978.

Marsh, George, "The Day the Pensions Stopped," *Canadian Business*, January 1978.

Marsh, Leonard C., *Report on Social Security for Canada, 1943*. Toronto: University of Toronto Press, reprint, 1975.

Marshall, Victor W., *Aging in Canada: Social Perspectives*. Toronto: Fitzhenry and Whiteside, 1979.

McQuaig, Linda, *Behind Closed Doors: How the Rich Won Control of Canada's Tax System...and Ended Up Richer*. Markham, Ont.: Viking, 1987.

McNaught, Kenneth, *A Prophet in Politics: A Biography of J. S. Woodsworth*. Toronto: University of Toronto Press, 1959.

Menzies, June, *The Canada Pension Plan and Women*. Ottawa: Canadian Advisory Council on the Status of Women, January 1974.

Mercer, William, "We're going haywire in our security plans," *Maclean's*, July 20, 1957.

Mercer, William M. Ltd., *Canadian Handbook of Pension and Welfare Plans*. Toronto: CCH Canada, 1956—.

Mercer, William M. Ltd., *The Mercer Bulletin*, 1980-1988.

Mercer, William M. Ltd., Submission Regarding Inflation Protection for Employment Pension Plans, 1987.

Morton, Desmond, "Resisting the Pension Evil: Bureaucracy, Democracy and Canada's Board of Pension Commissioners, 1915-1933," *Canadian Historical Review*, LXVIII, June 2, 1987, pp. 199-224.

Morton, Desmond, "Taking on the Grand Trunk: The Locomotive Engineers' Strike of 1876-7," *Labour/Le Travailleur: 2.* (1978).

Morton, Desmond and Margaret E. McCallum, "Superannuation to Indexation: Employment Pensions in the Public and Private Sector in Canada, 1870-1970." In *Task Force on Inflation Protection for Employment Pension Plans: Research Studies*, vol. 2. Toronto: Queen's Printer for Ontario, 1988.

Nagnur, Dhruva, *Longevity and Historical Life Tables 1921-1981* (abridged), *Canada and The Provinces*. Ottawa: Minister of Supply and Services Canada, 1986.

National Action Committee on the Status of Women, "Brief on Bill C-90: An Act Respecting Pension Plans Under Federal Jurisdiction," March 25, 1986.

National Action Committee on the Status of Women, "Extending the Spouses Allowance, Brief on Bill C-26 to the Standing Committee on Health, Welfare and Social Affairs," May 9, 1985.

National Action Committee on the Status of Women, "Pension Reform: What Women Want," March 1983.

National Action Committee on the Status of Women, *Women and Pensions*, September 1982.

National Advisory Council on Aging, *Family Role and the Negotiation of Change for the Aged.* Ottawa: July 1983.

Olive, David, *Just Rewards: The Case for Ethical Reform in Business.* Toronto: Key Porter, 1987.

Ontario. Ministry of Financial Institutions, *Building on Reform: Choices for Tomorrow's Pensions.* March, 1989.

Ontario. Ministry of Financial Institutions news release, December 9, 1986.

Ontario. Ontario Legislative Assembly Select Commmittee on Pensions, *Final Report,* 1982.

Ontario. The Royal Commission on the Status of Pensions in Ontario, *Report,* 1980.

Ontario. Task Force on Inflation Protection for Employment Pension Plans, *Report.* Toronto: Queen's Printer for Ontario, 1988.

Ontario. Task Force on Inflation Protection for Employment Pension Plans, *Research Studies,* vols. 1-3. Toronto: Queen's Printer for Ontario, 1988.

Ontario. Task Force on the Investment of Public Sector Pension Funds, *In Whose Interest?* Toronto: Queen's Printer for Ontario, 1987.

Ontario Chamber of Commerce, Submission to the Ontario Government Task Force on Mandatory Indexation in Employer-Sponsored Pension Plans, June 1987.

Ontario Hospital Association, "Information" bulletin, February 17, 1988.

Ontario Public Service Employees Union, Presentation to the Friedland Task Force on Inflation Protection, July 10, 1987.

Ontario Supreme Court, *Order of the Divisional Court Re Batchelor et al.,* Aug. 18, 1986 and September 8, 1986.

Pension Commission of Ontario, Consultation Draft of Proposed Regulations under Bill 170. Toronto: February 1987.

Peron, Yves and Claude Strohmenger, *Demographic and Health Indicators: Presentation and Interpretation.* Ottawa: Minister of Supply and Services, November 1985.

Perry, Robert L., "Through the Labyrinth: A plain man's guide to pensions," *The Financial Post,* April 1978.

Pesando, J. E., "Assessment of Alternative Formulas for Delivering Inflation Protection." In *Task Force on Inflation Protection for Employment Pension Plans: Research Studies,* vol. 1. Toronto: Queen's Printer, 1988.

Pesando, J. E., *Issues Regarding the Reform of Canada's Private Pension System.* Ottawa: Consumer and Corporate Affairs Canada, 1983.

Pesando, James E., *The Use of 'Excess' Pension Fund Earnings to Provide Inflation Protection for Private Pensions.* Toronto: Ontario Economic Council, 1983.

Pesando, J. E. and S. A. Rea, Jr., *Public and Private Pensions in Canada: An Economic Analysis*, Ontario Economic Council. Toronto: University of Toronto Press, 1977.

Regush, Nicholas, *Condition Critical: Canada's Health-Care System.* Toronto: Macmillan of Canada, 1987.

Reich, Robert, *The Next American Frontier: A Provocative Program for Economic Renewal.* New York: Times Books, 1983.

Retail Council of Canada, Submission to the Task Force on Inflation Protection for Employment Pension Plans, May 29, 1987.

Revenue Canada, "Information Circular 72-13R7," December 31, 1981.

Rhodes, Anne, "Women: Still the losers in pensions," *Chatelaine*, May 1982.

Romaniuc, A., *Current Demographic Analysis. Fertility in Canada: From Baby-Boom to Baby-Bust*, Statistics Canada. Ottawa: Minister of Supply and Services Canada, 1984.

Shiele, Robin, "Pension plan reform: It's here at last!," *The Financial Post*, June 1, 1985.

Sinclair, Clayton, "Control of pensions to be union's goal," *Financial Times of Canada*, Dec. 12-18, 1977.

Stone, Leroy O. and Susan Fletcher, A profile of Canada's older population, I.R.P.P. [Institute for Research on Public Policy], 1980.

Stone, Leroy O. and Susan Fletcher, *The Seniors Boom: Dramatic Increases in Longevity and Prospects for Better Health.* Statistics Canada, Population Studies Division: Health and Welfare Canada, Office on Aging: The Secretary of State of Canada, The Social Trends Analysis Directorate. Ottawa: Minister of Supplies and Services, 1986.

Stone, Leroy O. and Susan Fletcher, "Why We Should be Cautious in Accepting Forecasts of the Dependency Ratios in the 21st Century." In *Pensions Today and Tomorrow: Background Studies.* Edited by David W. Conklin, Jalynn H. Bennett and Thomas J. Courchene. Toronto: Ontario Economic Council, 1984.

Stone, Leroy O. and Michael J. MacLean, Future income prospects for Canada's senior citizens, I.R.P.P. [Institute for Research on Public Policy], 1979.

Townson, Monica, "Pension Reform for Women." In *Pensions Today and Tomorrow: Background Studies.* Edited by David W. Conklin, Jalynn H. Bennett and Thomas J. Courchene. Toronto: Ontario Economic Council, 1984.

Towers, Perrin, Forster & Crosby, Submission to the Ontario Task Force on Inflation Protection for Employment Pension Plans, May 1987.

United Steelworkers of America/District 6, Presentation to the Task Force on Inflation Protection for Employment Pension Plans, June 29, 1987.

White, Bob, *Hard Bargains: My Life on the Line*. Toronto: McClelland and Stewart, 1987.

Wilson, Michael, ed., "The Young-old: a new North American phenomenon," Canadian Institute on Public Affairs 24th Winter Conference, 1979.

Major reports on pension reform in the last decade include the 1978 Quebec report by le Comité d'étude sur le financement du Régime de rentes et sur les régimes supplémentaires de rentes (the "Cofirentes+ report"); the 1979 report of a special Senate Committee chaired by David Croll *(Retirement Without Tears)*; an examination of the future of the pension system by the Economic Council of Canada that same year *(One in Three: Pensions for Canadians to 2030)*; 1980's federal Task Force on Retirement Income Policy (the "Lazar report"); a 1980 Royal Commission on the Status of Pensions in Ontario (the "Haley report"); a 1982 federal-provincial report by the Canadian Association of Pension Supervisory Authorities *(A Consensus for Pension Reform)*; a 1982 federal Green Paper *(Better Pensions for Canadians)*; a 1982 Ontario Select Committee on Pensions report; a 1982 report by the Canadian Labour Congress *(The CLC Proposal for Pension Reform)*; a 1982 British Columbia report *(Developing a Pension Policy for the Future)*; a 1982 report by the Pension Committee of Manitoba; a 1983 report by the Business Committee on Pension Policy; a 1983 position paper by the Ontario Economic Council *(Pensions Today and Tomorrow)*; a 1983 Parliamentary Task Force on Pension Reform (the "Frith report"); a 1984 Ontario White Paper *(Ontario Proposals for Pension Reform)*, and the 1988 *Report of the Task Force on Inflation Protection for Employment Pension Plans* (the "Friedland report").

INDEX